Getting Started in

A FINANCIALLY SECURE RETIREMENT

The *Getting Started In* Series

Getting Started in

A FINANCIALLY SECURE RETIREMENT

Henry K. Hebeler

BICENTENNIAL
1807
WILEY
2007
BICENTENNIAL

John Wiley & Sons, Inc.

Published by John Wiley & Sons, Inc., Hoboken, New Jersey.
Published simultaneously in Canada.

Disclaimer: This document is presented "as is." The author and publisher make no guarantees or warranties of any kind regarding this document or the legality or correctness of any document or plan created herewith. They do not guarantee or warrant that this document will meet your requirements, achieve your intended results, or be without defect or error. You assume all risks regarding the legality and use or misuse of the document or plan created from it. The author and publisher expressly disclaim any and all implied warranties or merchantability and fitness for a particular use. Under no circumstance shall they be liable for financial outcomes or any special, incidental, consequential or other damages arising out of the use or inability to use this document, even if they have been advised of the possibility or such damages. Their total liability shall be limited to the purchase price. Some states do not allow the limitation and/or exclusion of implied warranties or damages. You may have other rights which vary from state to state. The author and publisher are not providing legal, investment, tax, or accounting advice. This document is not a substitute for qualified professionals. You should seek the advice of qualified professionals for all of your legal, investment, tax, accounting and financial planning needs. The user of this document agrees that any legal issue shall governed by and under the laws of the state of Washington.

For general information on our other products and services or for technical support, please contact our Customer Care Department within the United States at (800) 762-2974, outside the United States at (317) 572-3993 or fax (317) 572-4002.

Wiley also publishes its books in a variety of electronic formats. Some content that appears in print may not be available in electronic books. For more information about Wiley products, visit our web site at www.wiley.com.

Wiley Bicentennial Logo: Richard J. Pacifico

Library of Congress Cataloging-in-Publication Data

Hebeler, H. K. (Henry K.)
  Getting started in a financially secure retirement / Henry K. Hebeler.
    p. cm.
  ISBN-13: 978-0-470-11778-1 (pbk.)
  ISBN-10: 0-470-11778-8 (pbk.)
  1. Retirement income--United States--Planning. 2. Investments--United States. 3. Estate planning--United States. 4. Finance, Personal--United States. 5. Financial security--United States. I. Title.
  HG181.H34 2007
  332.024'014--dc22

                              2006034375

Printed in the United States of America.

10 9 8 7 6 5 4 3 2 1

I dedicate this book to my children and grandchildren whose generations will experience the things that I describe. May they show wisdom and properly prepare themselves for a lengthy period of adverse economic conditions that is an inevitable part of their future and, by so doing, gain comfort and health throughout their lives.

Henry (Bud) K. Hebeler

Contents

Chapter 7

About the Author

Henry "Bud" K. Hebeler earned three degrees from the Massachusetts Institute of Technology (SB, AerE, MB), and his academic career includes the Honors Program, Outstanding Student Award, Kuljian Humanities Award, Mead Prize for Aeronautical Engineers, Tau Beta Pi (engineering honorary), Sigma Zi (aeronautical honorary), Sperry Gyroscope Fellow, Sloan Fellow, MIT Sloan School Board of Governors and boards of several other colleges.

Bud Hebeler, as an aeronautical engineer, taught ballistic missile design at Cal Tech and has patents on an aeroelastic analog computer and reentry heat shield. In addition, he has managed several classified defense projects, developed the Short Range Attack Missile, led Minuteman Ballistic Missile systems engineering, and served as vice president engineering, vice president corporate planning, and president of Boeing Engineering and Construction. He then served as president of Boeing Electronics and president of Boeing Aerospace Company.

As an active citizen, he has been an economic advisor to the governor of the state of Washington and, at the federal level, a policy consultant to the secretaries of Commerce, Interior, Energy, and Defense as well as a consultant to the U.S. Congress on fusion. In his community, he is active on many church and local community projects.

A successful writer, Mr. Hebeler is the author of *On the Offense Against the Defense* (Arcata, CA: Humbolt State University, 1986); *J. K. Lasser's Your Winning Retirement Plan* (New York: Wiley & Sons, 2001); *Deception, Dynamics and Decisions* (a paper delivered for the National Association of Personal Financial Advisors at 2003 Philadelphia Conference); and numerous retirement articles on www.analyzenow.com, which are referenced in many national magazines and newspapers including the *Wall Street Journal, BusinessWeek, Kiplinger's, AARP, Money, Smart Money,* and *Financial Planning* as well as television and radio programs.

As a retired Boeing exective and working without compensation, Mr. Hebeler assists thousands of people with answers to retirement questions. When not doing this, he and his wife enjoy an active life of skiing, golfing, and church activities. They are high-handicap golfers but accomplished skiers who are not afraid to tackle deep powder and double-black expert slopes even though now in their 17th year of retirement. The Hebelers have four daughters and thirteen grandchildren, all skiers or snowboarders.

Foreword

Growing old is not an option. We don't have a choice. But we do have choices that will greatly affect our quality of life for the rest of our life. That in a nutshell is what this book is about; how to make the right decisions regarding our resources to maintain a retirement lifestyle similar to the one we have grown comfortable with during our income-producing years of employment.

As a financial advisor of 25 years, I have taken a keen interest in this topic, doing my best to make sure that my clients have enough dollars to sustain themselves for the rest of their lives. I have often felt that what is needed for people who are intent on meeting this challenge is a comprehensive and concise "how-to" retirement manual. I have hunted long and hard to find such a book. Thankfully, my hunt is over. Henry Hebeler has delivered—but first a little history . . .

In 1982 a cultural financial shift of seismic proportions took place. Corporate America began doing away with defined benefit plans by introducing self-directed 401(k) retirement accounts to their employees. Essentially, companies started unloading the burden of employee retirement saving off their own backs and onto the backs of their workers.

Instead of looking forward to a monthly pension check from their employer upon retirement, employees were now faced with the responsibility of first saving enough money, and second, investing it wisely so that eventually this account would sustain them throughout their retirement years, or what I more bluntly refer to as a 20- to 30-year period of unemployment.

As a result, millions of Americans began turning to the Wall Street crowd of stockbrokers for a little help and guidance and came face to face with an industry that was far more concerned about making the next commissioned sale than offering prudent, intelligent investment advice.

Unfortunately, for much of the 1980s and 1990s this problem was masked, largely because the stock market generated returns during this period almost *twice* that of its historical long-term average. As the saying goes, everyone is brilliant in a bull market, especially your stockbroker.

The good times of great returns came to a screeching halt in the spring of 2000 when the stock market bubble burst. 401k accounts plummeted, and investors started realizing they needed to get serious and start making some smart decisions about retirement planning.

Who do these investors turn to for commonsense, unbiased advice now? The financial industry is still intent on making the next sale, and the financial press is intent on meeting its next deadline, so not much help there. Providentially, Mr. Hebeler has stepped up and filled an enormous void with this book.

Relying on his expertise as a long-range planner for the Boeing Company, he brings clarity and wisdom to the individual investor, through his website www.analyzenow.com and through his frequent articles. Now he offers us a splendid little book that is packed full of common sense advice on all dimensions of the retirement planning process.

Make no mistake, preparing for retirement is still a daunting challenge. There are so many different topics to address, everything from Social Security payouts to replacement budgeting to reverse dollar cost averaging. This book addresses them all.

Despite the popular (and accurate) notion that Americans are woefully unprepared to embrace their retirement years, it has been my experience that many of these same folks have a keen desire to accept responsibility for their financial well-being; it is just that the task is so daunting that they don't know where to start and what to focus on. Hebeler's book is certain to become the definitive guide to long-term planning for investors who want to accomplish the elusive goal of a worry-free retirement.

Bill Schultheis,
Financial advisor, journalist, and author of
The Coffeehouse Investor

Preface

I've been rich and I've been poor. Believe me, honey, rich is better. —Sophie Tucker

Sophie, you were poor before being rich. It is even worse being poor after you've been rich—as too many people are going to learn! Today, most people are rich compared to lifestyles several decades ago. Yet in several decades in the future, a large contingent of our older people are going to be truly poor because they are not willing to pull back a little now so they will have some resources in retirement.

The problem is compounded because it is a social problem, not just an individual problem. In order to get elected, politicians cannot run on a platform advocating real fixes for future generations. Then, once in office, they promote public spending and consumerism that makes the current economy look good and keeps employment high.

The individuals who are attentive and motivated will do much better because they will have looked ahead and included some relatively simple things in their plans that will help them achieve a better lifestyle than the vast majority. This book will pave the way for those who heed its advice. Then, like Sophie, they can say, "Rich is better."

Introduction

If you have decided to read this book, we already share some things in common. When I was 55 years old, I started to look into retirement planning very carefully. Before then I always relied on a very competent financial advisor who was getting handsomely compensated for his effort.

Reaching the age of 55 was a critical point in my life because, like many, I started to consider when I could afford to retire and what other activities would replace those of my job. My financial planner said I already had accumulated enough to retire comfortably. In light of the fact that retirement is a one-time life-changing event, I decided to look into planning methodology very, very carefully, not only with regard to how the planner put the numbers together, but also with the same perspective that I had used for Boeing's corporate planning that I headed for six years.

I started attending seminars put on by other planners trolling for new clients. I went to an introductory class designed for people who were considering becoming professional financial planners. The professor outlined subjects and investments that I not only already knew much about, I had personally owned most of the types of investments that they would only read about. So I picked up some books on the subject to try and better assess the current state of the art in financial planning. In short order, I felt very uncomfortable about what I was learning.

Then I turned to the computer to help with solutions. I started to use some of the commercial retirement planning programs to see how close results were to my own planner's forecasts. I could not find any two programs that gave results that were even close, much less close to each other. So I started to do some reverse engineering—that is, try to deduce what was causing the differences. After a while, I could spot troubles just by inspection of the way they were assembling the entries. For example, many of the media sources asked people to add their Social Security projection to their pension projection. We were all taught that you could not add apples and oranges in grade school, yet here they were adding inflation-adjusted Social Security to fixed income pensions. It does not take many years before this addition is painfully off—and in an unconservative direction.

Further, neither the programs nor the books nor the magazine planning methods seemed to include or even hint at the fact that it was important to be conservative. It wasn't just the methodology, it was the default values for investment performance which almost universally did not include costs and fees and used national life expectancy for the length of retirement, after which the person would exhaust all investments. Never mind that one-half of the population would live longer than this, and that the life-expectancy numbers included a significant number of early deaths from murders and could be woefully low if you were an Asian or white woman. Nor was there even a hint that maybe you should not plan on using all of your investments for normal retirement expenses when, in fact, almost everyone has numerous financial surprises that were never planned.

I learned the importance of being conservative when planning long before my years in Boeing's headquarters. At the division level, we had to submit both one-year operating plans and long-range plans every year. Our compensation depended on our performance as measured against our one-year operating plans, but the long-range plans gave upper management some perspective about the amount of research and development money a division should get. These were actually conflicting objectives, in a sense. The operating plans motivated a conservative outlook while the long-range plans motivated an optimistic outlook.

Why do I bring up this history? The answer is because the same thing is true in the financial industry. When they want you to sell a product, the amount they charge must be conservative to cover their costs and make a profit. On the other hand, to sell their products, they promote very high long-term expectations such as booming future returns.

Few financial firms put planning methodology very high on their priority list. I have helped financial journalists expose flaws in numerous widely used programs developed by mutual funds, insurance companies, software houses, financial magazines, and nonprofit organizations supposedly dedicated to helping people do retirement planning. Some of the offenders have not changed their methods after years of prodding, and almost all are very slow to react.

If successful, the leading managers of financial companies often get compensated in excess of $10 million a year. This is just one part of what one firm estimates to be about $300 billion of annual financial companies' overhead that you and I pay through both disclosed and hidden costs in the products. My research concluded that my professional planner had done a good job recommending low-cost mutual funds, but I could never get anything very explicit on real estate partnerships. I do know that the general partner of several of these partnerships bought maintenance services from subsidiaries that the general partner owned, so the management decisions may not always have been in the best interest of the limited partners.

After some of this research, I agreed with my planner that I did have enough resources for my own fairly comfortable retirement, so I set a new goal. I would retire and devote a major effort in trying to help people do better retirement planning. I decided that I would do this on a not-for-profit basis not just to be charitable, but also so that I would be considered as objective and unbiased.

I now help several dozen financial journalists with articles that reach millions of people. I do not ask for credit, but often they will mention my website, www.analyzenow.com, or my J. K. Lasser series book. Sometimes newspapers and magazines publish an article I've written. For the past 15 years, I have provided these efforts without a request for compensation, and when the organization I helped insisted on paying me, I donated the money to charity.

I've come to respect authors who challenge the financial industry's conventional wisdom and those who provide practical help to their readers. Two of these are in my hometown of Seattle, Paul Merriman and Bill Schultheis. They not only write useful material, they help those in our community with seminars to motivate the audience. For the most part, I've never met my financial journalist heroes in person, although I've often had lengthy e-mail and phone conversations about challenging subjects. These are people like Jonathan Clements, Jonathan Pond, Tom Herman, Mary Beth Franklin, Jean Gruss, Lynn Asinof, Lynn O'Shaughnessy, Chris Farrell, Kelly Greene, Walter Updegrave, and many others, all of which help those in audiences far greater than I can reach.

I do not work alone to get my own material to the public. My website is supported largely by unpaid volunteers, many of whom I have never met in person. I have people that assist me in many states, Canada, and England. These vary from a volunteer who is my webmaster in Salt Lake City to a retired professor of finance from Oxford University who acts as a sounding board for many of my technical concerns. I get both ideas and help from professional planners and lawyers who like my work as well as a retired math professor who helps test my programs and an amazing retired Navy captain who almost daily e-mails me retirement planning news clips.

As the Getting Started title implies, this book has no pretense of being a scholarly treatise. Instead, its audience is intended to be those who know they would like to get started on a sound path to a financially comfortable retirement. It is my hope that the efforts I put into this project will provide a major improvement in the retirement lives of the Getting Started readers.

Chapter 1

Planning

The secret of getting ahead is getting started.

—Mark Twain

Planning is all about creating an image for the future and the path to get there. If you are planning on upgrading your home, you envision the revised structure, estimate its costs and revise the image to bring it into sync with the amount that you can afford. Then you enumerate the things you have to do to get to that position in the future.

So it is with retirement planning. You have to think about the future lifestyle that you want and the path to get there. You have to estimate what that will cost and bring the image of the future into sync with the sacrifices you have to make now.

The image we have of our retirement needs is far different than it was for our grandparents. Grandfather may have lived on a farm, depended on his children when he got old, had little use for a telephone, never saw a computer, had a few 78 rpm phonograph records, worked until unable, and, for the short time until he died, liked sitting on the front porch talking to neighbors and relatives.

planning
a strategy and actions to get to an objective. In finance, it requires a projection based on some assumptions about the economy, resources, saving and/or spending that provides an estimate of future financial status.

1

Now our retirement image is vastly different. We are influenced greatly by the lifestyles of friends and images portrayed by newspapers, magazines, movies, television, and so forth. We are living longer, retiring earlier, relying heavily on technology, and are well aware of the lifestyles of those around us. So let's examine some of these things.

The Joneses

Today, it is all about keeping up with the Joneses. The Joneses may be real people in your neighborhood, business, relations, friends, or even celebrities you have never met. They create the lifestyle goals you seek. Images from TV, advertisements, holiday cards from acquaintances, and visits to other homes or areas may sway you. You may also feel pressure from your children whose friends may set your children's goals. All of this is reflected in your choice of houses, automobiles, furnishings, electronics, club memberships, sports, vacation spots, entertainment, restaurants, colleges for children, and the like.

inflation

A measure of increasing costs for the same items. Inflation is usually measured by changes in the *consumer price index* (CPI), which is based on a "basket" of items that are supposed to represent the kind and proportion of things consumed by the average person. Specifically, inflation is the cost growth (this year's costs less last year's costs) divided by last year's costs.

By foregoing some parts of the Joneses' lifestyle now, you are likely to do better than the Joneses in the long run even if you have lower income now. This book is going to tell you what the future may well hold and the benefits you will be able to enjoy by lagging a little behind the Joneses, showing some restraint, and putting aside enough money for a decent retirement which, after all, could well be one-third of your life.

By the time some people will be reading this, they will already be retired. This book also is for retired people. Whether still working or already retired, the same principles apply. Everyone has to save, everyone has to invest, everyone is exposed to *inflation*, and everyone is subject to taxes. Retired people are not an exception, but they have a serious disadvantage compared to younger working people, namely, it is very hard for them to get back into the workplace after they discover that their financial problems force them to seek more income.

Don't forget, this is a *long-range* planning book. You will not likely see any of the effects that I forecast for a long time. This is to your advantage because the more everyone else spends, the better off you are as a consequence of greater investment opportunities and lower taxes. But someday, that will change, and you will be far ahead if you follow the advice in this book.

The Planning Path

The first step to do better than the aging Joneses is to develop a conservative financial plan that provides a reasonable lifestyle in your retirement, particularly your late retirement. We are looking for how much you will be able to spend in retirement, and, if you are not yet retired, how much you will have to save beforehand. It is an amazing thing to me that many people expect to live twenty to forty years in retirement and still have not made an attempt to reconcile how much they would have to save in order for their savings to support a reasonable retirement lifestyle without going broke in short order.

Eighty percent of success is showing up.—Woody Allen

The future environment, as influenced by massive overspending in the last few decades, requires forecasts of lower than historical returns, higher inflation, and higher tax rates. It also means setting aside some money as a contingency for unforeseen events, which could include things that could happen to your adult children or aged parents and at least partial provisions for long-term care.

You can make such plans yourself using the simplified approach in the appendixes of this book, use a competent computer program, or rely on the help of a professional planner. You may have to lean on the planner to use conservative inputs because less experienced planners often believe they can foresee the future—and they would have you believe the future is going to be glorious with their help. It is common to use historical data for things like inflation and returns, but it is very unlikely that the long-term future will be like the past. So don't let an apparently sophisticated planner have you believe that a comprehensive computer program with a *Monte Carlo analysis* will give you high confidence. Plan more conservatively than this.

Uncertainties in Forecasts

There are many uncertainties in long-range plans, but even an imperfect plan is likely to give a better basis for your economic decisions than no plan at all.

- Family emergencies
- Aging parents' care
- Adult children troubles
- Returns
- Inflation
- Taxes
- Social Security
- Pension viability
- Medical costs
- Years your money must last

Monte Carlo analysis

a statistical analysis involving a large number of trials of randomly drawn values. In financial analysis, the values are usually historical daily or monthly returns on investments. The result is the probability that investments would have been exhausted in a certain number of past years. Caution! It represents what happened in the past, not necessarily what will happen in the future.

There are many imponderables when doing planning including economics, health issues, and unforeseen events. Although you cannot be precise, every year that you redo your plan, you get closer to reality and build a financial base that hopefully gives you some resiliency to accommodate the unknowns.

There is a saying that expresses the other side of uncertainty:

"When nothing is certain, everything is possible." Our objective in this book is to show you some things that are possible and help you rise above the crowd. If you seize on the possibilities, you will succeed.

Overcoming Planning Uncertainties

No one can predict the future. We don't know how long we are going to live, what surprise events will develop, nor what is going to happen in the economic world of returns, inflation, and taxes. Yet all of these things need to be specified to develop a financial plan that determines how much you should be saving before retirement or how much you can spend after retiring. Fortunately, there are some things that we can do to provide some insulation from the uncertainties in planning.

> There are only two groups of forecasters—those who do not know and those who do not know that they do not know.
> —John Kenneth Galbraith

I would like to go back in my own history and give you an analogy that may help you understand some things that most financial planners do not. I started my working career in the Boeing Company in a stress group of a technical organization called *Structures*. My first project involved the design of a very advanced and highly classified new airplane. I was responsible for the preliminary design of the wing structure. In order to size the wing structural members and skin, we needed to know the loads and the strength of the materials. Our stress group computed the loads and we received "allowable" stresses for various materials from a group that specialized in the strength of materials.

The strength of materials was determined by testing many samples, mainly in "pull" tests where machines pulled at each end of carefully cut samples and measured how much stress the materials could take either before deforming unacceptably or failing completely. After many pull tests on the several test sheets, the materials group used the statistics from those tests to give us a design "allowable stress" that had a high probability of surviving an "ultimate load." We got ultimate loads by multiplying known loads by 1.5 to account for unknown loads and provide a "factor of safety."

The material "allowable stress" is analogous to a planner using the statistics of investment returns and inflation in preparing a plan. Planners call the results "success probabilities." You want a conservative success probability just as you want a high probability of getting to your destination in an airplane. Of course, no planner ever recommends the ultrahigh success requirements used in the design of an airplane. Retirees would be able to spend very little indeed.

Moreover, the financial planner cannot go as far as an airplane manufacturer because the planner cannot sample the future to determine the statistics of the future. Unlike a financial planner, a materials specialist sets up stringent material content and process specifications and confirmation requirements. But it does not end there because after the materials are produced and delivered, the materials are tested again to see that they meet the specifications. For example, they might require that a sheet of aluminum to be used for a wing skin have three pull specimens cut from the sheet and tested to see if the statistics of that sheet actually match the same kind of strength statistics that were used in the design.

The materials specialist then makes a technical calculation of the "confidence" that that sheet will survive by comparing the results from these samples with the more extensive tests used to develop the allowable stresses. If the confidence level does not meet the designer's requirement, the sheet is rejected. A financial planner not only cannot sample the future, he does not have the opportunity to reject the future if it does not meet the assumptions used in the plan.

Unfortunately, planners have become so enamored with statistical programs such as Monte Carlo analyses that, unlike the materials specialist, they fail to remember that they are not able to sample the future. So they blithely say that they have a certain success probability that a retiree can live on such and such income for a certain number of years. What they really should say is that *if* the statistics of future returns, inflation and taxes turn out to be very similar to those of the past, and *if* the reserves prove to be adequate for surprise events, then the chances of succeeding (or success rate) is some specific number.

Now that you have this background, the planner's qualified success statement is not likely to be very comforting. Of equal import is the fact that no one knows what financial surprises may confront you. Perhaps an aging parent needs some uninsured care and does not have sufficient funds, or perhaps a daughter with several children gets divorced and desperately needs financial help. All of these things point to the need to make a conservative plan by using less-than-average returns, higher-than-average inflation, longer-than-average life expectancies, and so on, as well as putting aside some reserves, even though arbitrary, for surprise events. Like the factor of safety used to get ultimate loads in airplane design, a reserve provides some cushion for unknown events that happen in everyone's life.

So how do we get confidence in the planning process? We do it by using conservative and repetitive analysis and by gradually shifting to the kind of investments that have much less uncertain performance. When young we can take risks and recover from stock and real estate volatility. When older, we shift to a larger share of fixed income securities like certificates of deposits (CDs), bonds, and immediate annuities. If we do a new conservative

Overcoming Uncertainties

There are numerous ways we can protect ourselves from retirement planning uncertainties:

- Conservative plans
- Reserves for unknowns
- Shift to fixed income investments
- Immediate annuities late in life
- Repeat planning process every year
- Fewer uncertainties as we age

plan each year, as we age we experience the surprise events and use some of the reserves. We get some of the event uncertainties behind us. Using the previous examples, aging parents finally die and the children of the divorced daughter finally become self-supporting adults.

If the economy goes awry, we have some cushion to accommodate it. If the economy turns out better, we raise our sights somewhat but still use conservative projection values. The plan will never be perfect so, unlike the theory, we will not spend our last nickel on our last day on earth—instead we try to have enough money to support us if we live longer than average. If not, we leave something for our children or some worthy cause.

Early in retirement, your forecast may change significantly from year to year. Plans change; that is the nature of planning. Don't believe that you can set out on a course where during the first year of retirement you spend a certain "safe" percentage of your income and then continue to simply increase that by the amount of inflation in every succeeding year until your death. Realistically, you have to change your outlook every year. If you don't, you overspend so much in bear markets that you cannot recover. Or, if you really get lucky in a bull market, you are at your planner's door asking why you cannot spend more. And you know what? Your advisor will give you a new plan which is what you should have developed each year yourself as a matter of course (see Figure 1.1).

immediate annuities
a contract with an insurance company that, in exchange for a lump sum of money, will make lifetime payments on a regular basis. These may be either fixed, have cost-of-living adjustments, COLAs, or be based on other kind of an index. Pensions are really immediate annuities, most of which have fixed payments and some have COLAs.

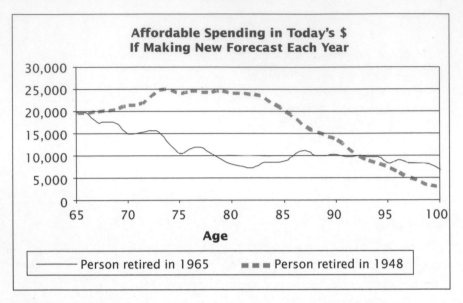

FIGURE 1.1 In real life, people do not spend a constant (inflation-adjusted) amount each year until death.

Source: Dynamics program from www.analyzenow.com.

One of my big gripes about the planning programs used by the vast majority of professionals is that these supposedly sophisticated programs do not make a new affordable spending calculation every year. Advisors would like you to come back every year for a new calculation anyway, so why don't they use models that include the mathematics to calculate affordable spending every year instead of just in the first year with an inflation adjustment for all of the following years? This is not hard to do. I demonstrated this by incorporating this feature in the professional program, *Dynamic Financial Planning Pro,* on www.analyzenow.com. This gives a more realistic perspective of human behavior. For example, virtually everyone who has any significant dependence on the stock market would modify their spending in the year after a market crash or increase spending following some years of extraordinary market growth. That is human nature. Your professional's model will not simulate this.

But, let's get back to confidence. We can improve our confidence too by the way we invest. Diversified investments reduce risk. The natural process of investing in more fixed income investments as we age reduces the risk. We might put some part of our investments in immediate annuities that will make payments until whenever our death actually occurs without exhausting investments on some assumed death date. We can reduce the uncertainty of inflation with inflation-adjusted government bonds or competitively priced inflation-adjusted immediate annuities. Many can sensibly reduce the uncertainty of tax rates by investing in tax-exempt bonds. Those that can meet the income requirements can avoid future tax increases by investing in Roth *IRAs* or Roth *401(k)s* that, unlike regular IRAs and 401(k)s, have no tax deduction on deposits, do not tax withdrawals, permit withdrawals of deposits before 59½, and do not have minimum distribution requirements..

The ultimate answer to the need for planning in spite of uncertainty comes from examining the alternative, that is, no planning. No planning is a disaster. President Eisenhower likened planning to his experiences as a general. He said you cannot enter a battle without a plan. Yet that plan may change every day or hour as the enemy modifies its tactics to counter yours. Retirement planning is no different. It just has a different time scale. Things do not change as fast in your life as they do in war.

No financial planning leads to little savings. Little savings ultimately make retirees reliant on relatives, charity and/or welfare. Think of no planning as being equivalent to a life dependent on Social Security, Medicaid, and a very restrained lifestyle that probably does not fit the image you may have of what you would like to do when you finally can get away from work and have an opportunity to broaden your horizons and pursue your hobbies or new activities. A plan provides an opportunity, though not totally assured, of a much better future.

IRA
stands for Individual Retirement Account. This is the most common of deferred tax accounts. They are administered by financial institutions such as mutual funds and brokerages. There are a number of stringent requirements subject to strict regulations such as the earliest age to take out money (59½) and age to start mandatory withdrawals (70½). (Roth IRAs have major exceptions to these rules.) IRS Publication 590 thoroughly covers associated regulations and life expectancy tables used for withdrawals.

401(k)
stands for the applicable part of tax code that authorized employers to offer savings plans with deferred-tax benefits. Deposits are tax deductible, but withdrawals are fully taxable and are subject to constraints similar to regular IRAs.

Planning Myths

pension
an annuity that makes lifetime payments to a retired employee and, as a lower-paying option, to a surviving spouse.

consumer price index (CPI)
a federal measure of inflation. This index is based on the price of a "basket" of items that is supposed to represent the purchases of the average person. The index is ratio of the current prices to the price in some past reference year.

There are a number of things commonly accepted, even by professionals, that may be far from the truth. Let's take a look at some of these.

Social Security is the foundation for the vast majority of people's retirement planning. The general belief is that Social Security is adjusted for inflation every year. In fact, it is adjusted in accordance with the *consumer price index* or *CPI*. The weighting of the constituents of the CPI are unlikely to match those of retirees, particularly as they age and incur larger medical, dental, eye, hearing, and service expenses. Not only do retirees incur an ever richer mix of these elements, the elements themselves are increasing faster than the CPI. Further, the government itself reduces the actual Social Security checks if you (wisely) sign up for Part B to cover many medical costs. Those deductions are increasing faster than inflation, so the net Social Security payment is growing even more slowly than the CPI.

Another common myth is that your pension is insured. Long before Enron, WorldCom, Arthur Andersen, and other debacles, I was asked to participate in a television program to ask questions of a panel of four professional financial advisors. One of my key questions and their reply was

---

Planning Myths

There are many things we accept as true that may be simply myths:
- Social Security is inflation-adjusted.
- Your *pension* is insured.
- There are "Safe" withdrawal limits.
- It is easy to get high returns.
- Inflation will be 3 percent.
- Any planning method works, but Monte Carlo programs are best.

edited from the show before airing because all four professionals made it sound like the proposition was preposterous. I asked, "What kind of assurance do retirees have that they will get their pensions?"

The panelists all responded that this was not a problem. They said that not only were the funds in trusts but there was a *Pension Benefit Guaranty Corporation* (PBGC) that backed them up. I knew that was the wrong answer because I had found some research showing the projections that the companies were using for future returns in their trust projections. These projected returns were all near 10 percent at a time when they not only were not making 10 percent, but also they had a large percentage of fixed income investments with much lower returns. Further, I knew that the PGBC had a cap on the most the PBGC would pay each person and severe reductions if a person retired before age 65.

> **Pension Benefit Guaranty Corporation (PBGC)**
>
> a quasi-government corporation set up to insure employee pensions in case the employer fails to fund its pension trust. It collects insurance premiums from employers and makes pension payments if necessary in accordance with its own rules.

Well now anyone who can read a newspaper or has paid any attention to the news on television knows that numerous large companies have defaulted on their pension promises, and the PGBC is paying a lot less than retirees expected. Furthermore, the PBGC itself is essentially bankrupt, something the U.S. Congress will try to rectify at some point with an infusion. Firms have started to be a little more conservative in their trust projections, but many are getting out of pensions entirely and now leaving the responsibility for saving to the employees themselves. Unfortunately, only a small number of employees are now saving at a rate that would equal the benefits that they would get from a pension.

Still another myth is that there are "safe" withdrawal limits. What is meant by this is that if a retiree withdraws the "safe" amount in the first year, the retiree can increase that withdrawal amount each succeeding year by the amount of the previous year's inflation—and not exhaust the retirement investments until death. In my view, this is nonsense, and the only ways that this could be safe would be to either use zero for the safe amount, or have planned so conservatively that no unforeseen event would have otherwise depleted investments, or that the retiree would be assured to be in the 50 percent of the population that lives less than the life-expectancy used in the initial calculation.

Now it is common to say that the "safe" amount is 3 percent to 5 percent of a balanced portfolio. Figure 1.2 shows that these would not be safe for a long-lived person who retired in 1965 or somewhere within that period because of significant market failures and inflation far higher than 3 percent.

In 2000, a highly respected and well-written scholar advocated that retirees use an all-stock portfolio and draw 7.5 percent the first year and increase the amount every year by inflation. He based his conclusions on a million Monte Carlo statistical simulations per case. He concluded that there was only a 10.4 percent chance of failure for a male and 15.6 percent chance of failure for a female if they retired at age 65. (Note the accuracy down to 0.1 percent.)

I wrote a counter for the advocates of high withdrawal rates on AnalyzeNow.com, which turned out to be prophetic. Anyone who retired in 2000 and followed that author's advice for three or four years without realizing the folly would now be in dire straits indeed as the stock

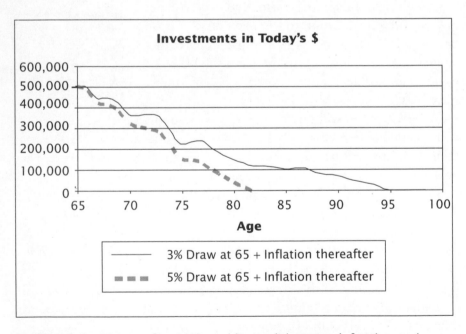

FIGURE 1.2 These safe withdrawal limits did not work for those who retired around 1965 and had 50 percent S&P 500 stocks plus 50 percent AAA-corporate bonds, 15 percent tax and about average (1.25 percent) investment costs.

Source: Dynamic program from www.analyzenow.com.

market plummeted. It would take some absolutely incredible market performance in future years to make his prophecy ring true.

Figure 1.3 shows what would have happened to an all stock portfolio for those who retired around 1965 and made large withdrawals in the first year followed by inflation adjustments thereafter.

Another planning myth is that a person can calculate an affordable spending amount at retirement and increase the amount thereafter by the amount of inflation. That is an inherent assumption even in the most expensive commercial planning methods using Monte Carlo analysis. Nevertheless, no retiree who uses a financial planner or has the capability of doing an affordability analysis would ever do such a thing. Normally, retirees should make a completely new calculation each year—not simply increase last year's budget by last year's inflation. If investments drop precipitously, even those who do not make a regular new calculation would do so after seeing their investments plummet. And conversely, those who find their investments growing far faster than predicted would certainly want to spend some of this largesse.

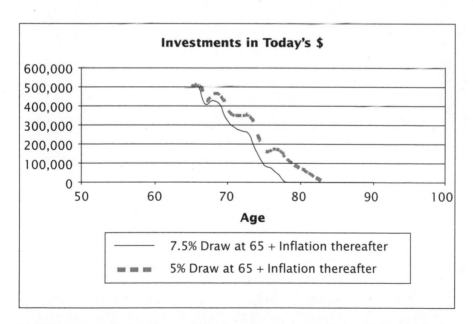

FIGURE 1.3 The highly touted safe withdrawal limits would have failed miserably for these 1965 retirees who had 100 percent of their investments in stocks (S&P 500), 15 percent tax and only 0.3 percent investment costs.
Source: Dynamic program from www.analyzenow.com.

Figure 1.4 shows the huge difference between the common assumption of constant inflation-adjusted spending and that based on making an entirely new calculation each year. It illustrates that no practical person would continue with such a spending program when seeing that investments would soon be depleted.

The planning myths do not end with the assumptions about Social Security, pensions or safe withdrawals from investments. They frequently extend to the basic assumptions. It is commonly accepted that stocks will return 10 percent to 12 percent over long periods of time. I personally don't feel that the future will be as good as the past, but independent of that, even if such growth would persist on a long-term basis, it may well have crucial dips early in your retirement when large withdrawals will take disproportionate amounts of the remaining investments. Those who retired in 1965, like my father, understood this well—as probably do those people who retired in 2000 and saw the investment world fall apart the next year.

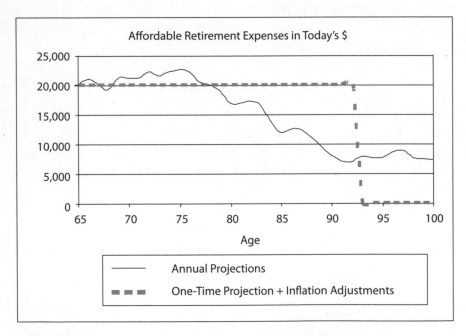

FIGURE 1.4 The contrast between the assumptions used in almost all planning programs and that which happens in real life is startling as illustrated by this typical case beginning in 1955 for $500,000 investments starting with a 45 percent stock allocation and a 1 percent reduction every year thereafter.

Source: Dynamic program from www.analyzenow.com.

Consider also that the very common assumption that inflation grows at 3 percent is based on a period in history that includes the *Great Depression*. The statistics starting shortly thereafter and extending to current times show that inflation has averaged over 4 percent, and there were periods of extraordinary inflation that were devastating to virtually all retirees.

Virtually all retirement planning programs assume that inflation will be constant throughout your retired life, even those that use Monte Carlo simulations to represent statistical variations of returns. Those that use "real" returns, that is, statistics for returns adjusted for the inflation in the same period as the return, would provide a more realistic simulation of what would have happened in the past, but still

Great Depression
the most tragic economic situation in the United States that followed the stock market collapse in October of 1929. Numerous companies failed, prices plummeted, unemployment was widespread, and many people went hungry.

offer no promise that the future will be like the past. I think that the most honest representation of the past is to review what would have happened to retirees if they retired in each successive year in the past. That is what I do in the *Dynamic Financial Planning Pro* application available at www.analyzenow.com. Then you don't have one period's return mixed with another period's inflation and the return from, say, 1933's depression loss back to back with a return from 1999's booming market (see Figure 1.5).

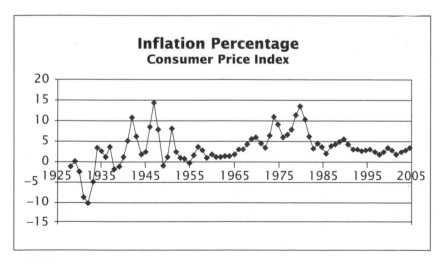

FIGURE 1.5 Inflation has been far from a constant 3 percent.
Source: Dynamic program from www.analyzenow.com.

Not all planning methods would give honest results even if both future returns and inflation were perfectly constant. (This is the most common assumption for simplified computer programs and magazine type retirement tables.) Many of the simplified programs use a gap-type analysis in which they ask you to subtract your forecasts for Social Security and pension from the amount that you would like to have for retirement income. Then they proceed to calculate how much savings you would need to fill the gap between what you want and the amount Social Security and the pension will provide.

cost-of-living adjustment (COLA)

wages or benefits may be adjusted according to an index, usually the consumer price index (CPI) or some other index that measures inflation.

Sounds simple. Only one problem though. Social Security and the amount you would like to get are inflation-adjusted. But the pension is not for most people. The equation works for those with a *cost-of-living-adjusted* (COLA) pension but not the fixed pensions that are common for non government employees. COLA pensions and expenses are apples while fixed pensions are oranges—and you cannot just add or subtract apples and oranges as everyone knows. It does not take many years for the value of the oranges to fall far behind the apples.

The other thing that very few simple programs take into account is that retirees suffer from *reverse-dollar cost averaging*. Savers generally benefit from regular deposits in volatile markets so that they effectively are buying more shares when markets are low and less shares when markets are high. That is just the thing needed to make a greater return. The poor retiree is forced to do just the opposite and so loses return.

reverse-dollar cost averaging

the opposite of dollar cost averaging. This generally adverse effect on returns is the result of regular withdrawals that cause selling more shares when prices may be down and fewer shares when prices are high. Few projection methods alert users to this common problem in retirement.

The last myth that I would like to discuss is that propagated in "get rich quick" seminars. One of the most infamous series of these was offered by a very well-known person in Seattle. He got thousands of people to attend his expensive seminars, buy his materials, and use his advisory services, never mind that his own firm could not successfully manage its own investments. He even trademarked one of his trading momentum schemes so that I cannot use the term here, but an incredible number of people fell for it. Now he is facing numerous lawsuits and criminal charges, and his clients are far poorer.

So the lesson from all of this is that if it sounds too good to be true, it likely is not true. Sound concepts for saving and investing elude the vast majority of people. Even the government does not do it well for the Social Security system. You and your employer are each docked 6.2 percent for a total of 12.4 percent. If you are not saving at least that much in addition yourself, then it is not likely that you will supplement Social Security with a comparable sum in retirement unless you are more savvy than the average individual or even our elected officials.

Put Details in Perspective

Most people that do their own planning give little thought to the kind of program that they use and the details they enter for personalized values. Yet both the methods as well as the entries may well give radically different results.

Let's consider planning methods first. There are two extreme financial planning methods: (1) those that are oversimplified and (2) those that are detailed beyond common sense. In between, you can find a few that may serve you well, but you still will have to think carefully about the inputs.

The oversimplified planning methods include those that do not ask any questions about the kind of pension (COLA or fixed) and whether the quote is a future value (escalated dollars) or present value (*today's dollars*). Most often they suggest returns that are considerably above those most people can achieve, especially in retirement when subject to reverse-dollar cost averaging. Further, they assume that all of your present investments are used for normal retirement expenses—something that is generally far from the truth.

The programs that are detailed beyond common sense are those that pretend to be able to foretell the future from the return statistics for your detailed list of investments and may even do a

today's dollars
a measure of future values that adjusts for inflation. In financial terminology, today's dollar is the present value of a future value that has been discounted at the rate of inflation. It generally takes more future dollars to buy something than it does in today's because inflation reduces the value of each future dollar.

> ## Garbage in, Garbage Out!
>
> You will be surprised by the different results you can get from different programs with the same inputs or the same program with different inputs. Make sure you question both.
> - Is your program too simple or impossibly detailed?
> - Are you confident about your inputs?
> - Are there external events that might upset your plans?
> - Put things in perspective by considering plans with alternative inputs as well.

detailed tax analysis for every future year—assuming the current provisions of our tax laws will stay the same when they change almost every year. Further, the vast majority of these programs fail to account for investment costs and assume that, despite all of the other detail, inflation had no affect on the statistics of past returns.

Of course, there is no perfect program, no matter how detailed, and even if it were perfect mathematically, it still cannot predict the future. All any program can do is to give you an estimate based on the assumptions that the economics of the future will be statistically similar to the past and that there will not be any surprise financial events later in your life. So, be sure to give your planner a quizzical look when the planner tells you that your plan has an 81.5 percent success rate! (No kidding, I've seen technical reports from financial scholars that show success rates down to the tenth of a percent.)

Therefore, I believe that the best thing to do is to use a program that is not at either end of the spectrum unless you ask the right questions and view the result with some overarching perspective. The methods in this book, though fairly simple, will not give perfect projections either, but I believe that the accompanying text will make you think about the input and thereby improve your perspective of the final result.

There are hardly any inputs to any program that do not require some thought. Consider the amount of investments that you enter. It cannot be the total of what you have already accumulated, because, both before and after retiring, you will bump into events in your life that were unplanned. In addition, if your plan did not make provisions for known replacement expenses, high inflation budget components, and terminal life expenses, then you have to assume that part of your investments will either go for such items or that your normal retirement living affordable spending projections will be overstated.

Another input that is often oversimplified is the value for a pension. The most important thing you should consider is whether you will get any significant pension at all. That is because an early change of employers will reduce whatever you vested to a very small amount both because of the formulas used to calculate pensions as well as the inflationary losses that occur between leaving the job and actually getting the pension. If it is a COLA pension, is it capped? If so, you may want to enter a slightly lower value to account for the years that inflation may exceed the cap. If it is a fixed pension, does the program specify whether it wants today's values or future values and is the quote itself in future or present dollar values.

There are probably no inputs that do not require careful consideration; but two real imponderables are life expectancy and investment growth rates. Insurance sales people are inclined to get you to consider early death. Security sales people are inclined to overstate growth prospects. From the standpoint of calculating how much you should save before retirement or how much you can spend after retiring, it is usually better to assume longer lives and lower returns.

It is very important to do more than one analysis to get the details in perspective. Almost all plans (except *Dynamic Financial Planning Pro* at www.analyzenow.com) are very sensitive to the year assumed for death. So calculate the result if you would live somewhat longer. Or, conversely, change your retirement spending rate and see how that affects the time when you exhaust your investments. You might try different returns and see how that changes your impressions and investment course. Try a different inflation rate, too. And, if your program permits, consider what will happen if the stock market tanks the year after you retire, or if already retired, tanks next year.

Planning Apathy

I know many people who have not done any retirement planning—even among some of my associates and closest friends. There are a number of reasons they cite, but I call them excuses. They blame procrastination, but after a while, a better description is apathy.

Man must sit in chair with mouth open for very long time before roast duck fly in. —An old Chinese proverb

So here are some of the excuses.

Time

The most common reason some people give is that they do not have the time to plan. Isn't this interesting? Those who have not yet retired do not have an hour or two to plan for what could easily be 30 years of retirement. They have no idea how much they should be saving. Those who have retired generally are flying by the seat of their pants and get into trouble pretty quickly as they begin overspending too early because they do not understand that a plan relates their resources to the amount they can afford.

Timing

Another common reason is that the market is too high now, so it is not a good time to start saving and investing. Many studies have shown that deposits made only at the top of market peaks over a number of years do quite well, thank you. It is not the best, but it is not a reason not to start putting some money away. Better yet, if they would start saving some out of every paycheck, sometimes they will be making deposits when the market is low and make gains that far outstrip their investments made at the high points.

Don't Know How

This is often cited by many people. They don't know enough or are too frightened to show their ignorance and call one of the lower-cost mutual fund companies like Vanguard, Fidelity Investments, T. Rowe Price, or TIAA-CREF and ask for some general investment education information. Instead, when they pass age 50, they start attending financial seminars, some advertising get rich schemes. At this point they have saved too little and are taking a chance on the advice they get unless they have thoroughly researched the speaker's background.

Savings Plan Questions

Another reason for apathy is that people do not understand their *employer's savings plan* choices. Well, even if they picked a fund at random, put a little in every fund offered, or chose some of the funds their friends liked, the chances are that over a period of years they would accumulate enough to help retirement. After getting some involvement, they would start to get interested in some of the investment topics such as those in this book and get smarter about allocations and diversification.

Numbers Not Available

Another reason is that people do not know how much their investments are worth. This may sound bizarre, but there is an element of truth to this in some cases such as real estate partnerships. But you know what? Even if they guessed at inputs for a

> **employer's savings plan**
> this may be a 401(k), 403(b) or a number of other plans that are "qualified" by the IRS as tax-deferred accounts for employees to save for retirement. These have age requirements similar to IRAs but differ in allowable contributions.

plan, they would be better off than not having a plan—and they would understand where to put their next savings deposit to come to a more rational allocation.

Had a Bad Experience

These people called a broker for some recommendations. They watched their balances fall instead of growing gloriously as forecasted by the broker. I had a similar experience; but a professional planner pulled me up short when he said individual stocks were for gambling, not investing. Index and mutual funds were for investing.

I Don't Have the Money to Save

There are not many people that are really in this boat. I've heard this story from people who interrupted the conversation with a cell phone with a camera from a child with the same. At home they had a computer on broadband and had cable for their flat-panel television. They had cars for their teenagers and let them buy numerous CDs and DVDs. More often, it is all a matter of priorities, is it not?

I'm Going to Have to Work in Retirement Anyway

That is certainly going to be a self-fulfilling promise if there ever was one. Sure, many are going to have to work because they have too little savings, but how long will their bodies hold out, their minds stay sharp, and their skills stay current? This may have worked in the agrarian economy of the last century, but will there be the equivalent of a farm with their children and grandchildren helping in the field, doing the chores, and caring for the bedridden parents?

Kids to Support

This is a tough one, but it is surprising how once you start a payroll savings plan, you really don't miss the money—and it is a tax deduction. The kids have to learn that they cannot have everything they want or that the neighbor's kids have. You have to learn that, as ugly as this sounds, your retirement takes precedence over anything other than the basic needs for the children.

I Have Children in College

This is often common with middle-aged people who have not learned that their children can earn a significant part of their college expenses, that they can get scholarships if they apply themselves, and that they can get loans and sometime grants. Further, your own employer's savings plan balance or IRA may not be a factor in determining the need for scholarship support.

My Kids Will Help Me

Your children may give you some help, but it is unlikely it will be such that you will be comfortable—either physically or emotionally. There will always be financial worries and conflicts. Also, you should ask if this will be fair to your children, who should be putting that money aside for their own retirement as well as not worry about how much to give you.

The Government Will Support Me

You better think this one out carefully. First think about what your life will be like if you have to live on Social Security and Medicaid versus the additional freedom you would have if you had some savings. Then think about what has to be inevitable: Those are cuts in benefits and services in order to bring some balance with tax revenues, especially as the number of workers compared to the elderly keeps going down and the promised benefits keep going up.

> Success is not the result of spontaneous combustion. You must first set yourself on fire. —Fred Shero, Canadian hockey player and coach

Be Aware of the Environment

Confidence is the feeling you have before you really understand the problem.

—Ogden Nash

Before you start planning anything, it is important to have some understanding about the environment you will face. For example, a building contractor tries to be aware of materials availability, loan interest rate trends, trade union effects on costs, and so on. An airplane manufacturer works hard to project airline market trends, fuel prices, technology improvements, political factors that may affect trade or landing rights, and many other things. The government tries to project things that might influence tax receipts as well as its own future expense growth.

As individuals, we too must develop some perspective about the future. This may relate to personal things such as our health, housing needs, expenses, taxes, inflation, potential growth of our savings, and other family members' financial situations. In this part of the book, I will try and stimulate your thinking about long-range elements that have a major effect on the financial environment that you likely will encounter in retirement.

Demographic Shifts

We are talking big changes here: People are living longer, and the elderly part of our population is increasing both as a consequence of greater

25

The Increasing Burden of the Elderly ...

... part of the population is falling on a proportionately smaller working population. This is how the burden comes down:

- **Past.** When Social Security began, there were five workers for each Social Security beneficiary. Few people lived to 65.
- **Present.** We now have 3.4 workers for each Social Security beneficiary and generous provisions for health care of longer living elderly.
- **Future.** Before 2030, demographers tell us that there will be only 2.1 workers for each Social Security beneficiary. The tax burden will be enormous.

longevity as well as a low birthrate. Virtually unlimited illegal immigration has strained major cities along our southern borders. All of these things have profound implications, especially economically. Most notable right now is the increase in health care costs for older people that currently consume about one-third of the federal budget. In 10 years, that will grow to almost half the federal budget according to the Congressional Budget Office.

Most notable, only a decade or two in the future, we will see many older people with inadequate savings. The net result is that the elderly cohort will have considerably less to spend, and a good part of their income will come from support of a proportionately smaller working population.

When Social Security was started, there were five workers for each person who was over 65. By the time the younger people in our workforce today reach retirement, there likely will be two workers for each person over 65 instead of three workers today. If we look ahead, this translates to each working person having to carry 50 percent more of the current welfare burden, which itself will be larger considering the growth of Social Security, Medicare, Medicaid, tax credits for the poor, public housing, and all of the other welfare for the elderly.

This phenomenon is not limited to the United States. Europe has already faced up to part of the problem by beginning to cut benefits for the elderly and increase what are already debilitating taxes. Germany is increasing its value added tax to 19 percent from 16 percent and has a 28-hour workweek which helps keep the elderly employed, never mind the fact that the short workweek is a serious competitive disadvantage internationally. Japan employs many of its "retired" executives as instructors for young employees, which helps keep some of their elderly employed. Many countries that previously encouraged lower birth rates are now offering incentives for families to produce more children. When foreign countries have these problems, the prices of their exported goods go up thereby exacerbating inflation here.

Although the birthrate of our nation is low, it is not so among certain parts of the population. In particular, the Spanish American cohort has a much higher than average birthrate that nevertheless fails to compensate for the birthrate decline in the major part of the population. Combine this with large life-expectancy growth and you end up with more and more people whose parents are alive when they retire and, later, whose children also retire. Unexpected financial events in any one of these generations, retired or not, can easily affect the others as the financially challenged seek family support for their troubles.

The fact that we don't require immigrants to learn English hurts cities such as my own—a Seattle suburb—even though we are far removed from the border. Our local schools have to provide translators for 85 languages or otherwise teach students in their native tongues. These students have to be bussed to their special classes. Communication with their parents is very difficult. Letters to their homes have to be written in their native languages. This is a major financial burden on the schools and reduces funds for teaching those who learned English before they came to school.

Demise of Pensions

Employers are becoming increasingly unwilling to assume the financial obligations and risk of funding pensions. The working environment for Americans has changed appreciably. In 1980, 84 percent of workers in large and medium sized companies were earning a pension. Twenty-five years later, only 33 percent are included. Employers that were once paternalistic have shifted from the concept that *employees are our most important asset* to an unbridled drive for profit and executive compensation. The labor force is now more of a commodity to be purchased at the least possible cost—often from suppliers who are overseas.

Workers have been forced to shift their allegiance from an employer to a trade or profession. Pensions are largely determined by multiplying a percentage such as 1 to 2 percent times wages late in employment and multiplied again by the amount of cumulative service in a company. Those who stayed with the same employer and retired after 30 years of service might expect to get a pension that could be anywhere from 30 percent to 60 percent of their working wages for retirement. This, together with Social Security, would almost replace their working wages. However, with the exception of the large number of public workers supported by our taxes, pensions are rapidly disappearing leaving retirees from industry or commerce to rely on Social Security and personal savings.

Then there is the ever-increasing number of employer pension trusts that were inadequately funded. The government has an insurance program using the Pension Benefit Guaranty Corporation (PBGC), but for many, especially those who are forced to terminate employment before age 65, the PBGC pays only a fraction of what would otherwise have been their pensions.

There is one very large segment of employees who may not have to worry about their pensions. Those are long-term federal government employees and military personnel who have cost-of-living-adjusted (COLA) pensions. Not to be left behind are the ever-increasing number of state and local government employees many of which also have COLA pensions. The fly in the ointment here, however, is that a number of states have promised far more than their tax receipts may ultimately provide. Unlike the federal government, the state governments often have to operate on a balanced budget as opposed to deficit financing.

The amount of underfunding of pension obligations is improving in this bull market. Some estimates had put private pension trusts at almost a $500 billion shortfall. The public pension promises are at least that much as well and may well be twice the deficit of the private sector. This just cannot go on this way for another generation without major changes in the plans and their funding sources (see Figure 2.1).

One way or the other, the working population is going to have to pay some part of the pension problem with increased taxes to support the additional welfare costs or the PBGC's deficits. The rest of the burden will fall on those whose pensions end up being far short of the amounts they once envisioned.

There are numerous examples of reduced benefits today. Most prominent are a large number of airline pilots who have been hit three times: once from the loss of their pension due to airline bankruptcy; second from the maximum insured amount the PBGC will pay, which is

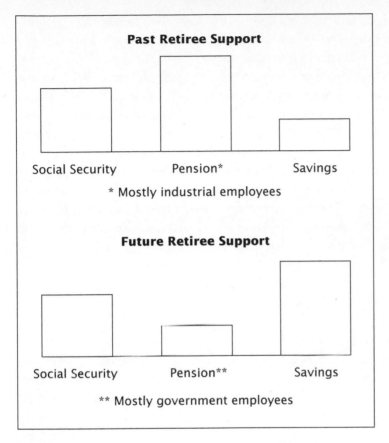

FIGURE 2.1 Future retirees will have to depend on personal savings to a much larger degree than generations in the past.

about one-fourth of the amount that they would have otherwise received; and third from the severe reduction in that maximum because pilots are forced to retire at age 60, five years before they would even be eligible for the insured maximum amount. The net result is that many retired pilots will get only about 10 percent of the pension that they had planned on.

There are serious concerns about funding the PBGC. Its obligations are already greater than the funds it can collect from insurance premiums paid by firms that offer pensions. As more firms opt out of pension programs, the revenue of the PBGC falls, thereby exacerbating the problem for its existing obligations as well as covering the overhead of the organization itself. There is little doubt that the PBGC will have to increase the cost of its insurance premiums that, in turn, will discourage more firms from offering pensions. Even that is unlikely to be enough. Congress most likely will have to bail out the PBGC with huge sums. This will add more to the tax burdens of everyone.

Bad as these problems may seem, they pale in comparison to the current wave of companies abandoning pension plans and freezing current values. When pension plans are frozen, the residual pension is very small unless the worker is already very near retirement. That is because the pensions are based on what has already been vested and have no gain from future years of service nor wage growth. The pension formulas are such that the last few years of employment increase pensions far more than earlier years. Frozen pensions are particularly devastating to older workers who can't possibly save enough to make up for what they will lose in pension benefits.

Unbridled Consumerism

The desire to have the latest and best products has driven Americans to spend all they have and more. This is encouraged by massive advertisements on TV and popular media. Our children *must* have the latest electronics, media, and other goods that all of their classmates have. A high priority for the younger generation is audio equipment. Most certainly we are going to see huge numbers of people who will have difficulty hearing after spending their youth constantly listening to loud music with earphones or from riding in cars with speakers playing so loudly that the thump, thump, thump can be heard a block away.

Not only is cell phone and iPod ownership on their way to being universal among children and young adults, but their use seems never-ending, often leaving little time for more productive pursuits. Parents exercise little restraint and *must* have the most recent developments in technology themselves. These are accompanied by very large phone, cable, and Internet costs that would shock those a generation ago. Flat panel TVs and gas-guzzling SUVs take money at the expense of deposits to retirement accounts for their old age.

When we stay in Park City, Utah, we have an annual invasion of New Yorkers and folks from Hollywood for the Sundance Film Festival. All of these people have a cell phone glued to their ears and are talking loudly to drown out the voices of those nearby whether in a bus, grocery store, or just walking down the street. Many of us doubt whether there is really a person on the other end. Taxi drivers pick up people using their phones at 2:00 A.M. and wonder who would be willing to listen at 4:00 A.M. in New York.

Parents looking to save money should consider whether their children really need cell phones. Presumably the parents want to be able to call if their children's school is in a lockdown or if they are late coming home. For such purposes, they may not need a camera on the phone, text messaging, or e-mail service. When television is commonly available on cell phones, the additional service charges may be another burden.

High-technology products are a boon to their industries and an everlasting outpouring of money from their users. There is a repetitive "need" to repair and upgrade. New generations of devices are smaller and have more features. Software gets to be more comprehensive. The stack of CDs, DVDs, and downloads never ceases to grow, much to the delight of their producers and much to the chagrin of parents at bill-paying time or those watching their spouses fritter away money that should be going to savings.

We Gotta Have It!

We have got to have it all, now! At the expense of retirement savings deposits! Here is just a partial list of the high-tech stuff we are buying:

- Large flat-panel TVs
- Cable or dish for TV reception
- Multiple computers
- Computer games
- Multiple cell phones
- Cell phone camera
- Cell phone games
- Portable DVD players
- WiFi
- High-speed Internet
- Personal digital assistant (PDAs)
- PDA games
- iPods, Zunes, and other kinds of downloadable music players
- Game boxes and games
- Theater sound systems
- Subwoofers for the car
- Digital cameras
- Global positioning devices (GPS)
- And so on

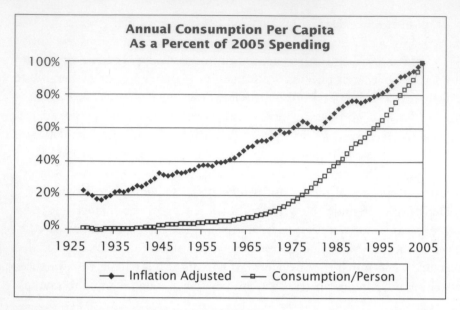

FIGURE 2.2   Consumption is increasing at an alarming rate. Unless this stops, personal debts will continue to soar.

Source: Department of Commerce, Bureau of Economic Analysis, www.bea.gov.

The increased spending is growing at a staggering rate. In the last few years it is been 2.2 percent per year faster than inflation and has been accelerating (see Figure 2.2). Unless this abates, the average person will continue to save nothing and personal *debt* will soar.

Large Homes

The standard size home for any economic class has grown enormously in the last few decades. Grandma's house was about 1,100 square feet only 55 years ago. The average now exceeds 2,300 square feet—and it is increasing every year. In part, this is driven by the desire to live like the Joneses, but also by easy credit, often with no money down and/or temporarily low interest rates. Incredibly, there are more new retirees buying larger homes than those who are (or should be) downsizing. This is not only contrary to good economic sense, the average household size has gone from 3.3 to 2.6 persons per house and the number of single owners has gone from 16 to 27 percent. These McMansion homes are augmented by an increasing number of second homes, often in the form of a time-share—generally a decidedly poor investment.

In recent years, the rapid increase in home values has made home ownership equivalent to retirement investment in many people's minds. This logic helps justify the need to have special rooms for special purposes or additional space for just-in-case needs. Massive kitchens and master suites are now the objective of many families. Family, media, and great rooms do not seem to eliminate the need for living rooms. Large garages add to the need for larger lots. The net result is massive home debt with an illusive promise of great wealth. Since 1975, homes have appreciated only 2 percent above inflation—and that is hardly enough to cover the additional property tax and maintenance cost of a larger home.

> **adjustable-rate mortgages (ARMs)**
> a mortgage with an interest rate that is adjusted periodically, often starting with a very low teaser rate that is soon followed by adjustments according to some interest index.

Those who have taken on *adjustable-rate mortgages* (ARMs) may be the first to realize the trouble they are in. As interest rates increase, so do payments. Over a couple of years, it is certainly possible that mortgage rates could increase by 2 percent. A 2 percent rate hike can increase the payments by 30 percent or more. Those who cannot make the payments will lose it all—both house and credit rating.

Those with ARMs that reset every year at 2.75 percent above one-year Treasury bonds have probably already felt some of the sting. Those with "option" ARMS may be in the worst trouble of all. This kind of mortgage lets the borrower opt a very low interest payment that is below the actual interest payment due on the mortgage. The difference between these two payment values is added to the mortgage balance every month. Many of these mortgages are now "upside down," meaning that the loan value exceeds the value of the house.

Of course, property taxes and maintenance costs increase with house size. A house that has twice the dimensions of another house is likely to have four times the cost to furnish and maintain. And bigger closets beg for more clothes and possessions.

TIP

Is a large home now worth poverty in retirement? It is a question you are likely to ask a number of times in your life.

But the real financial trouble may come when it is necessary to sell the house. If the price is lower than the mortgage value, you will have to pay money to get the house off your hands. Many people have made good money selling houses—but it all depends on market values at the time and whether any buyers are interested in the architecture that you thought so quaint when you made the purchase or had it built.

Multiple Automobiles

The one-car family is obsolete. Not only must each spouse have a vehicle, but so do most high school seniors. Parking lots in schools are jammed and ever expanding. The cars of students usually exceed the number of cars for the high school staffs. Many seniors would not be seen dead on a school bus. The car has become a status symbol for American youth, and parents seem supportive, not resistant to this in spite of often staggering insurance, gas, and maintenance costs. Children with cars give the parents more freedom themselves because they no longer have the burden of driving the youth from one activity to another.

Do you have a teenager who wants to drive? Brace yourself for doubling your insurance costs if the teenager is a boy or about 50 percent more if a girl. It gets worse after their first (very common) accident report and unbearable after the next (also common). It is important to check with several auto insurers to find out what is required to reduce the costs such as special driver's education courses, raising deductibles or eliminating collision coverage. Of course, some of these things mean that you bear the financial risk instead of the insurer. And while you want the teenager to get a clunker with a broken radio, the teenager wants a supercharged new convertible with thousand-watt speakers.

There are now almost three times as many cars per adult as there were in 1960. Of course, things like a large house and multiple automobiles come at the expense of reduced saving for the parents' retirement, never mind that retirement could well mean 30 years of living on little savings.

When I was young, most families could not afford more than one car. Children drove the family car, not one of their own. Later on, I was a

---

NOTE

Many modern high school children would not be caught dead in a school bus or let their parents drive them.

highly compensated executive, but I still saved money by buying two-year old cars for more than 20 years. My boss, the company president, drove his inexpensive Chevy until it practically fell apart. That was exceeded only by the chairman's obvious penchant for saving money by driving his Ford long after the bottom of the trunk rusted out and had to be replaced. Of course, things have changed a lot. Now senior executives have large expensive cars of their own that inspire protégés to try and keep up. The difference in cost between then and now is staggering.

Record Debts

If you want to find the value of money, go and try and borrow some. —Benjamin Franklin

We are building massive *debts*, not just from large homes, multiple automobiles, or unbridled consumerism. Our debts include our personal debts of all kinds, state debt, national debt, and international trade balance—all at record levels and all of which influence the costs of things we buy and our taxes. Even worse are the promised, but unfunded, benefits of Social Security, Medicare, Medicaid, pension trusts, government employee pensions at both state and federal levels as well as obligations of the government's Pension Benefit Guaranty Corporation.

debt
an obligation to someone else usually backed by collateral. A debt is equivalent to a negative investment, often at a rate that is higher than most people would get from their portfolios.

Lawrence Kotlikoff, Boston University economist, estimates that the government would have to either double taxes or cut Social Security and Medicare benefits by two-thirds to solve the unfunded problems of just these two programs. Others report smaller, but still devastating impacts.

Virtually everything is leveraged with the hope that the future will be better than the present. The financial industry and government often act as if debts do not have to be paid. Perhaps the government can stave off their debts by continually draining the tax payers. But we not only have to pay the taxes, we have to make our personal debt payments or lose what we have. In spite of that, both the government and security dealers would have you believe that consumerism will defy the demographic changes, international outsourcing will not affect job and wage growth, economic growth will continue unabated, and interest rates, inflation and taxes will remain low.

It is possible for this whole deck of debt cards to tumble all at about the same time, although it is not likely to happen in the near future as long as people continue to spend and pay their mortgages. A large dose of inflation also ameliorates debts at the expense of lenders; but debts mean leverage that can either enhance during a boom or destroy during a recession. Therefore, we could have serious trouble right now should a significant set back in real estate prices occur. There will be many people with home loans that exceed the price they paid, and those who have little equity in their home will either have to abandon them or pay money to the buyer instead of the other way around.

It is not just home borrowers with ARMs who will be in trouble, but they will be at the leading edge. The lenders, banks, mortgage brokers, purchasers of mortgage debts, and hedge funds that speculate in mortgages may all tumble together creating a problem requiring another government bail out to solve banking system problems. Fidelity Investments, the largest provider of employer savings plans, reports that 20 percent of these plans have outstanding loans. Those who lose jobs will have the seemingly impossible problem of paying off these savings plan debts and their associated penalties.

Virtually All Debts at Record Levels

Virtually every type of debt is at a record level as we leverage our homes, business, and country expecting that the future economy will save us.

- Medicare
- Medicaid
- Social Security
- National debt
- Credit cards and mortgages
- International trade
- State and state pensions
- Pension trusts Pension Benefit Guaranty Corp.
- 401(k) retirement savings plan loans
- State health care unfunded obligations

Low Savings

The flip side of spending is savings. What you do not consume, you save. What you save is not consumed. For the last three decades, the national savings rate has steadily declined to the point where it was less than zero in 2005. The last time this happened was during the Great Depression. The national savings rate from 1940 to 1985 averaged 10 percent of disposable income. Ten percent was the advice my dad gave me. This was enough to sustain the relatively small number of retirees at that time. But they retired later (if at all), lived shorter lives, *and* had significant pensions to sustain them. Think about it: We have to save more than 10 percent now—a *lot* more considering lower pensions and longer lives (see Figure 2.3)!

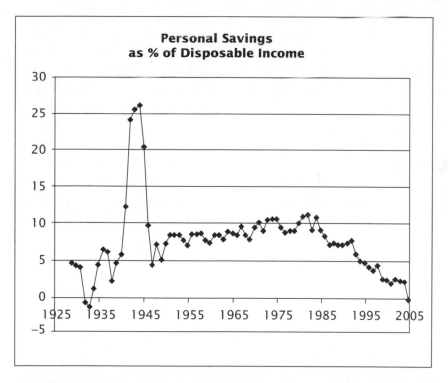

FIGURE 2.3 The loss of savings over the last 20 years has been so great that it is now virtually impossible to recover—especially considering the great reduction in pensions.

Source: Department of Commerce, Bureau of Economic Analysis, www.bea.gov.

Low savings rates have gone on for such a long period now that it would be virtually impossible to increase personal savings balances to the point where the average person could achieve a savings level suitable for our times, much less the lower amount that was required to accumulate in previous generations.

Let's suppose that all we wanted to do was get the same total investment as if we had averaged 10 percent savings from 1985 to 2025. We use the actual national savings rate for the years between 1985 and 2005 and then see what the savings rate would have to be from 2006 to 2025 in order to give the same total investment as if 10 percent had been saved the entire period.

To get the same total savings in 2025 as saving 10 percent of wages every year, everyone would have to start saving 23 percent of their income from 2006 until 2025 if invested at 8 percent interest and wage growth was 3 percent.

Even at that level, the general population would not have enough savings to be able to offset the decline in pensions. It is absurd to pretend that pensions will once again promise to replace 30 percent to 60 percent of the average worker's income. Therefore, employees would have to save a *lot* more than 23 percent of their income! Starting instantly!

Now let's suppose that the general population had to save an average of 20 percent of their income over their lifetimes in order to both get average historical savings plus compensate for the loss of pensions. Then those people would have to save 60 percent of their income from 2006 to 2025 to compensate for the miserable savings rate from 1985 to 2005. After paying income taxes, payroll taxes, and health insurance costs, there would hardly be enough left for hamburgers at McDonald's.

TIP

Obviously, the general population is not going to start saving 23 percent and precious few souls will be able to save 60 percent of their income from 2005 to 2025, so we are just going to brace ourselves for many people having to work almost until their death. Only those with significant savings or government workers (who most likely will still have pensions) will escape this fate.

Escalating Health Care

Lots of things are driving health costs to increase much faster than inflation. People are living longer as a consequence of better medical care early in life. In turn, the longer lives exacerbate the need for medical care late in life. Better medical care requires more costly diagnostic equipment, facilities, and trained personnel, particularly specialists. Hip and knee replacements are now common and even heart and lung transplants are not unusual. *Medicare and Medicaid* have paperwork that often requires more people in the back office than those actually applying the care. Visits to the doctor increase with age to the point where those in their 80s average a visit almost every month, but the largest costs may well come in the final days of life as extreme measures become more common and both medical personnel and relatives try and add some more time to the life of a dying person.

Medicare and Medicaid
these are government insurance programs to partially assist people with medical bills. Medicare is automatic for 65 year olds who register with the Social Security Administration. Medicaid is free care for the indigent.

Then there is the ever increasing cost of drugs. Expensive drugs help the elderly to live longer or more comfortably. Some drugs are so exotic that costs of well over a thousand dollars a month still do not reduce their use below the drug industry's ability to produce them. The drug costs may be covered by health insurance; but retirees seldom get little help for eye, ear, and teeth care. These costs are often in the thousands for the elderly. Most dental costs are uninsured, and many dentists make larger incomes than the average physician.

Long-term care costs continue to escalate as costs for care, service, facilities, and insurance grow. Many people bought *long-term care insurance* believing that they would pay a fixed rate until the need for long-term care. Insurance companies, however, have increased their rates to the point where many people had to abandon their policies without recovering past premium payments.

long-term care insurance
an insurance policy to cover living and medical expenses in an approved facility (and sometimes home care). Important considerations are amount per day, possible premium increases, inflation protection, home care alternative, total days covered, and pages of fine print.

The shame of all of this is that health care costs could come down dramatically if more people (1) exercised and (2) lost weight. The evidence of these two factors is overwhelming.

There is a growing shortage of geriatric doctors ahead of us, which will exacerbate both the costs and availability of medical care. Before you reach 65 or try to find a new retirement community, you had better find out if any available doctors will take Medicare patients. Many will not. You might find yourself in a "heal thyself" mode using www.TelaDoc.com or www.WebMD.com.

Hopefully, you won't have to do this; but you may have to search quite a while for someone to help the elderly. Neighbors may have some suggestions. Or you can try to locate a doctor using www.CareManager.org, a site run by the National Association of Professional Geriatric Care Managers. Often, if you get started with a doctor before you are 65, the doctor will keep you as a patient after you enroll in Medicare. But that is not always the case as a number of our friends have found. It is not a great feeling when they hear that they are too old to be worth caring for.

Health Care Costs Increasing

There are many reasons why health care costs are increasing faster than inflation and will continue to do so.

People living longer
- Proportion of older people growing.
- Older people need more care.

Medical research developments
- New highly specialized drugs.
- New high-tech equipment and facilities.

Uninsured care increasing
- Long-term care for middle income.
- Dental care for most retirees.
- Ear and eye care for many retirees.

Political forces
- Government paperwork and regulations.
- Proportionately fewer people paying income tax.

Geriatric doctor shortage growing
- Geriatrics not financially attractive field now.
- Medicare limits time per patient & technology.
- Allowable Medicare charges will have to increase.

Misleading Wealth Conceptions

There are those that say the savings rate does not matter. This argument was voiced when investments grew so much during the late 1990s. In an effort to keep consumerism going, some economists said that people did not have to add to savings because investments had grown so much on their own. Then the market fell, and we did not hear from these economists for several years. Using the same logic, they should have complained that the market drop meant people had a large negative saving rate.

Now these same economists have again come out of their scholarly cubicles with the same story based on the theory that home prices will continue to grow, and equity growth will be recovered sometime in the future as people downsize their homes or take out additional debt using their homes as collateral. Never mind that homes as "investments" are equivalent to illiquid highly leveraged long-term securities that would be shunned by the average person if they had a name other than "home." No broker will sell stock with a margin account with so little collateral.

> **downsizing**
> selling a more expensive home and buying a less expensive one in order to get cash and less expensive operating costs. This is often a better alternative than getting another loan on home equity.

Further, not everyone owns a home, or certainly not the behemoths that would be great for *downsizing*. Many still live in apartments and others have little, if any, equity.

Another major wealth misconception is that the baby boomers are going to inherit millions of dollars each. Such statements assume that current assets are going to continue at a significant growth rate, the money will all be left to heirs, and, importantly, the wealth will be evenly distributed. Nothing is likely to be further from the truth, especially the even distribution. The top 10 percent of the population owns about 70 percent of the nation's net worth while the bottom 50 percent owns less than 3 percent. I don't expect that my children will get anything from Bill or Melinda Gates, Warren Buffett, or all of those overcompensated CEOs. If you are one of the very few who is in line for a big inheritance, and you will invest and spend your personal massive good fortune, you don't need to read any further.

These kind of statistics from those trying to rationalize that low savings rates are acceptable are like the man who went swimming in a stream and drowned in an average of one inch of water. For a while the

> **NOTE**
>
> "Feel-good" economists won't put food on the table of retirees.

average of investments was high, in another period the *average* of home prices was high, and in still another period the *average* inheritance was large. Just like the stream that goes up and down in various seasons, many will drown despite these *average* proclamations.

Reduced Welfare

Although welfare benefit reductions are likely to be small because of political pressures, there will certainly be efforts to contain costs, especially medical benefits. If the same thing happens in the United States as in Europe and Canada, this will translate to long waits for care as well as more stringent constraints on the type of care that may be given. Look for greater family support until your turn for government assistance is available.

AARP

formerly called the American Association of Retired Persons, but now just known by its initials. This is an organization that lobbies for the elderly as well as offers newsletters, insurance, and other products.

Inflation constraints for Social Security adjustments and higher taxes on or for Social Security benefits are virtual certainties. Worse yet must be the constraints on Medicare and Medicaid benefits. At some point, the working populace will support political positions to make large cuts in current promised benefits, but it will be at a time when the elderly population also has a major voice in politics, and organizations such as *AARP* and the Seniors Coalition will vigorously oppose such actions.

Many of the baby boomers and following generations believe that they will not get any Social Security benefits. That casual attitude will turn to serious opposition to Social Security benefit reductions as they get near retirement and realize that their current savings levels will be far short of what they will need for retirement.

The federal government will continue to try and unload more of its health care responsibilities on the individual states. This is already a problem with Medicaid, but it is just the beginning. There may come a time when many people select the state where they will retire based on the welfare available.

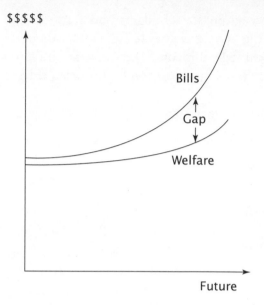

FIGURE 2.4 The government's promises for the benefits of future retirees are so over committed that it is impractical, if not impossible, to fulfill. The gap between people's actual expenses and welfare like Social Security and Medicare will increase.

Watch for Medicare to increase the age when benefits start from the current age of 65 to 67. This alone might force many people to delay early retirement because they will have very large medical insurance costs between the time they retire and age 67. The gap, illustrated in Figure 2.4, will be unbearable for many.

Significantly Higher Taxes

> The taxpayer: That's someone who works for the federal government but doesn't have to take the civil service examination.
> —Ronald Reagan

Since it is unlikely that the government will make huge reductions in promised future welfare benefits, much less current spending outlays, it is very likely that tax rates will increase significantly at both federal and state levels—especially for higher-income people who have little weight at the ballot box. The current promises for Social Security and Medicare benefits are unsustainable and therefore need much greater tax support as well as the need to offload some of the responsibilities to states.

These offloads will further strain state budgets and result in the need for higher tax revenues at the state level as well. Remember there are a lot of taxes other than state and federal income tax. Consider building permits, business and occupancy taxes, cigarette and liquor taxes, driver's

Lots of Ways to Tax

There are many ways the government gets money from us.

- Federal income tax
- State income tax
- Capital gains tax
- Tax on interest and dividends
- Tax to fund Social Security
- Tax on Social Security income
- Medicare tax
- Alternative minimum tax
- Estate tax
- Trust tax
- Gift tax
- Phase out of deductions and exemptions
- Sales tax
- Property tax
- Licenses and permits
- Excise taxes
- Gas tax, vehicle tax, and road tolls
- Gas guzzler tax
- Cigarette and liquor taxes
- Telephone tax
- Cable tax
- Power tax
- Water tax
- Corporate tax
- Inventory tax
- Use tax
- Workers compensation
- Employment tax
- Unemployment tax
- Duties and tariffs
- Import tax and export tax
- Compulsory insurance
- Hotel tax
- Entertainment tax

licenses, fuel taxes, inheritance taxes, luxury taxes, licenses of all kinds, Medicare tax, property tax, road tolls, sales taxes, unemployment tax, federal excise tax, telephone taxes, utility taxes, vehicle registration, and workers compensation tax, and so forth.

Unless you have a lot of gray hair like me, you probably don't remember how high tax rates have been in the past. During World War II the highest tax bracket was 90 percent. During much of my working career, I was in a 50 percent tax bracket. Of course, there were many more things we could do in those days than now to get allowable deductions to income. Now it is very hard to get much of a deduction for income tax. The combination of limited deductions, higher state and federal income tax rates, and almost uncountable hidden taxes provide some of the help needed to satisfy the federal and state obligations. However, higher taxes will hurt all of the other economic aspects such as personal savings, personal and industrial debt reduction, job growth, and the like.

You can get an interesting perspective of both federal and state taxes from the Tax Foundation at www.taxfoundation.org, which shows both historical and sources of taxes as a percent of income. Taxes now take about 30 percent of our income. I have read that the Government Accounting Office estimates that if federal spending isn't cut by 60 percent, the government will have to increase taxes by 100 percent to balance the budget by 2040.

Inflation Reduces Past Debts

One way to make debt seem smaller is to reduce the value of currency. Not only does it make the debt seem smaller, say in relation to the gross domestic product (GDP), it makes it possible to pay the debt with less valuable dollars.

As an example, during the first 10 years of my retirement that occurred in a period of less than average inflation, the value of the dollar reduced by almost 30 percent. So the holders of bonds, mortgages, and loans effectively took a beating both by getting cheap dollars back for interest payments and effectively 30 percent less principal on a ten-year note or bond.

The government debt will be the major beneficiary of inflation. If welfare programs are constrained so that they do not increase as fast as inflation, they too will be effectively reduced, probably with less vocal opposition because the average person does not understand that inflation compounds just as investments compound.

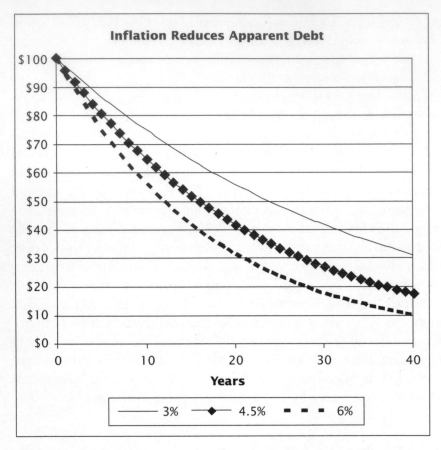

Inflation Reduces Apparent Debt

Legend: 3%   4.5%   6%

X-axis: Years

FIGURE 2.5 Inflation compounds, but unlike compound interest, it destroys value exponentially.

To illustrate the power of inflation, let's look at an example (see Figure 2.5). The commonly quoted historical 3 percent per year inflation includes the devastating Great Depression. For most history after that, inflation has averaged closer to 4.5 percent. With 4.5 percent inflation, every dollar loses the following amount of purchasing power: 36 percent in 10 years, 59 percent in 20 years, 73 percent in 30 years, 83 percent in 40 years and 89 percent in 50 years. So, if you bought some of the government's debt with a 30-year Treasury bond, the principal you would get at the end of the period would have lost 73 percent of its purchasing power!

Sustained Economic Boom Unlikely

> The election of Hoover ... should result in continued prosperity for 1929. —Financial statistician and founder of the Babson Institute, one year before the Great Depression

Considering all of the aforementioned conditions, it seems unlikely that the ultimate solution will come from a steady state of doing more of what we are already doing. Still, that is the argument used by both the government and the financial industry. Remember, though, that both of these sectors rely on such notions. The government needs industrial and personal economic activity (i.e., employment and spending) to get the taxes for its commitments. Industry needs people to buy its goods. The financial industry needs an upbeat view of the future to sell stocks, one of the most profitable of its security transactions.

In fact, such conditions may well go on for a significant period of time. Of course, they also continue to dig a deeper hole due to overspending, increased international trade deficits, national and state debts, industrial debt, personal debts, and increased unfunded liabilities for Social Security, Medicare, Medicaid, and government pensions. Even more people nearing retirement will be far short of funds to sustain them. When the country wakes up to reality, the needed changes will be even more devastating.

Nevertheless, those who recognize these things and take actions during the good times will benefit greatly. By comparison, these few are likely to end up comparatively wealthy. If the consumerism binge ends too early, it will be hard to make significant returns on any savings. Consumerism keeps the factories engorged, employment full, tax burdens low, and the stock market strong.

What Wall Street and the Feds Want You to Believe

Let the good times roll!
- GDP will go everlastingly up.
- Stocks will continue to go up.
- Interest will stay low.
- Inflation will stay low.
- Tax rates will stay low.

War Won't Save the Economy this Time

World War II helped bring us out of the Great Depression. People were fully employed, made sacrifices, had rationing instead of consumerism, and saved more money than ever before. People saved a lot because (1) there was not much to spend money on; (2) all able-bodied people were earning wages; (3) the separation of husbands and wives by thousands of miles meant fewer children to support; and (4) it was considered patriotic to invest in savings bonds, an almost mandatory act in many parts of industry.

War is an unlikely solution to our current economic problems in this age not only because we are already essentially fully employed, but also because of reduced national resolve for things such as patriotism, nationalism, and particularly, a war. Political parties can hardly agree on anything, much less who our enemy is or might be. It is extraordinarily difficult to maintain policies that protect our country from subversive activities as well as to keep troublemakers from crossing our borders. Defense spending used to be the biggest federal budget item. Now it is a very small percentage of our expenditures which are largely committed to social programs. So many people have become dependent on government for their sustenance that they pose a formidable voting block opposed to anything that would reduce their benefits.

Of course, another major factor is that the enemy today does not require massive defense plants employing those who would otherwise be homemakers. Most spouses must be in the workforce now just to support their families to say nothing of the cultural change where many more women have working career goals.

It is inevitable that terrorism will continue to be a part of our future. It not only affects where we go abroad now, it may well effect where we go inside our country in the future. A significant number of suicide bombers in shopping malls could spell the end of casual shopping within large multistore complexes. Bombing of transportation hubs, communication facilities, power distribution grids and many other things could bring irreparable damage to many businesses that depend on daily commerce.

The politicizing of the proper reactions to a terrorist threat both within our country and the world as a whole makes us all the more vulnerable by impeding policies and programs that would lead to more protective actions. Religious zealots will not be silent; academia will continue to challenge conventional wisdom; the media will continue

> **NOTE**
>
> It is unlikely that a modern worldwide war would produce the same kind of economic solutions as provided by Rosie the Riveter in World War II.

substituting biased editorials and headlines for objective reporting, and politicians will still display highly polarized positions to attract attention and votes independent of some overall thought of what might be best for our nation in an environment where public safety is truly at stake.

Count on Energy Problems

Our energy problems will not go away—at least in our lifetimes. Our dependence on foreign oil is too great and our political process too weak to permit mobilizing solutions. It is virtually impossible to develop domestic oil fields, increase refineries, build dams, construct power plants, lay pipelines, string high power lines, open coalmines, dispose of depleted uranium, and the like.

Industrial and commercial growth has always demanded more energy. We have seen it here, and we are starting to see it in developing countries. China by itself is going to be a massive user of energy—even bigger than the United States. India is going to add to the problems.

These developing countries are just at the forefront of people being able to enjoy the mobility of automobile ownership. I can remember being in both China and the former Soviet Union in the 1980s. Then the only cars on the streets were those of high level officials and the streets were nearly empty. Now the major cities have some reasonable amount of traffic. It will not be long until urban areas start having traffic jams. There will be more competition for the mideastern oil supplies as well as those from all over the world. Do you think that is going to reduce the price of oil?

Of course, conservation will help, but the implementation is slow and often costly. High-efficiency furnaces have numerous sensors and more parts than lower-efficiency units and take more maintenance. Hybrid automobiles still have a long way to go to justify their additional costs even at today's gasoline prices. One of the more cost-effective changes has been in home insulation requirements, but the trend to much larger homes trumps the efficiency gains.

For a number of years, Boeing had a focus on helping this nation with its energy problems more directly than just more fuel efficient airplanes. This had its origin with George Stoner, a Boeing vice president and very forward looking person who also got Boeing into the space business. We formed a new company, and the chairman asked me to head it. I reported to a special board that, in turn, reported to the chairman.

Our mission was to help the country solve the energy problems that we saw at the time. Twenty-five years have passed since then and the problems that we foresaw have deepened. Part of this is a political problem, but most of it is simply the result of more people and more affluence, not just in this country but worldwide. Either more people or more affluence by themselves would increase the demand for energy, but we have both. This causes a compounding demand for conventional and easily obtained natural resources. However, these resources have a finite limit and practical restraints on their extraction.

Our company's research work was spread over many technologies from generating electrical power with solar cells to nuclear power improvements. Our developmental work was funded mostly by the federal government with some help from private Boeing and energy company funds. During my tenure, we had lots of exciting projects.

We built the largest windmills ever made. They had blades the size of a football field. We installed several of these experimental units in the windiest parts of the country. Though the technology was successful, commercialization was impractical because of the cost relative to oil or gas and because windmills do not produce power when the wind does not blow—even in the windiest parts of the country. Therefore, windmills often require energy storage facilities which are another expense and not always practical.

We worked with producers of solar power cells to make improvements, both in reducing the unit costs of the cells as well as alternative ways of using the cells including focusing the solar energy and maneuvering the arrays to follow the sun. We worked on projects that varied from home roof top units to acres of cells for utility companies. None proved practical although we were able to use some of the technology in our company's space programs. Dust and rain do not degrade the sensors in space vehicles. They can see the sun twenty-four hours a day. The power requirements are relatively small. And high costs are tolerable in space applications.

We had projects that tried to exploit hydrocarbon technologies even going back to one of the earliest coal gasification projects in Scotland. We looked at lower cost ways to extract oil from tar sands. We did the systems engineering on the deepest oil platform in the North Sea for the British National Petroleum Company and others including an oil platform that had to withstand the shifting sea-bottom sediment in the Mississippi delta for Shell Oil. We did the engineering for the offshore gas wells in the loneliest spot in the world, the seas off the west coast of Australia. We managed the Strategic Petroleum Reserve for the Department of Energy. We built water treatment equipment for many of the western coal fired generating plants in the west. We invested in trash separation and burning. Our van fleet ran on natural gas.

We had extensive efforts in nuclear power projects. Under contract to the Department of Energy we compared the French breeder reactor to the Westinghouse design. We participated in research on the glassification of nuclear waste. Our construction unit, together with other large contractors, worked on nuclear power plants and fuel processing. We developed centrifuge enrichment machines for the national facilities at Oak Ridge, Tennessee.

We worked on hydroelectric projects. We developed and built the power control system for the Bonneville dams. We did research work on more efficient ways to transmit high-voltage electricity including cryogenic means. And we studied harnessing energy from the ocean tides and other areas I've now forgotten.

We explored the use of hydrogen as a commercial energy source because we knew a lot about it from our space work on hydrogen powered rockets. We concluded that the practical problems of handling hydrogen would make it economically infeasible unless the cost of other forms of energy would increase many fold. Promoters of hydrogen power show little understanding of the real problems with hydrogen. This is a very dangerous gas, and it is not free. It takes energy to produce hydrogen. It takes more energy to transport it. And it takes incredibly sophisticated equipment to use it. In gaseous and liquid form, pumps, valves and pip-ing have to be ultra clean, pressure vessels extraordinarily well protected, and users highly trained.

Boeing's efforts lost motivation after George Stoner died and I left and took on a bigger job of running the majority of Boeing's military and space work. It was a time when the nuclear industry was taking a beating, the Washington Power Supply System's bonds failed, and our Board of Directors, which included some prominent oil industry executives, de-cided that the opportunities for Boeing in the energy business were small compared to airplane, military and space efforts. It was also a time when our commercial airplane company needed cash and our military space and arm was tripling in size.

I know firsthand many of the problems that alternative energy sources face. It is not pretty. Biomass and alcohol will offer some relief, but this will not come cheap and is subject to climatic changes and agri-cultural subsidies. We can get some energy from the wind and maybe some from the sun that will reduce hydrocarbon burning, but these are partial, not total, solutions. Few people realize the practicalities of getting good sites and storing the energy when the wind is not blowing or the sun not shining.

The countries that are basing their basic power supplies on nuclear power plants are going to have far fewer problems with uninterrupted and predictable power costs than countries like our own. It is my judg-ment that the generation of those who blindly opposed nuclear power with roadblock after roadblock will ultimately be replaced by those who see nuclear power as the primary answer to the earth's greenhouse effects and its subsequent warming. Then the long process of building can be-gin. Until then, look to many periods with energy shortages and high prices that will add to economic woes.

NOTE

Our political inertia is going to be a drag on practical new energy sources for generations of time.

Saving Will Save Individuals

I maintain that personal savings should be the first priority for those individuals who want to rise above this mess. It is going to take a lot of other things too, but only the foolish will not examine their own situation and try to find ways to save well over 15 percent of their income when they are young. If this sounds high, consider that you and your employer have been saving 12.4 percent for Social Security since you started working—and that is insufficient to meet promised benefits. Those who have already saved little and are already middle aged may have to more than double or triple these amounts if they expect to retire at a relatively normal age.

Still, every age group has lots of opportunities to save more once the importance is understood. The best thing to do is to make an analysis with the appendixes in this book or with the help of a computer program or professional. Many people will not do this. They have the ostrich head-in-the-sand mentality. The net result is that they are likely to live like ostriches, scratching out a bare existence with little prospect of a varied and useful retirement.

The amount you should save while working or retired is dependent on many factors including your aspirations in retirement, how long you might live, returns you may get on investments, inflation and tax rates. Of course, any analysis, even with a very comprehensive computer program or with the help of the best professional, is only an estimate because no one can foresee the future and whatever surprises it may bring—including financial demands from elderly parents or adult children. Nevertheless, an analysis will give you an anchor point, and, if you do a new analysis each year, you will get closer to the truth each time. It is not hard. You can do a quite respectable job with the simplified methods in the appendices of this book.

Saving more money is going to come slowly for the spendthrift, debt-laden Joneses, so they are going to have to look elsewhere for their meager retirement livelihood (see Figure 2.6).

Money is better than poverty, if only for financial reasons.
—Woody Allen

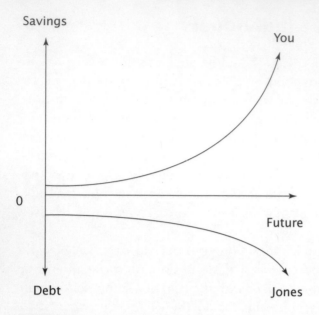

FIGURE 2.6 By spending a little less now, your retirement is going to be lots better than the Joneses who will have to work longer and live largely off Social Security—which has a shaky future that politicians are unwilling to face.

Pre-Retirement Planning

Go directly to Chapter 5 if you are already retired. However, if you have adult children, you may want to review this chapter and recommend to them that they do this as well to see if they are really on their way to being prepared for retirement.

N umerous and very detailed planning programs exist that depend on many factors to make projections for your future retirement. I am going to present you with a very simple method that is quite suitable for most people who are not very close to their retirement already.

If you are close to retiring, then it is important to switch to post-retirement planning in this book or elsewhere. In fact, it is a very good practice to spend a year or so trying to live on the budget from post-retirement planning to verify that you are comfortable with that lifestyle for what might otherwise be decades of impoverishment. *After* you have done that, it is a lot safer to tell the boss and your friends that you are going to retire.

There are several reasons that I have chosen a simple method here. Of course, one reason is that this is a book about getting started. The most important reason is that you are more likely to do the analysis right now and several times more in the future as you get closer to your anticipated retirement age.

If you have Microsoft Excel, you can download the *Simplified Financial Planner Plus* at www.analyzenow.com. This detailed but simplified program gives some perspective about how stock and bond market variations can affect your future as well as account for some future lump sum expenses that you may see as part of your retirement. The method that I describe in this chapter is far better than most of the simplified programs that you can download from financial sites on the Internet but not as comprehensive as the Simplified Financial Planner Plus.

You could go straight to the Pre-Retirement Worksheet in Appendix A of this book and start filling in the blanks to help determine how much you should really be saving, but I suggest that you skim the material in this part to see if any of the subjects pertain to your situation. I'll be very much surprised if they don't.

Deciding How Much You Need

You can be young without money but you can't be old without it.
—Tennessee Williams

Various professional retirement consultants suggest that in retirement you need 70 percent to 80 percent of your current income. Some say 100 percent. Certainly you would want to lean toward 100 percent of your current expenses if you are an empty-nester and you exclude the amount you are saving from "income." Still, 100 percent may understate the amount somewhat because higher potential lifestyles with more free time will beckon you later in life. As you age and your income increases, so does your image of the income that you think you need in retirement. Start with 100 percent for want of a better number, especially if you are quite far away from retirement. If you are currently paying full college expenses for several children or supporting a large mortgage that will be paid before you retire, you may be satisfied with a lower goal. But you want to think carefully about the difference.

It is very hard for someone who is not retired to know how much money will be needed for retirement. You have to relate to what you think you need in retirement versus what you are spending now. When you are young, it is even difficult to do if you examine your current budget carefully for things that you might give up, not need, or want to add. That is why we are going to work in terms of retirement income as a percent of your current wages.

The projection in Appendix A, the Pre-Retirement Worksheet, is in terms of today's dollar values so that you don't have to try and estimate what future dollars may be worth today. People are often misled by the financial industry's description of future growth. The fact is that you should be viewing the projections in terms of what a dollar buys today, not the much smaller amount it will buy after years of inflation. You may remember grandparents or even parents' comments about what one dollar used to buy. In a few decades, you will be able to tell similar stories.

Working in today's dollars is no great trick. We simply use current values of Social Security, which are always stated in today's dollars. To analyze the growth of investments, we use "real" returns that are approximately the anticipated actual return minus inflation. Technically, real return is (Actual return minus Inflation) divided by (1 plus Inflation), and that is what is used to generate the tables here. Fixed pensions are more difficult to relate to today's dollars, but we will show you how to do that when we get there.

Another good reason to look at pre-retirement projections as related to income instead of expenses is that income ignores the subject of income tax. You will be comparing pretax income both before and after retiring. No one can predict precise income tax rates for the future, so if you are a long way from retiring, a detailed analysis does not necessarily give you a better result. Still, when you get closer to retirement, it is better to look at after-tax results by using our post-retirement analysis or to use a more detailed computer method such as *Simplified Financial Planner Plus* at www.analyzenow.com.

I ask you to record your values in a copy of the Pre-Retirement Worksheet in Appendix A. Save each year's analysis so that years later you can look back at your original projections and see the values you used as well as the results. Of course, you should record later year entries on their own separate pages.

The Mysteries of Social Security

If you are a legal worker in the United States with a Social Security number, your wages will be docked 6.2 percent of your gross wages up to a maximum limit, which changes every year. In 2006, the maximum is $94,200. Your employer also contributes 6.2 percent to the Internal Revenue Service (IRS) so that the total is 12.4 percent. It turns out that this is not enough to support the benefits promised by the Social Security Administration (SSA), so at some point in the future either the benefits have to come down and/or the Social Security taxes have to go up.

Your ultimate benefits depend on your working wage history. Higher-income workers get more Social Security than lower-income workers; but this is not proportional to income. The higher-income values are capped and the lower-income values get proportionately more benefit per dollar earned while employed.

Every year you get a report from the SSA listing (1) the benefit you will get at age 62; (2) the benefit you will get at your *full-retirement age* (FRA) that is between 65 and 67 depending on your birth date, and (3) the benefit at age 70. Age 62 is the earliest you can start the benefit and 70 is usually the latest. Naturally, you get more, a lot more, at age 70. All values are in today's dollars and are based on your past earnings history and an extrapolation of your future earnings.

full-retirement age (FRA)

this is a Social Security reference age that now depends on your birth date. It used to be known as your normal retirement age when it was fixed at age 65 but now extends all the way to age 67 for younger generations. The change was one of what ultimately will be many ways the government reduces its unsupportable obligations to the elderly.

• *If you are a long way from retiring,* You might simply enter your FRA benefit from your latest report. If married, enter the FRA benefit for the higher-income spouse plus the larger of (1) the other spouse's FRA benefitor (2) 50 percent of the higher-income spouse's benefit. So a married couple would have a total value that is at least 1.5 times the higher FRA benefit if they both retire at their FRA ages.

If you have misplaced the annual report on your Social Security forecast, you can get another by submitting Form SSA-7004, Request for Social Security Statement. I've found that the SSA tries hard to be responsive. However, if you go to your local SSA office, you may have some substantial wait before your turn arrives.

• *Close to retirement or want to be more accurate?* I'm going to describe the rules as they stand now; but things change, so check with the Social Security Administration (SSA) for cases not in your annual report from the SSA. Contact the SSA at 1-800-772-1213 or access rules at www.ssa.gov. A useful website for unusual conditions is www.socialsecurity.gov/retirement/retirechartred.htm.

- *If a working spouse starts Social Security at age 62.* The FRA benefit is reduced 20 percent if born before 1938, and 30 percent if born after 1959. If a working spouse starts Social Security after the full retirement age, the FRA benefit is increased by 0.4583 percent for each month over the FRA benefit if born before 1935 or 0.6667 percent per month if born after 1942. For retirement or birth years in between, see the SSA for your particular case.

- *A nonworking spouse.* A nonworking spouse can get up to 50 percent of the working spouse's benefit up to a maximum of the working spouse's FRA benefit if the nonworking spouse retires at the nonworking spouse's own FRA. This is true even if the working spouse has not yet started taking Social Security but has passed the working spouse's FRA. If the working spouse chooses to delay Social Security past the working spouse's FRA, then the working spouse should go the SSA and "file and suspend."

  If a nonworking spouse starts benefits earlier than the nonworking spouse's FRA, then the amount a nonworking spouse can get is less than 50 percent of the higher-income spouse's FRA benefit. As a guide, if the nonworking spouse starts Social Security before the nonworking spouse's FRA, say starts draws at age 62, then the nonworking spouse will get between 37.5 percent (if born before 1938) and 32.5 percent (if born after 1959) of the working spouse's FRA Social Security.

- *A low-income spouse.* A low-income spouse will get the greater of (1) the amount credited for the low income, or (2) the amount calculated for a nonworking spouse based on the high-income spouse's benefits.

- *A low-income spouse that is older than the high-income spouse.* This person can apply for benefits at her/his FRA, and file again when the high-income spouse reaches his/her FRA to get the additional benefit.

- *Upon death of either spouse.* The surviving spouse will get the greater of (1) 100 percent of the amount the survivor was previously getting, or (2) 100 percent of the amount the other spouse was getting—but not both.

- *What if spouses start taking Social Security in different years or if one or both retire before age 62?* Don't worry about this now because we will account for this later when you make your own calculations using the Pre-Retirement Worksheet in Appendix A. In essence, we take money from your investments to cover the gap between retirement ages and the ages to start Social Security. However, you will have to worry about it a lot if you have not saved enough money to cover the gap.

- *Optimum age(s) to start Social Security.* This is not an easy decision considering all of the various rules and your own personal circumstances. You can get some substantial help from Chapter 4, Final Commitment to Retire, and Appendix B, Age to Start Social Security.

Medicare and Medicaid

These are also Social Security programs. Medicare starts at age 65 and Medicaid only applies to the indigent. When you sign up for Medicare at 65, you automatically get Part A, which covers hospital insurance but will be faced with choices for Part B, which largely covers doctor bills and Part D, which partially covers drugs. If you are still employed at 65 and have an employer sponsored group policy, you can sign up for Part B within a month after you retire.

Your choices here may depend on the kind of private or group "Medigap" policy you have for personal medical insurance. Most people, however, elect Medicare's Part B plus a Medigap policy. You can compare various Medigap policies with some Internet research and materials from the Social Security Administration that force Medigap insurers to classify their policies within a limited number of options labeled A through L. For the same level of care, prices can be very different. Also, compare alternatives with health maintenance organizations (HMOs) or preferred provider organizations (PPOs)—either of which can limit your choice of doctors.

Medicare Premium Increases. *Medicare Part B's* costs have been increasing at a rate far faster than the basic inflation adjustment rates for Social Security itself. Congress not only just increased the rates appreciably, it made the rate increase larger for higher-income people, thus abandoning the previous principle of a common program for all citizens. After the automatic deduction for Part B, Social Security checks will lag inflation increases appreciably. In fact, the programmed increases are so large that our family will be getting lower net amounts from our Social Security checks in each successive year of the next few years as the phase-in of higher Medicare rates begins.

Social Security Handbook Social Security Online provides a great wealth of Social Security information in the *Social Security Handbook.* You can read it for yourself at www.ssa.gov/OP_Home/ handbook/handbook-toc.html.

Medicare Part B coverage of most doctors' services. Its costs are deducted from Social Security benefits. Until recently everyone had the same monthly amount, but in the future Part B costs will be higher for higher-income people.

Pension Mysteries

When I started working, most employees expected to get a significant pension, probably more than their Social Security. That is no longer the case. Far fewer employers now offer pensions. Instead, they have shifted the responsibilities for retirement saving to the employees themselves— who it turns out, are doing a very bad job of putting enough money aside.

Traditional Pensions

Traditional pensions depend on years of service. But even employers who offer a pension end up having to pay out significantly less than the promises foretold on their employee's benefit forecasts. That is because many employees leave their employer long before they have vested any significant amount. Pensions usually are based on a formula such as:

(1% to 2%) × (Years of service) × (Highest wages over some period)

So, employees who change employers before retirement get hurt in two ways: (1) They have not accumulated many years of service; and (2) they miss the wage growth of subsequent years. Let's illustrate with an example comparing results for John and Bill who have the same wage history but significant pension differences. See how John gets almost 50 percent more even though both have exactly the same pension formula.

John stays with the employer until retirement after 30 years of service and has wage growth of 4 percent per year. He began work at $20,000 a year and ended at $65,000. His annual pension, assuming 1.5 percent per year would be about $29,250. On the other hand, Bill started at the same wages and had the same wage growth but quit after 10 years at a wage of $29,600. Bill's annual pension would be only $4,440. Now let's assume that Bill goes to another employer, starts at $29,600, has the same wage growth, and quits after 10 more years with a wage of $43,800. He gets a pension from that employer (using the same formula) of $6,570. Finally, he goes to work for a third employer at $43,800 and stays there for 10 more years before retiring with a final wage of $65,000, the same wage that John had just before retiring. Bill's pension from his third job is $9,750. Bill's total of three pensions is $4,440 plus $6,570 plus $9,750, which is $20,760. That is far less than John's $29,250 even though he got a pension using the same formula from three different jobs.

Social Security May Reduce the Amount of a Pension   In practice, both John and Bill are not very likely to have earned even that much because many employers subtract an amount from the pension calculation equal to one half of the expected Social Security. Employers often feel it is their right to subtract one-half of Social Security from a pension because they paid one-half of Social Security's cost. Both John and Bill had the same wage history, so suppose that they each had earned enough for $15,000 per year Social Security. John's final pension would then be $29,250 − 0.5 × $15,000 = $21,750. That in itself is a big hit. If Bill's employer also subtracted one-half of Social Security, he'd get virtually no pension for his first two jobs and $2,250 from the third job.

It Can Be Worse   Job hopping may well mean going to an employer with no pension plan. That is the most devastating blow to a person who spent many previous years in firms that promised pensions. All of a sudden, the retiree is expected to retire on a tiny residual pension and non-existent savings from those previous years of employment.

TIP

So, unless you are really sure that you are going to be a long-term employee, you may not want to use the full quote from your employer in a retirement calculation. Further consider that your employer's pension trust may go belly up with insufficient insurance from the Pension Benefit Guaranty Corporation.

What Kind of Quote Do You Have?   It will be either a quote of what you have vested so far or a projection of what your pension would be at certain retirement ages. The latter requires an employer's assumption of your wage growth which might be, for example 4 percent per year. It is important to know which kind of quote you are getting because many programs want the present value of the pension (i.e., today's dollar value), not the forecasted future dollars. Ask you pension administrator whether the quote (1) just represents your current vested value; (2) a projection based on wage growth until retirement in future dollar values; or (3) today's dollar value of the amount projected at retirement. Most retirement programs want you to enter the value of (3), but the method in Appendix A, Pre-Retirement Worksheet, makes an adjustment for the value in (2) as well.

Cash Balance Plans

This type of retirement plan is rapidly replacing the traditional pension. These plans are a benefit to employers and therefore a reduced benefit for employees when compared to traditional retirement plans, especially for long-time employees. Cash balance plans help those who change jobs often because employees can take a lump sum when they leave a job. On the other hand, they offer little incentive to stay with an employer. You can get a pension or a lump sum when you retire, but the values are likely to be quite a bit less than traditional pensions.

Severance Package Pensions

If you will have a pension that comes from a severance package that adds to the pension you would otherwise get, the additional amount from the severance agreement will be subject to Social Security and Medicare tax deductions until you die. Therefore, in any analysis including the one in the Pre-Retirement Worksheet in Appendix A, you should reduce the severance input by at least 7.65 percent.

COLA Pensions

COLA pensions (cost-of-living-adjusted pensions) are much more valuable than fixed pensions because over a 20- or 30-year period they can increase payments by 100 percent to 150 percent or more. That is why we have to adjust the value of a fixed pension in a retirement plan so that you don't spend too much too early. Roughly, a fixed pension is worth only the payment value times your age divided by 100. (See Appendix E, Pre-Retirement Assumptions.) COLA pensions are very unusual in industrial or commercial businesses, but often are the basis for government pensions such as those for retired military personnel. COLA pensions are almost always quoted in today's values, just like Social Security quotes, but you still have to know whether the quote is based on just your current years of service or a projection of future years of employment.

COLA Caps   Many COLA pensions and virtually all COLA immediate annuities have a cap that limits the amount that will be paid when inflation is very high. For example, there might be a 3 percent cap. This means that if inflation goes over 3 percent, the payments will not increase above 3 percent. A 3 percent cap would suggest that you might only want to use about two-thirds of your COLA quote in a pre-retirement planning analysis. A 5 percent cap could justify using only 80 percent of your COLA quote while a 10 percent cap would mean you might use only 95 percent of the COLA quote.

Figure 3.1 shows the power of COLA caps. That is why financial institutions apply them.

You should consider multiplying a capped COLA quote by one of the percentages in Figure 3.2 if your COLA pension has a cap that limits the inflation adjustment depending on life expectancy in retirement.

> **TIP**
>
> If you are using a program that does not ask whether you have a fixed or a COLA pension, or does not ask whether the quote you have for a fixed pension is in today's dollars or future dollars, there is a very high probability that the program will misuse the pension value you enter.

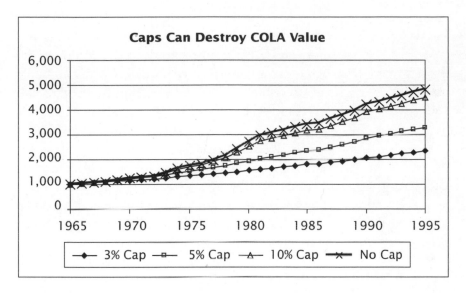

FIGURE 3.1 This shows the growth of a $1,000 COLA pension that started in 1965 and the reductions caused by capped inflation adjustments.

**COLA Benefit
as a Percent of Uncapped Pensions**

Life Expectancy	COLA Caps			
	3% Cap	5% Cap	10% Cap	No Cap
10	93%	97%	100%	100%
20	71%	82%	96%	100%
30	60%	75%	95%	100%

FIGURE 3.2 The table shows the sum of all of the capped values divided by the sum of the uncapped values based on scenarios starting in 1965.

You Need Reserves, Too

It is extraordinarily important to have savings reserves—that is, money that is readily available for both unforeseen financial surprises that occur in everyone's life as well as for those high value items that you try not to buy on credit. The amount you need for reserves may not be hard to estimate but can be very hard to accumulate.

Even though an event is relatively far in the future, you can use its value in today's dollars because the math we are using assumes that the prices will increase as fast as the after-tax return you can make on the savings. This is fairly simple to do if you could use deferred tax accounts, but few deferred tax accounts are assessable for the kind of things that will use reserves, especially if you are younger than age 59½.

after-tax basis
the value of something as if you had to pay taxes on it today. If wages, it is your gross pay less state and federal income tax. If it is a deferred tax investment, it is the total amount less the taxes that you would pay if you liquidated the account now.

So, as a practical matter, we are talking about growing taxable investments at the same rate as inflation. Since the money has to be readily available, it should not be in real estate which is not liquid nor stocks which are volatile and could be down when you need the money. That means you need some short-term fixed income accounts that will grow to offset inflation—and that is where the rub comes. To do much better in retirement on an *after-tax basis* than inflation is not always easy, especially for those who know little about investing.

Reserves for Unknowns

It is difficult to know how much to set aside for surprise events, but I suggest that it should be at least 10 percent of the current balance of your investments unless your assets are already at stratospherically high values. The truth is that most people should have either more than 10 percent or have the strength to vehemently say, "No," even to a relative who is pleading for help.

I say this because some of the largest assaults on what should have been retirement funds come from relatives—either elderly parents who have run out of money or adult children who are going through some kind of crisis and have no easy way to get money. It is really hard to say no in these circumstances as I and most people I know can attest.

If 10 percent of your investments is not enough to be able to support you for three to six months if you lose your job, you should first work to accumulate emergency reserves at least at that level.

Reserves for unknowns should not be in deferred tax accounts. That is because there is always some kind of a penalty for withdrawals before age 59½. A simple withdrawal will cost you both the income taxes on the withdrawal as well as a 10 percent penalty. If you borrow the money from your employer's savings plans, there are onerous rules that apply to paying off the loan.

Reserves for Known Future Events

Almost every working person has some known large expenses in the future. Perhaps they are college expenses for children, the marriage of a daughter, or building an extension on the house. These things consume savings that would otherwise go into retirement accounts, so they should not be counted in a calculation to determine how much you can otherwise spend in retirement.

Replacement Reserves

Replacement reserves are something that most young workers have to ignore because they are just starting their first major expenditures in getting a household together. This is not something that more mature workers can ignore. The math is simple as shown in Chapter 6, Implementing Your Plan, and Appendix H, Replacement Reserves Worksheet. The results can be discouraging. However, when you are getting close to retirement or in retirement, you don't want to have to buy almost anything on credit. You want to *make* interest, not *pay* interest to someone else.

We are talking about building up savings to replace high-value items like automobiles or the roof on your house. Let's take the roof as an example: Say that it will cost $20,000 to replace a roof in today's dollar values, and that its expected life is 20 years. That means its annual cost is $20,000 divided by 20 or $1,000 per year. If the roof is already 15 years old, you should have $15,000 in an account and be saving $1,000 a year. You should

replacement reserves
cash or other investments set aside to replace major items that wear out and have to be replaced infrequently such as a roof or automobile.

subtract the $15,000 from the total of your investments for retirement because that money cannot be used for normal retirement expenses. (If you are past 59½, you could take the money from a deferred tax account, but you will also have to take out the money to pay the tax on the withdrawal.) On the other hand, the $1,000 is part of your normal budget, not as a payment to someone else, but as a payment to your savings.

When you know that you are going to have a series of such replacements, such as automobiles for the rest of your foreseeable life, then for the purpose of a pre-retirement calculation, you need only subtract the amount that you should have already saved from your investments, and not the cost of every future car. That is because the budget that you finally calculate for retirement will have to provide for the annual payments (to yourself instead of an automobile credit company) for as long as you have automobiles.

This sounds simple in theory, but young people in particular have real trouble coping with replacement reserves. One thing they can do to gradually work into a more responsible position over a long period of time is to try and put down perhaps one-third of the purchase price and save one-third of the annual amount that they should be saving for a full replacement. Then, when buying the next car years later, they should try to put down perhaps two-thirds of the purchase price and save two-thirds of the annual amount that they should be saving for a full replacement. Finally, when it comes time to get the third replacement car they may be in a position to make the purchase entirely from savings and save the full annual amount each subsequent year.

When young people and older poor savers make reserve calculations for the first time, they often conclude that they are going to have to work longer and save more. Still, it is better to learn this before you give up your job than after you have retired and try to find the money for that roof and replacing an automobile.

Accounting for Inflation   You should redo your replacement reserve calculation each year using the current prices of the items to be replaced. This will increase the amount you must save each year by about the amount of inflation. The amount you have already saved should also have grown, depending on your return for the year. Nevertheless, the amount of the replacement reserve you should use for retirement planning should be the result of the new calculation. (See the illustration in Appendix H.)

Reserves for Gaps

Those who are planning on retiring before taking Social Security or pension payments will also have to use some of their savings to cover the gap period where they have no Social Security and/or pension. We make that adjustment in the projection method that is included in Appendix A: Pre-Retirement Worksheet. However, if you are using one of those oversimplified methods from a magazine or the Internet, you have to account for these with a reserve.

Savings Contributions to Retirement

You save for many things, one of which is retirement. The first thing you have to do is to decide how much of your savings is for the normal expenses of retirement. By normal expenses, we mean the kind of things you would pay for regularly every week, month, quarter or year, but not large singular expenses like buying a time-share, automobile, or money you have saved for a new roof. We will help you account for normal retirement expenses in the Pre-Retirement Worksheet in Appendix A.

For many people, most of their retirement income will come from savings that have been invested and grown over the years. Be forewarned that projections of the future of investments are very speculative, so you want to be cautious about the values you use for return (growth) assumptions in any program. In most retirement programs that I've seen (and I've seen a lot), the suggested return entries are much greater than most people actually attained in the past, and there is little reason to expect that returns in the future will be a lot higher than they have in the past.

In the simplified approach here, we are going to assume that before and after retiring you maintain a *nominal* allocation of 50 percent stocks, 40 percent bonds, and 10 percent money markets and incur typical mutual fund and/or broker costs. (See Appendix E, Pre-Retirement Assumptions, for related investment cost and other assumptions.) However, we are going to give you a choice of using the *nominal* results from this analytical model or increasing returns or decreasing returns by 1 percent.

There are several ways that you might get 1 percent higher returns. For example, you could use mutual funds that averaged 0.5 percent less costs than the 1 percent assumed for the nominal case and get another 0.5 percent increase either by increasing the stock allocation to 60 percent or by splitting the stocks into part large company stocks (used for nominal case) and small company stocks.

Assuming a larger stock allocation, of course, increases the risk. And you want to keep in mind that we are already assuming that the future will be the same as the past. This could turn out to be an optimistic assumption if it is likely that tax rates increase to respond to a reduction in workers relative to the elderly as well as the massive government debt and unfunded future Social Security and Medicare benefits. The case for 1 percent less than nominal returns is persuasive if you believe the economy will turn down or if your investment costs are higher than 1 percent.

In other words, from an historical perspective, if you used 1 percent less return, you would either be a conservative investor or less bullish about the future economy. If you would use 1 percent more return, you would be an aggressive investor by historical averages. You should note the substantial difference between being conservative and aggressive, but remember there is also a significant difference in risk.

There are those that are willing to take a lot more risk, particularly when young, but as they get near retirement, even the vast majority of those people become more conservative. Review Appendix E, Pre-Retirement Assumptions and see if you really want to add more than 1 percent to the nominal case in light of impacts from higher taxes, aging population, low savings, and diversion of public resources to health care.

From risk considerations, many people may have a somewhat higher stock allocation early in life and a lower allocation later in life. *Dynamic Financial Planning Pro*—which you can download from www.analyzenow.com—allows you to vary allocations throughout your life, but considering all of the other imponderables, you might do just as well with the simple assumptions used here, especially if you are more than ten years from retiring.

Saving for Things Other Than Retirement?

The savings part of the Pre-Retirement Worksheet in Appendix A, steps 17 through 25, is intended to give users an estimate of retirement income from (1) current retirement investments and (2) future annual savings for retirement. If you are saving for college expenses, that part of your total savings does not belong in your entries. The same this is true if you have already accumulated some reserves for emergencies or replacements, so we provide step 18 to remind you to take those out of the analysis. If step 18 is larger than the investments in step 17, you exceed the intent of this kind of analysis. If you want to do an analysis accounting for saving for other things at the same time as saving for normal retirement expenses, I suggest that you use either *Simplified Financial Planner Plus* or *Dynamic Financial Planning Pro* from AnalyzeNow.com. They show you a way to reduce what might otherwise be overburdening savings while you are young.

Contribution from Part-Time Work

Many people nearing retirement recognize that they are far short of the savings needed to provide a comfortable retirement. Therefore, they often decide to assume that they will work part-time for a few years in retirement, or perhaps one spouse will continue to work and the other retire completely. Either way, the idea should be to add to the savings and not just supplement retirement in the years they are working.

Part-time work is not the panacea many believe is the substitute for too little savings. You will see that to be the case when you do an analysis in Appendix A, Pre-Retirement Worksheet. For part-time work to be effective, you need both high part-time wages and many years of part-time work.

The reason for this is simple. You don't have the benefit of compounding interest working for you as you did when you put away money many years before retiring. This is exacerbated when people work part-time to earn money for a special purpose. Once spent on something else, there is nothing left of the part-time work contribution for other things later in retirement.

Of course, there are other factors that reduce the value of part-time work. It is subject to Social Security, Medicare and income tax. There may well be other deductions too. Further, if you started Social Security before your full-retirement age (FRA), you may get a penalty tax until you get to the FRA. You have to account for these things in your plan.

Don't be so overconfident that you can work part-time most of your retired life. There are far too many things that can happen to your health, energy, and employability. Furthermore, you will see others your age doing the kind of activities you wished that you had saved enough to do as well.

Summarizing Results

In the Pre-Retirement Worksheet presented in Appendix A, we total the contributions from Social Security, pensions, part-time work and savings. Each contribution is stated as a percent of your current gross wages. That makes it easy to relate the results to the income you now have.

But we don't stop there. There is a final adjustment needed if you plan on stopping work before starting Social Security or a pension. This is often neglected in very simple retirement planning programs.

Retiring early leaves a gap that has to be filled until Social Security and pensions are available. Further, retirees often benefit significantly by delaying Social Security until age 70 while they would like to retire earlier.

The theory behind the gap adjustment in the Pre-Retirement Worksheet is that you will be able to invest gap savings in retirement at a rate that equals inflation. Since the kind of investments needed to fill the gaps must be liquid and not volatile, this requires prudent investment allocations.

Further, when you finally get to the point where you are near retirement, you will want to make sure that your savings are sufficient to fund the gaps as well as to support whatever you consider appropriate reserves at the time. Otherwise, you will have to retire nearer the years when you can take Social Security and your pension(s).

It is possible that you have a more complex case than the analysis in this book offers. For a more refined estimate that may be better tailored for the kind of expenses, debt, investments, and retirement ages for your own situation, see one of the programs from www.analyzenow.com, which you can download to determine if the extra detail is warranted in your case.

Final Commitment to Retire

ife is full of important decisions and choices, such as whether to get married, have children, or get a divorce. Add to these your retirement date. There is a lot of finality associated with the act of retiring, and it is a difficult one to reverse without some significant injury.

Going back to work after retiring is difficult in many respects. It is difficult to get into the swing of things again. You forget how much energy it takes. It is hard to find work when you are older, and your experience may be obsolete. The available jobs may pay significantly less and benefits may be nonexistent.

For all of these reasons, it is really important to keep the considerations very confidential between you and your spouse until you are *really* sure you want to make the commitment and the retirement date is *not very far away.* Telegraphing your thoughts on this subject may get you emotionally committed and too embarrassed to reverse the decision. Furthermore, your employer may forgo a raise or promotion that might make a significant difference either in your decision or the amount of retirement benefits that you will ultimately receive.

However, sometimes you may have to act fast, as when an employer offers what appears to be a tasty severance package to encourage a large group of people to retire voluntarily. *Beware.* Those packages are designed to better help the employer rather than you. Nevertheless, it could be in your own best interest, too, depending on the circumstances. We will show you how to find out.

> The best time to think about your retirement is before the boss does. —Author unknown

Should I Retire Now?

There are two basic situations:

1. You make the decision yourself.
2. Your employer makes the decision for you in which case you then have to decide whether to retire or to seek work elsewhere.

In either case, you want to be very careful and consider your retirement decision on as broad a front as you can. You must take into account financial matters. Also, you must think through the activities that you will pursue, your role in the home (especially if the other spouse continues to work), what you will do with your house, the location in which you intend to live, associations with relatives and old friends, your medical support, and so forth.

Perhaps the more difficult retirement decisions come if your employer decides that he no longer needs your services. Then you have a lot of work trying to compare potential jobs with other employers and perhaps the alternative of retiring prematurely.

It makes it easier if your employer offers a severance package that is attractive, but it is a lot more difficult to know what to do when the employer offers a severance package with a voluntary choice to take the severance package and leave or reject the severance package and stay. You know that there may still be a chance that the employer may terminate your service, and you will have missed the opportunity to benefit from what might have been attractive in retrospect.

There may be choices within a severance package. For example, you may be offered a lifetime annuity *or* a lump sum. A lump sum requires that you manage the investment using principles such as in this book, while an *annuity* offers lifetime income. The annuity itself may have some choices such as a choice of 0 percent, 50 percent, 75 percent, or 100 percent for your surviving spouse.

Whether you take a lump sum or lifetime payments, severance income is subject to 6.2 percent Social Security tax and 1.45 percent Medicare tax while your regular pension or other savings plans are not. These taxes are usually much more painful from an annuity than from a lump sum because it is likely that the combination of your earnings for the year plus the lump sum will be over the maximum amount that is taxable in one year—so part of your severance pay would then escape the Social Security tax. Further, if these tax rates increase, you will be subject to the higher rates in future years if you choose an annuity.

When insurance salespeople hear about a group severance package offer, they salivate and are quick to encourage you to take the lump sum (foregoing any survivor option) and use the money to buy an annuity from them and/or a life insurance policy to assist the survivor. Be cautious because their offer may not account for an after-tax comparison of your choices, particularly when the taxes increase abruptly after the exclusion period ends.

Such situations call for trying to make analytical comparisons of your alternatives. You may want to make the financial comparisons using the materials in this book or the Excel programs on www.analyzenow.com or you may need some *professional help*. Either way, you want to compare both quantitative elements such as your finances as well as quality of life issues. Make a column for each alternative and start the list. There should be rows to compare retirement income, what you will do about your home, how you will get medical help, medical insurance costs, the activities you will pursue, the effects on your children, lifestyle changes, risks, and so on. Get your spouse to participate and add additional considerations.

When making your retirement decision, give some thought to part-time work and voluntary help within your community. Even though neither may contribute much to your financial success, work may give you the pleasure of still other accomplishments. I know that it has for me.

annuity
a tax-deferred investment issued by an insurance company and often marketed by mutual funds. Investment selection and withdrawal rules vary, but unless you withdraw the funds before some specified age, all eventually annuitize, that is, convert to periodic payments as with an immediate annuity.

professional help
assistance from a person certified and licensed. The central figure in financial planning is usually a Certified Financial Planner (CFP), but may also be (or assisted by) an accountant or lawyer.

Free Sites for Stimulating Retirement Thoughts

- Living to 100 Life Expectancy Calculator, www.livingto100.com
- Speeches by John Bogle at Bogle Financial Markets Research Center, www.vanguard.com/bogle_site/bogle_speeches.html
- The Coffee House Investor, www.coffeehouseinvestor.com
- Bylo Selhi, Smart Mutual Fund Investing, www.bylo.org
- Right on the Money!, www.rightonthemoney.org
- Fund Advice, www.fundadvice.com
- Analyze Now!, www.analyzenow.com

It is very important to discuss your potential retirement life thoroughly with your spouse, particularly if one retires substantially before the other. Remember that a nonworking spouse may also want a different lifestyle during retirement years.

Consider not just your activities, but also the roles you will each play and how you will divide responsibilities. Cover such subjects as household chores, cooking, bill paying, and investment controls. Talk about one spouse assuming the duties of the other in the event of a disability or death.

Discuss possible social relationship changes that may occur, particularly if most of your social activities are with those with whom you work or if you will be moving to an entirely different area of the country. Too often I hear relocated friends say that they are having difficulty establishing new social relations. Sometimes they feel like they are intruders injecting themselves into a social structure that does not have room for them.

And integrate some intellectual and physical activities in your plan so that you keep your mind and body well tuned. It is well known that mental stimulation can offset dementia and physical activities can delay the effects of arthritis and other physical problems.

Successful retirement is the result of marrying financial capability with the lifestyle you envision. If you are like most people, you will have to go through several iterations of capability and desires before you settle on your final plan.

What Can I Afford?

> When a man retires, his wife gets twice the husband but only
> half the income. —Chi Chi Rodriguez

Almost any retirement decision requires that you make a financial assessment of your future prospects. First, you have to project retirement income; and then you have to determine whether you can live within that income comfortably. If you cannot say confidently that you have a little surplus of income over expenses, you probably should not retire.

After you have made an analysis that keeps spending below income, step away and ask yourself about the reality of the numbers. You want to be able to answer all of the following questions. If you cannot answer these and other questions pertinent to your own situation, you may not be able to retire.

Key Questions: Income Forecasts

- Am I far enough from starting Social Security that I should discount the projections that I get each year from the Social Security Administration?
- Have I accounted for the fact that the deductions from my Social Security payments for Medicare's Part B, for example, are likely to continue to escalate far faster than inflation?
- Are my pension payments either based on a solidly financed pension trust or otherwise fully insured by the Pension Benefit Guaranty Corporation (PBGC)? The PBGC will not insure pensions above a limit that changes every year but currently is less than $50,000 annually. If you retired before age 65, the PBGC makes serious age related reductions as well.
- Are any of my income payments such as deferred compensation or severance pay dependent on the solvency of my former employer? You don't want to outlive the ability of your company to pay.
- Are my withdrawal rates from investments realistic? Are they based on optimistic future returns or a conservative estimate based on a slowing economy?

- Did I keep enough savings in reserves so that I could cover known future lump sum expenses, special needs of my family, replacement of items nearing the end of their useful lives, and something for unforeseen emergencies?

Key Questions: Expenses

- Does my list of budget items include all categories for my future expenses?
- Can I reconcile the future budget with the expenses that I have actually incurred over the past several years?
- Have I made provisions for annual savings for an automobile and other large-cost items?
- Have I used a conservative value for inflation when projecting expenses?
- Will other family members need additional financial support?
- Do I have adequate medical insurance and provisions for long-term care? Can I support uninsured costs related to dental, ear, and eye care?

The B Word

We all know about the dreaded B word. Everyone hates to make a *budget*. Budgets take time to make and are difficult to implement. There are few people who can make a retirement decision without making some kind of analysis of how they are now spending their money—and foreseeing the changes once they do retire. The generations after yours will have an especially difficult task because pensions are disappearing and savings are low.

Spending Analysis

Long ago I used Intuit's Quicken and finally quit when I found that I had become a slave to it. I have to admit, however, that programs such as Quicken and Microsoft Money do help you better understand your spending patterns. Some people find they can do some of the same things with financial firms such as American Express, which break down your credit card purchases into categories that you choose. There is the free *Pre-Retirement Savings Planner* that you can download at www.analyzenow.com. It has a budget breakdown that is part of an elementary planning program that some also find helpful.

If you don't want to do the B business, another approach is to just look at elements that you believe can be changed to make the bottom line numbers work out, that is the difference between your current pay-check deposits and the amount you can afford in retirement as determined by Appendix C, Post-Retirement Worksheet, or some other retirement program. Adjust for the costs that you won't have in retirement like the deductions you have for Social Security, Medicare, savings, union dues, or expenses such as child support.

Discretionary Spending

If the changes in deductions and other factors do not cover the difference between your current take-home pay and retirement spending, you know that the next place to look is discretionary expenses, that is, spending for such items as entertainment, restaurants, vacations, clothes, etc. Even with significant reductions, this too might not be sufficient, especially since you want some measure of these in retirement or it won't be any fun.

That means that you have to get down to items that really are discretionary, but you have trouble admitting it. Wives often can see things that husbands don't need and vice versa. Financial counselors see things that neither spouse can see. Let me suggest that you start with utility bills. Then ask if there are not ways to reduce things like charges for multiple phones, internet services, cable for television, and the like. Next examine automobiles and their related costs.

Mortgage Payments

A large item for most people is mortgage payments. If these stop at some point early in your retirement, you possibly can spend more in retirement than a simple budget analysis shows. Take advantage of the optional debt calculation in the Post-Retirement Worksheet in Appendix C to see if this will help.

Downsizing Aspirations

You will find other things too, but often it will come down to some rather large things like finding a less expensive home in a less expensive neighborhood or even a different state. The latter may require that you do some really thorough investigations, though. As an extreme, we have known people who decided that they could spend their retirement in a RV or trailer home wandering around the country—and discovered before long that they had made a very bad mistake. They were far from old friends and support groups, had expenses that they grossly underestimated, and simply tired of that lifestyle quickly.

Replacement Budgeting

If you are not well on your way toward building a reserve for items that wear out and are expensive to replace, you may not be ready to retire. Financially successful retirees are able to purchase such items out of their savings, not by buying them on credit. To build such reserves, you must budget an amount to save each month. (See Chapter 6.) Instead of making payments to someone like a car dealer or credit firm, you have to make payments to an investment account. It has to be part of your monthly budget. By making regular deposits to such reserves in a balanced account, you may well benefit from dollar-cost-averaging. Or by periodically buying bonds or CDs in ladders, you can gradually increase the overall return as the years go by. (See Chapter 7.)

When to Start Social Security

breakeven age

the age when there is no economic advantage of one choice over another or the age where the better choice switches between two alternatives.

Some financial planners recommend taking Social Security early if you retire early. This is based on the assumption that you will save and invest your early Social Security money and live shorter than or equal to the breakeven age, that is, the age where you will accumulate the same present value of payments no matter when you start. The *breakeven age* is usually a little over age 80. In fact, taking early Social Security when retiring early is the best answer if:

1. You and your spouse believe that you both will die early in retirement.
2. You have not saved enough to even consider taking Social Security at a later age.
3. You are not concerned about the amount your spouse will get on your death.
4. You believe that the government will soon default on future payments.

    If you are retiring in your early 60s, be sure to read the mysteries of Social Security in Chapter 3 and review the details of your and your spouse's Social Security options with your local Social Security office.

Other than the exceptions above, those who have saved enough will generally do better by starting Social Security at a later age. It is not hard to do your own comparative analysis by using Appendix B, Age to Start Social Security, or you may download the *Social Security at 62, 66 or 70* free Excel program at www.analyzenow.com and use the free Social Security calculator there that covers more conditions.

I have entered some illustrative numbers in Appendix B, Age to Start Social Security, as an example. Of course, you would want to enter your own numbers starting with the last estimates that you got on your annual report from the Social Security Administration.

Single Person with Return Equal Inflation

Let's consider the three different ages in a retirement report for someone who has just reached age 62 and is deciding whether to take Social Security of $1,500 per month at 62, $2,000 at 66, or $2,723 at 70. Assume initially that this person can invest $500,000 from a deferred tax account so that returns just equal inflation. (Later we look at the case when returns exceed inflation by 2 percent.) We use a ballpark 15 percent tax rate assumption except that only 50 percent of Social Security will be taxed. We use the Social Security calculator at AnalyzeNow.com—*Social Security at 62, 66 or 70* for the illustrations that follow.

Figure 4.1 shows what would happen (in today's dollar values) to lifetime spending if the retiree spent $3,000 per month or $36,000 each year until running out of investments. Figure 4.2 shows the savings history in today's dollars for all three Social Security ages.

What we learn from this example is that the retiree is better off from his own personal considerations if she delays starting Social Security until age 70 because she could continue to spend $36,000 (plus inflation adjustment) all the way until age 94 at which time her investments were exhausted and spending would be completely dependent on Social Security.

By way of contrast, if she started taking Social Security early at age 62 and began with $500,000, she would have exhausted investments at age 84, after which she would have only about half as much income as if she would have started Social Security at 70.

On the other hand, if she dies shortly after retiring, her heirs would be better off if she started Social Security early. However, if she lives past age 80, then the heirs would be better off if she delayed taking Social Security until age 70. See Figure 4.2.

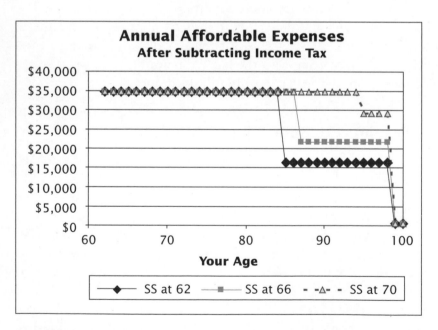

FIGURE 4.1 Delaying the start of Social Security until age 70 provides the best solution for this 62 year old.

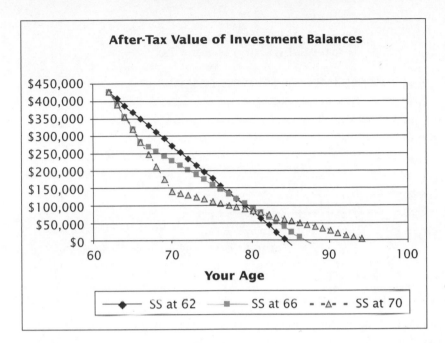

FIGURE 4.2 Investment histories.

Single Person with Return 2 Percent above Inflation:

Figures 4.3 and 4.4 show what would happen if the retiree could earn a 2 percent real return. Some people think this is easy. But real retirees experience investment costs and reverse-dollar-cost-averaging that can give a punishing blow to retiree's investment returns. Those who invest in currently taxable investments will find it even harder.

The primary difference between the Figures 4.2 and 4.4 cases is that the money lasts longer with the higher return. Nevertheless, you would come to the same conclusions.

CAUTION

If you think there is a chance that you might have to work when taking Social Security between the ages of 62 and 66, be aware that you will lose $1 of Social Security for every $2 of wages above $12,480 annually in 2006. Check www.ssa.gov for current limits or call 1-800-772-1213.

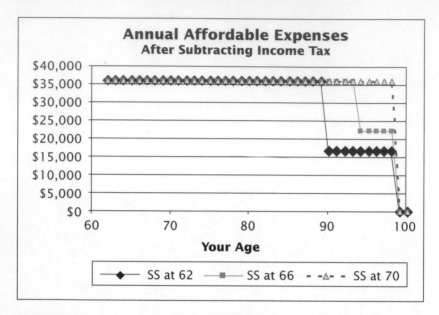

FIGURE 4.3 Two percent additional return increases the age for exhausting investments but does not change conclusions.

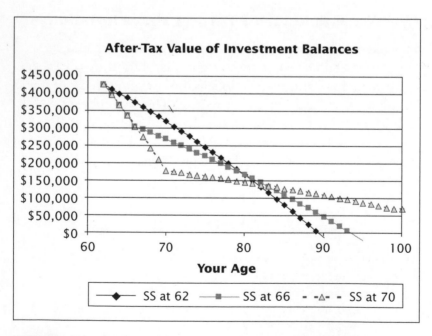

FIGURE 4.4 Investment histories with 2 percent more return.

If Married, Pay Attention to Spousal Benefits

A spouse gets whichever is the larger of (1) the benefit from the spouse's own working career or (2) up to 50 percent of the higher wage earner's full retirement age (FRA) benefit which occurs between ages 65 and 67 depending on the birth year. If the spouse starts taking payments after the higher earner is taking payments and after the spouse's own FRA, then it is the full 50 percent, but if the spouse starts taking Social Security early, say at 62, then the amount is only 37.5 percent (or less at larger spousal FRAs) of the higher earner's FRA benefit. You can get particulars for your situation at the Social Security Administration website (www.ssa.gov).

The Social Security rules put pressure on the lower-income spouse to wait until the lower-income spouse's FRA. Since the lower-income surviving spouse gets 100 percent of the higher earner's Social Security after the higher earner's death, there is also additional pressure for the higher earner to delay taking Social Security as long as possible.

The mysteries of Social Security in Chapter 3 may help with many alternatives you are considering. Whatever the alternative, it is a good idea to review your considerations with a representative from your local Social Security office before making the actual commitment.

Married Couple with Return Equal Inflation

If a couple has sufficient savings, it is almost always better to delay Social Security even if one dies before the breakeven age. That is because the survivor's benefit is likely to be significantly better if the survivor lives longer than the breakeven age.

It is more difficult to analyze results for married people, particularly when one spouse has not worked at all or has a significantly lower earnings history than the other spouse. We illustrate this with an example in which we assume that the husband is the high earner and dies at age 75. We further assume that the surviving spouse can live on 67 percent of the inflation-adjusted income that they had when they started retirement. Both spouses are the same age.

All of the other assumptions are the same as with the single person—for example, $500,000—in a deferred tax account, the husband's Social Security at age 66 is $2,000 per month, 15 percent ordinary income tax, 50 percent of Social Security is taxed, and so on. Because there are now two people contributing Social Security, we increase the spending to $4,000 per month or $48,000 per year.

Again we look at starting Social Security at three ages. In the first case, both start Social Security at age 62. In the second case, both start at age 66. In the third case, the higher earner starts Social Security at age 70, but the lower-income spouse starts at age 66 since that provides the maximum Social Security income.

Again we use the Social Security calculator in the *Social Security at 62, 66 or 70* program for the illustrations. The results are in today's dollar values. Figures 4.5 and 4.6 illustrate what happens when the higher earner dies at age 75 and the survivor can live on 67 percent of the income when both were living.

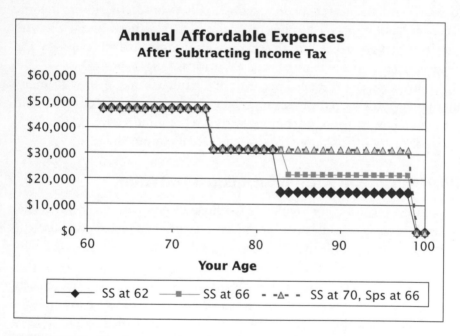

FIGURE 4.5 The best results are when the higher earner starts Social Security at 70 and the low-income spouse at 66.

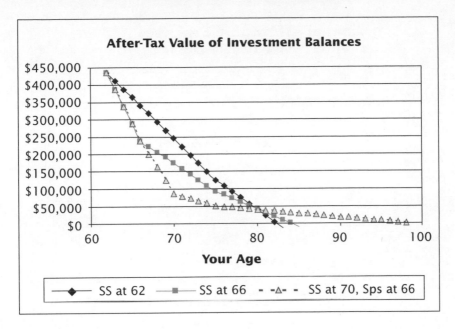

FIGURE 4.6 This couple exhausted their investments relatively early that puts a premium on delaying Social Security.

Married Couple with Return 2 Percent above Inflation

In this illustration, we assume that the retirees start off spending the same amount, that is, $4,000 per month or $48,000 per year. The higher earner will still die at age 75. The only change is that we increase the real return from 0 percent to 2 percent.

Just as with the case of the single person, the additional return in Figures 4.7 and 4.8 pushes out the age where investments are exhausted, but you would largely reach the same conclusions, namely, that the survivor is generally better off if the higher earner starts Social Security at age 70 providing they have sufficient funds to support them until Social Security income begins.

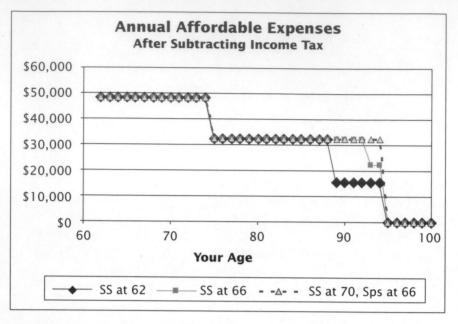

FIGURE 4.7   Two percent more return stretches the results.

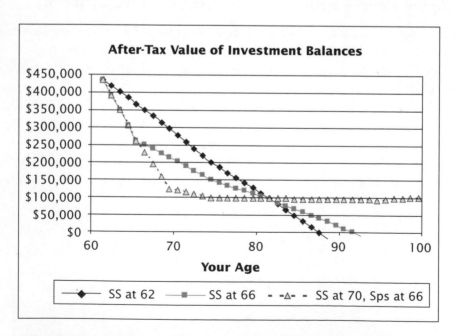

FIGURE 4.8   Investments last longer with 2 percent more return.

Making Your Own Calculations

If you don't have access to a computer program that can help you compare results for different ages to start Social Security, you can use an abbreviated method in Appendix B, Age to Start Social Security.

The first thing is to help you decide whether you have saved enough money to delay the start of Social Security. I often feel that those who have not saved enough should probably not be retiring so early.

It is not hard to make the calculations as you see. Simply multiply the annual amount of Social Security you will get at the later age to take Social Security by the number of years between retirement and when you start Social Security. Then do the same for your spouse. Add the spouse's to yours to get the total amount needed to fill the gap until Social Security starts. We do that in the Age to Start Social Security worksheet.

Given that you have saved enough to delay the start of Social Security (and still have some reserves for emergencies), we can go on to compare the results of starting Social Security at several ages, usually the three ages quoted in your annual Social Security report: Earliest retirement (62), full retirement age (between 65 and 67 depending on your birth year), and latest age (70).

The Age to Start Social Security worksheet also helps you to consider the effects of one spouse dying before the other. Most analyses assume that both spouses die at the same time or the primary wage earner dies after the other spouse. Our analysis accounts for the very important, and most common case, when the higher-income spouse dies first.

TIP

With few exceptions, the best choice is to delay the higher earner's Social Security to age 70 and the other spouse's Social Security until that spouse's full retirement age (e.g., 66)—if savings are sufficient. To implement this, it may be necessary for the higher earner to "file and suspend" just before the higher earner's full retirement age. If you already started Social Security at age 62 and want to do better by waiting till your full retirement age, you can pay back the money you have already received with no penalty if you file a "withdrawal of claim." See the Social Security Administration for the necessary paperwork for either of these filings. You can also get back the income taxes on these Social Security payments when you file your income tax the next year either with a negative 1099-SSA or by filing a claim per IRS publication 915. Discuss this with a tax professional.

It took a long time to get many professionals to recognize the real importance of delaying Social Security as long as practical. I helped Jonathan Clements write articles about this for the *Wall Street Journal.* He said he got huge numbers of hate mail from the articles from both professionals and others, but now most planners agree. In fact, insurance companies have now come to a similar conclusion and have started to sell policies to cover the gap period with an annuity. My father did not take Social Security until age 70. He was smart enough to figure this out without the math in the Age to Start Social Security worksheet in Appendix B and without an insurance sales person!

Review Insurance

Any time is really a good time to review your insurance needs. This is especially true just before retiring for this is when you can probably drop life insurance—unless it is part of your estate plan—and go for increased deductibles on your auto and home insurance. You may also be able to reduce your liability insurance. On the other hand, you need to make sure that your home is fully insured because once you stop working your ability to recover from a fire, flood, wind, or whatever is limited to what you can draw from your investments.

Medical insurance after retirement may be the most confusing, expensive, and important insurance question you face at this point. Perhaps your employer will offer a less expensive group medical insurance policy. At age 65, Medicare helps immensely, but you most likely want to sign up for Part B as well as consider either a health maintenance organization (HMO), preferred provided organization (PPO) or a Medigap health policy and perhaps some drug insurance with Part D of the Medicare plan.

Whether or not to take Part D of Medicare is a difficult decision. Unfortunately, the government does not give you a lot of time to decide. In general, if you choose a Medigap policy that has drug coverage, you won't need Part D, but that is not always true. Read the descriptive material about your medical policy alternatives carefully before committing. Further, call the insurance company's representatives and discuss the Part D issue with them.

This is also the time to consider buying a long-term care (LTC) policy. You won't need this if you look like you are going to be impoverished and have to use Medicaid anyway or are in a position where you are confident that your children will care for you. Also, you don't need it if your normal retirement income will be sufficient to support those kind of costs that today are about $75,000 per person per year. Or, possibly, you can use your home equity to assist. Most people are in between the situation of being impoverished and wealthy enough to support the costs.

Furthermore, most people don't have to buy a LTC policy that provides full coverage. You may not have to pay for the full amount of the care if you can augment the costs at the time with your Social Security, pension, investments, and home equity or reduce service costs with the help of a relative. No matter the amount, it is good to have some inflation protection in any LTC policy. An excellent Internet site for long-term care information is www.longtermcare.gov. Also see Google "long-term care quotes" for specific reference prices.

If you have a large estate that is likely to be subject to inheritance taxes, or you want to ensure that certain heirs will get a certain amount of money, you may want to consider a life insurance policy that is owned by a trust. Many people are reluctant to take this step because it implies that they know the future of tax laws and feel that a trust established by their will after their death will take care of the children and the surviving spouse. You want to make sure that you understand all of the alternatives before committing to a life insurance policy either for inheritance or to direct funds to certain beneficiaries.

There is more on insurance in Chapter 6 on Smart Insurance, so be sure to read that before analyzing your insurance needs.

Part-Time Employment

In another decade or two, retirement at age 62 or less will be much less common than today. The average person will be considering employment until age 70 or beyond. The best jobs may well be full-time employment in a firm that has both good medical and retirement benefits. The best positions for retirement benefits may be government jobs supported by tax payers. Many will seek part-time work which may mean cottage industries, odd-hour or odd-season jobs, handyman businesses, sales clerks, and so on.

I cannot even count the number of people who have e-mailed me asking for help because they retired too early and/or spent too much early in their retirement. Their only real choice has been to try and return to the workforce, but it is really tough. They gave up, or were relieved of, jobs that paid decent wages and had good medical, retirement, insurance, and other benefits. Now most end up with much lower-paying jobs with few benefits, if any. They also return to the Social Security tax rolls often compounded by penalty taxes if they started taking Social Security before their full retirement age. Taking Social Security early is a mistake many learn because the lifetime inflation-adjusted income from Social Security is far more starting at age 70 than earlier considering increased life spans.

There are three major problems that face the elderly when seeking employment:

1. They must be healthy enough and have the physical capacity to work.

2. Many employers do not want the burden of elderly workers, who use more sick leave and increase exposure to discrimination suits.

3. The workers may not have the education, training, and experience that the employer expects.

So people may be rather glib when they say, "I'm not worried about saving for retirement because I'm going to have to work anyway." More likely than not, they'll rue the life they will ultimately have when they look back and consider the alternatives they had at the time.

Elderly Find It Difficult to Get Jobs in Spite of Laws that Prohibit Age Discrimination

There are many reasons why it will be hard to work during normal retirement ages:
- Lack training
- Lack education
- Lack stamina
- May be hearing impaired
- May have poor eyesight

Employers know their health insurance costs may be higher and sick leave time greater if they employ older workers—and the age discrimination laws further add to the problems of employing them.

Professional Consultation

It is possible that you may not need any professional help if you understand the concepts in this book. Before I became involved with this subject, I had personal help from a professional before making my own decision to retire. He got most things right—and a few things wrong in spite of being very bright and up to speed on the latest in technical analysis at the time.

There is no better time to see a professional than before you tell the boss and the world that you are going to retire. You are seeking a critical review of your plan, not someone to manage your money for you. This is an important distinction. The vast majority of planners want to make money from your savings, so you want to get the right kind of help here. You probably want someone who will work for a few hours at a specified fee.

Whether you use a professional or not, you want an orderly file of your information on sources of retirement income, last income tax return, investment details (account names, amounts, and percent of total), insurance, recent monthly spending compared to recent monthly working income, and how you arrived at the amount you will be able to spend in retirement.

You want to ask the professional whether he or she thinks you have the resources to retire with a reasonable lifestyle. You also want comments on your plan for future investment selection and allocations. (You don't need estate considerations for this review.) See the information in Chapter 10, A Critical Review, on finding professional help. It is not easy, but the diligence may make a big difference in the results.

CAUTION

Beware of investment advisors who try to convince you they can select investments that will beat the market averages. Most of the time they cannot, as demonstrated in many studies. Look for someone who recommends a mix of low-cost index funds where your performance will be very close to the market averages and not have to overcome the burden of high costs and fees.

Informing the Boss

How and when you tell your boss is a strategy question that depends on a lot of things including fairness to both you and your employer. Unless you are very easy to replace, your employer most likely will need a lot more than two weeks of notice. On the other hand, if you notify your employer a year or so in advance, you could be making a big mistake. So someplace in between is what may be fair to both you and the boss.

There are a number of reasons that you do not want to make your declaration too early. First and foremost, you might change your mind. Unless you have thoroughly wrung out a comparison of the differences between retiring on a specific date and continued work until another date, you are not ready.

Another reason is that there may be events that make a difference. Perhaps there is an organization change coming, and you would be up for a big raise and promotion. Maybe the company will offer a severance plan to alleviate its cost problems. Perhaps your spouse gets sick, and you would get better medical care under your employer's health insurance than a policy of your own if you are not yet 65. Or maybe the government will announce a major change in Social Security or taxes for savings plans.

It is really important to keep the considerations very confidential between you and your spouse. Rumors about forthcoming retirements spread fast. Again, telegraphing your thoughts on this subject may get you emotionally committed and embarrassed to reverse the decision. So label this subject *Top Secret!*

You probably should not tell your children and certainly not your barber, hairdresser, or other service people who might leak the rumor. These tidbits spread fast, especially when you don't want them to.

Converting Savings Plans and IRAs

It is now very common for professional planners to rush retirees from their employer's savings plan into an IRA. Often, that is in the best interest of the planner if the planner sees an opportunity to get you to buy some of his securities or is able to convince you to turn your investments over to him or her to manage for you. There is also good logic in that there generally is a wider range of investment choices and, in the event of death, your IRA alternatives may be better for heirs than if the money remains in your employer's savings plan.

If you decide to transfer funds from an employer's savings plan to an IRA, be sure to first open the IRA and then have the employer send the check directly to the IRA provider, not to you. If the check is made to you it will be for only 80 percent of the amount in your savings plan because there is an automatic 20 percent tax withholding. It will take you a long time and lots of effort to get that 20 percent back into your IRA.

I chose to keep my money in my employer's savings plan against the recommendation of my professional because it had a guaranteed income fund that was an attractive alternative to investing in a bond fund. (A bond fund goes down in value when interest rates go up.) It has turned out that I did the right thing because my employer started allowing contingent beneficiaries, and the government changed the tax law so that beneficiaries of my 401(k) could, after getting the money into their own IRAs, stretch the payouts over their entire life.

A stretch IRA is one that allows an heir to take payments from the IRA using their own life expectancies. This allows the money to continue to grow in a tax advantaged account. So without converting my 401(k) to an IRA, I get the benefit of higher returns for the amount of risk I'm willing to accept in the fixed income part of my portfolio because the employer's savings plan has a better fund for this purpose than I can find elsewhere.

It is possible to convert an employer's savings plan to a *Roth IRA* if you first transfer the money from the savings plan to a regular IRA and then make the transfer to a Roth IRA. There are a number of restrictions, so you want to talk to your IRA administer or competent professional planner about this. This may be a good idea if you expect your tax rate will be higher later in life than it is now or if you want more flexibility in withdrawals. Because Roths have no required minimum distributions for the original owner, you may be able to leave more to your heirs. It is not a good idea to convert to a Roth if you don't have enough money outside the IRA to pay the income tax on the conversion.

Roth IRA
tax-exempt investment with special rules. With few exceptions, Roth IRAs are limited to lower-income workers. They are not subject to required minimum distributions (RMDs) after age 70½, but they are subject to early withdrawal penalties. Some employers offer Roth savings plans.

If you are eligible for a Roth IRA, seriously consider converting (also called, *rolling over*) a regular IRA to a Roth IRA. However, there are so many twists and turns associated with a conversion decision that someone just about has to model your particular situation to see what would be the best course of action. Even this is dependent on the assumptions for the fickle IRA tax rules and other income elements that may affect your tax rates. If considering a conversion, you can gain additional insight by going to the Roth IRA website Home Page at www.rothira.com or additional perspective from the Rollover IRA Distribution Calculator under Investment Guides and Tools: in www.troweprice.com. It is also important to get advice from your IRA provider or tax professional.

As with many investment tax situations, the rules can and do change often, so make sure that you understand the income, timing, and tax restrictions before you attempt a conversion.

It is a good idea to get advice from a professional or your IRA administrator on designating beneficiaries in order to best help your surviving spouse or heirs. Since the IRA will bypass your will, this is a good subject to cover with an estate attorney. For example, on the death of an IRA owner, the attorney might recommend that the surviving spouse retitle the IRA in order to be able to most effectively further pass it on when the survivor dies. In such a case the new title might be "James Jones, IRA (deceased August 12, 2006) for the benefit of Mary Jones, beneficiary."

Of course, there are cases when it may be better to draw most of the money out of an employer's savings plan or IRA shortly before death instead of trying to pass it on. That way the estate is reduced by the amount of income tax paid on the savings plan or IRA withdrawals. Such might be the better choice if the survivor is subject to a large inheritance tax, particularly if most of the estate tax would have to come from the savings plan or IRA. This is another area where professional advice could be useful.

Debt Considerations

Debts are a negative investment. Often, the best investment you can make is to pay off those debts.

CAUTION

Caution: Paying off any debt with funds from a deferred tax plan may have serious tax consequences. Do a tax analysis first.

Most certainly, you want to address the question of whether you should pay off any debts before retiring. Almost always you should pay off debt before making additional savings if the debt has an after-tax interest rate more than the after-tax rate that you can get on your investments. Theoretically, if you have enough investments to pay the debt, debt interest that is lower than your investment returns can enhance your overall returns. Good real estate investors take advantage of this, and it is the reason that developers can make so much money—or lose so much when real estate markets turn south. But there are other considerations too. Let's first look at debts on your home.

Home Mortgage

Whether it is better to pay off your home mortgage or not before retiring is always a subject for hot debate. It is very comforting to pay off your home mortgage before, or not too many years after, you retire. However, when inflation is rampant, you may do better by not paying a home mortgage off early.

If you have something other than a conventional long-term mortgage, you may have additional reasons to pay down the mortgage quickly or refinance. You certainly don't want to carry an adjustable-rate mortgage (ARM) into retirement, nor should your mortgage be a very large part of the current market price for the house. In the extreme, you don't want to purchase a home with close to zero down just before retiring. A drop in market value of the house at the time you might need to sell could be disastrous.

A long-term mortgage that extends well into your retirement is not necessarily a bad thing as long as the mortgage payments, taxes and upkeep are a good value compared to renting a home, and you are sure that the total expenses are not above your ability to support them. A large mortgage may be a signal that you should consider downsizing, that is, selling your home and buying a less expensive one. We cover this in Chapter 6, Implementing Your Plan.

Home Equity Loans

There is little justification to enter retirement with a loan on your home that is in addition to your mortgage. Once in retirement, you should only consider this as a possibility if the after-tax interest on the loan is confidently lower than the after-tax return you can get out of the total of your investments. Even then, a long period of poor market performance would prove a home equity loan a bad choice.

reverse mortgage

a contract with a lender that allows you to recover part of your home equity. It may make regular payments to you or give you a line of credit. The debt against your home increases with each payment and time as interest accumulates. These are subject to stringent government rules and often have costly provisions.

Reverse Mortgages

If the only way that you can retire is to take out a *reverse mortgage* on your house, you are already in trouble. These have high costs (2 percent of home value and possibly another 2 percent for mortgage insurance) and are typically subject to interest rate readjustments annually. Reverse mortgages are a last resort that you can use if you prematurely run out of retirement savings. Beginning retirement with a reverse mortgage means that you are probably destined to welfare roles at some point in retirement. Also, consider that if you are forced to live away from your home for 12 consecutive months, you will have to repay the reverse mortgage, and your payments will end. For more limitations be sure to see the information that AARP makes available at *www.aarp.org/revmort.*

Credit Card Debt

Having a credit card balance is bad thing to carry when entering retirement, especially when you cannot pay it off in its entirety. If you cannot afford to pay off your credit card balances, you should not consider retiring.

Automobile Loans

Early in life you probably have to purchase automobiles with borrowed money. This is not a good idea in retirement. In retirement, you want to be earning interest, not paying interest. Therefore, it is almost always better to buy a new car with cash that has been saved in advance. Divide the cost of a new car by the number of years it will last, and then budget to put that amount in savings every year from your Social Security, pension or by means of taking that much less from investments for your other expenses.

Investment Debt

Unless your principal investments are in real estate, and even then unless you are very good at real property investing, it is best to enter retirement with very little, if any, investment debt. If you have a stock margin account, get rid of it. Retirement is no time for gambling, particularly gambling with leveraged highly volatile securities. When I was in my 40s, my professional planner wisely advised me to get into low-cost *index funds* and forget about investing in individual stocks unless I just wanted to do this with a small amount of "play money." I've never regretted this investment advice.

Choosing a Lump Sum or a Pension

Before you retire, you may be faced with a choice between a pension (annuity) or a lump sum from your employer's savings plan, from a *severance package* or from a cash balance plan. I feel that the best way to make the comparison is with the use of a comprehensive computer program that allows you to model each choice and then compare the amounts you can afford to spend from each. The programs at www.analyzenow.com are well suited to this.

index funds
a fund with the same distribution of securities as the index it represents. The first index fund was one that had the same percent distribution of stocks as the S&P 500 index that represents the 500 largest capitalization stocks in the United States. Costs are very low because the fund does not have to do any stock or bond picking, which is done by the publisher of the index. Now indexes are published for many different kinds of securities. Mutual fund companies emulate many of these.

severance package

an offer or contract for supplemental retirement benefits. This might include a lump sum of money or an annuity and/or medical or other benefits. These are fully taxable as earned income and so have Social Security and Medicare deductions.

If you don't have access to such a program, you can use the Post-Retirement Worksheet in Appendix C in this book. First, do an analysis as if the lump sum were part of your savings. Then do another analysis with the employer's pension quote. From a financial standpoint, you would choose the one that gives you the larger retirement income.

Another alternative is to go to one of the larger mutual fund company websites and look for an immediate annuity. That way you can tell whether you would get a better pension from the mutual fund company than from your employer. However, make sure that you understand the tax implications. If you get the lump sum as cash, you can only buy an annuity for the after-tax value of the lump sum. Also, unless your annuity is in a deferred tax account, annuity payments are not fully taxable. You get an "exclusion" quote, which is the amount of your payment that is not subject to income tax. Be aware, however, that this tax exclusion disappears when you have recovered the amount of your original investment.

Another complex element in this evaluation is the choice of a survivor benefit. With a pension or annuity, you have a choice of perhaps 0 percent, 50 percent, 75 percent, or 100 percent survivor benefit. You get the largest payment with the 0 percent choice, but your survivor gets nothing. With 100 percent, your survivor receives the same payment as you had while living, but it will be a smaller amount for you than with any of the other choices.

You might decide to not take an annuity or pension and just manage the lump sum investment and subsequent draws yourself. This provides the most flexibility and the possibility of purchasing an annuity later in retirement when your expenses are more stable. Go back to Chapter 3 and stay tuned for Chapter 7 to get more information on pension and annuity subtleties.

Chapter

Post-Retirement Planning

If you are still a long way from retirement, you do not have to review this chapter, but if you are getting within a few years of that crucial retirement date, it is a good idea to work your way through this and see if you will be relatively comfortable with the resources that you anticipate having at that point.

Post-retirement planning must be done in more detail than pre-retirement planning. This is not just because the results are more crucial to survival, but because it requires more detail to determine how much you can spend after taxes than it does to estimate how much you should be saving before taxes.

Some planners presently build retirement plans on the basis that older retirees do not spend as much as younger retirees. They base this on the theory that when folks get into their 70s, 80s, and 90s they morph into couch potatoes and do not spend their savings. These planners justify themselves by citing statistics that show that older people spend less.

Of course, the statistics do show this. The average person overspent early in retirement and is severely strapped later on. These analysts don't look at people who *can* afford to spend more, lead more *active* lives, and actually spend *more* money. That is the category you want for your retirement life. My wife and I are in our 70s and ski three months out of the year on expert slopes. My father golfed until he was 95. Many participants in cruises are those late in retirement. And medical costs late in life can jack up expenses immensely, so you want to be prepared for this and not have to live as paupers.

The fault of most simple planning programs is partly due to the way they calculate affordable spending for a retiree with a pension as though the retiree can spend the entire after-tax pension every year. That by itself leads the retiree to spending less inflation-adjusted income later in life. It is a terrible fault in these programs. I have been trying to get financial magazines and financial websites to make this correction for years without success. They have to know that it is not right, but they don't know how to make the correction simply. I make the correction in the Post-Retirement Worksheet in Appendix C—and you will see that it is not hard.

Another problem is that very few programs caution users to withhold some of their investments for emergencies or potential future expenses. This also saps real retirees and is an important element in reducing investments to the scary point late in life when a retiree tends to be very cautious about how much he or she can draw from investments. During this time, retirees often avoid taking principal draws and draw instead only interest and dividends.

Because I don't want you to start retirement with a plan that is based on being inactive for the last half of your retirement, I assume that your expenses in retirement will be constant in today's dollar values, not diminishing. Said another way, expenses increase with inflation and you will exhaust your investments after a long life. And because I don't want you to get caught with unplanned expenses later in life, I am going to ask you to set aside a reserve.

The post-retirement analysis in Appendix C is fairly comprehensive. If you feel that more detail is needed or there is something unique about your situation, I suggest that you use one of the retirement planning programs from www.analyzenow.com.

Retirees should do an analysis at about the same time each year and *not* rely on just using last year's affordable spending increased by an inflation amount as seems to be almost universal elsewhere.

Before going to the appendix, at least skim the other subjects in this chapter to see which one applies to your case. You will see that entries such as Social Security shortfalls, pensions, home equity, returns, and reserves all require some thought. Other big judgment factors are what happens to future tax rates and how long you live. Therefore, we start with those two subjects. You will see that everything is not as black or white as some would have you believe when they say that you will have a certain success rate if you limit your retirement spending to a specific number.

Estimate a Future Tax Rate

The most exquisite folly is made from wisdom spun too fine.
—Benjamin Franklin

You can buy some very expensive programs that make a detailed tax calculation each year using this year's rates, inflation-adjusted deductions, and the like. That is an exercise in needless detail. During my lifetime, I've seen maximum tax rates all the way up to 90 percent, and I've seen allowable deductions anywhere from virtually nonexistent to a large number of items being deductible. I'm sure that the future will change at least as much as it has in the past, especially as the government tries to fund Social Security, Medicare, and all of the state and federal pensions that have been promised.

We base income taxes on the following equation using last year's tax return information or your own estimate instead of a detailed annual calculation based on deductions, exemptions, type of income, and tax tables.

State and federal income taxes / Adjusted gross income

This is because of our model's income construction and the way it better captures what happens over a long period of time than does an estimate based on current rules and rates on different kinds of income, deductions, exemptions, and credits that change almost every year.

Nevertheless, on the Post-Retirement Worksheet in Appendix C, there are optional entries for deductions, exemptions, and taxable income. We ask for this only to encourage you to consider whether these were extraordinary values last year and therefore might give you misleading tax rates when you make your estimate of future tax rates. For example, if you had a very large one-time medical deduction or capital gain last year, you might want to recalculate last year's income tax to give you a better estimate of future taxes based on more representative deductions and income.

Estimate Your Life Expectancy

life expectancy
the additional years to live for a specified group of people all the same age. This is the number of years where 50 percent of the population dies earlier and 50 percent lives longer. The older the person, the shorter the life expectancy. The way it is defined, you cannot outlive life expectancy because you still have a life expectancy no matter what your age may be.

I like to use *Living to 100 Life Expectancy Calculator* at www.livingto100.com for a personalized life expectancy estimate that accounts for many health related factors. You can, however, use the politically correct values from IRS Publication 590. The latter are used principally to determine required minimum distributions from IRAs and other deferred tax investments. Figure 5.1 may change with time, so use whatever is the current official IRS information for any distribution calculation. Before the IRS rules changed to the simplified version with longer *life expectancies* shown in Figure 5.1, you had to work through a form that is even more complex than the form I developed from IRS data shown in Figure 5.2. (You still do if your spouse is more than 10 years younger than you.) Nevertheless, there are a lot of lessons from the latter such as the significantly longer life span of a survivor in a marriage than a single person.

First, it is important to understand that life expectancy is dependent on your age. When you add life expectancy to your current age, you get the age the average person is expected to die. Your expected death age increases as you age. Half of the population that is the same age will die before that death age and half will die after that death age. In fact, the spectrum is fairly broad so that almost 40 percent of the population will live more than three years past the death age.

The IRS recognized this in their newer table illustrated in Figure 5.1, where it added a number of years to their politically correct, unisex life expectancies in Figure 5.2 to cover a wider variety of situations. In fact, women live longer than men, Asians live longer than European Americans, European Americans live longer than African Americans, and so on. Furthermore, the surviving person in a marriage is likely to live longer than the life expectancy of either person when single.

Required Minimum Distributions
Divide last year's ending balance by the divisor.

Age	Divisor	Death Age	Draw	Age	Divisor	Death Age	Draw
70	27.4	97.4	3.6%	93	9.6	102.6	10.4%
71	26.5	97.5	3.8%	94	9.1	103.1	11.0%
72	25.6	97.6	3.9%	95	8.6	103.6	11.6%
73	24.7	97.7	4.0%	96	8.1	104.1	12.3%
74	23.8	97.8	4.2%	97	7.6	104.6	13.2%
75	22.9	97.9	4.4%	98	7.1	105.1	14.1%
76	22.0	98.0	4.5%	99	6.7	105.7	14.9%
77	21.2	98.2	4.7%	100	6.3	106.3	15.9%
78	20.3	98.3	4.9%	101	5.9	106.9	16.9%
79	19.5	98.5	5.1%	102	5.5	107.5	18.2%
80	18.7	98.7	5.3%	103	5.2	108.2	19.2%
81	17.9	98.9	5.6%	104	4.9	108.9	20.4%
82	17.1	99.1	5.8%	105	4.5	109.5	22.2%
83	16.3	99.3	6.1%	106	4.2	110.2	23.8%
84	15.5	99.5	6.5%	107	3.9	110.9	25.6%
85	14.8	99.8	6.8%	108	3.7	111.7	27.0%
86	14.1	100.1	7.1%	109	3.4	112.4	29.4%
87	13.4	100.4	7.5%	110	3.1	113.1	32.3%
88	12.7	100.7	7.9%	111	2.9	113.9	34.5%
89	12.0	101.0	8.3%	112	2.6	114.6	38.5%
90	11.4	101.4	8.8%	113	2.4	115.4	41.7%
91	10.8	101.8	9.3%	114	2.1	116.1	47.6%
92	10.2	102.2	9.8%				

FIGURE 5.1 The divisors for required minimum distributions are life expectancies plus some extra years to cover those who live longer and/or married to a somewhat younger spouse.
Source: IRS Publication 590.

To get a very personalized life expectancy, you can use the *Living to 100 Life Expectancy Calculator* at www.livingto100.com or the table in Figure 5.2. You can even make an arbitrary assumption. It is wise to use a value that is higher than those in Figure 5.2, which gives the average number of years until death for a large group of people because you want

Age of Single or Older Person	Single Life Expectancy	JOINT LIFE AND LAST SURVIVOR LIFE EXPECTANCY TABLES (YEARS) Other Spouse Is Younger By										
		Equal Ages	1 Year	2 Years	3 Years	4 Years	5 Years	6 Years	7 Years	8 Years	9 Years	10 Years
55	29.6	35.6	36.1	36.6	37.2	37.7	38.3	38.9	39.6	40.2	40.9	41.6
56	28.7	34.7	35.1	35.7	36.2	36.8	37.4	38.0	38.6	39.3	40.0	40.7
57	27.9	33.7	34.2	34.7	35.2	35.8	36.4	37.0	37.6	38.3	39.0	39.7
58	27.0	32.8	33.2	33.7	34.3	34.8	35.4	36.0	36.7	37.3	38.0	38.7
59	26.1	31.8	32.3	32.8	33.3	33.9	34.5	35.1	35.7	36.4	37.1	37.8
60	25.2	30.9	31.3	31.9	32.4	32.9	33.5	34.1	34.8	35.4	36.1	36.8
61	24.4	29.9	30.4	30.9	31.4	32.0	32.6	33.2	33.8	34.5	35.1	35.8
62	23.5	29.0	29.5	30.0	30.5	31.1	31.6	32.2	32.9	33.5	34.2	34.9
63	22.7	28.1	28.5	29.0	29.6	30.1	30.7	31.3	31.9	32.6	33.2	33.9
64	21.8	27.1	27.6	28.1	28.6	29.2	29.8	30.4	31.0	31.6	32.3	33.0
65	21.0	26.2	26.7	27.2	27.7	28.3	28.8	29.4	30.0	30.7	31.4	32.0
66	20.2	25.3	25.8	26.3	26.8	27.3	27.9	28.5	29.1	29.8	30.4	31.1
67	19.4	24.4	24.9	25.4	25.9	26.4	27.0	28.2	27.6	28.8	29.5	30.2
68	18.6	23.5	24.0	24.5	25.0	25.5	26.1	26.7	27.3	27.9	28.6	29.2
69	17.8	22.6	23.1	23.6	24.1	24.6	25.2	25.7	26.4	27.0	27.6	28.3
70	17.0	21.8	22.2	22.7	23.2	23.7	24.3	24.8	25.4	26.1	26.7	27.4
71	16.3	20.9	21.3	21.8	22.3	22.8	23.4	23.9	24.5	25.2	25.8	26.5
72	15.5	20.0	20.5	20.9	21.4	22.0	22.5	23.1	23.7	24.3	24.9	25.6
73	14.8	19.2	19.6	20.1	20.6	21.1	21.6	22.2	22.8	23.4	24.0	24.7
74	14.1	18.4	18.8	19.3	19.7	20.2	20.8	21.3	21.9	22.5	23.1	23.8
75	1.4	17.6	18.0	18.4	18.9	19.4	19.9	20.5	21.0	21.6	22.3	22.9
76	12.7	16.8	17.2	17.6	18.1	18.6	19.1	19.6	20.2	20.8	21.4	22.0
77	12.1	16.0	16.4	16.8	17.3	17.8	18.3	18.8	19.4	19.9	20.6	21.2
78	11.4	15.2	15.6	16.0	16.5	17.0	17.5	18.0	18.5	19.1	19.7	20.3
79	10.8	14.5	14.9	15.3	15.7	16.2	16.7	17.2	17.7	18.3	18.9	19.5
80	10.2	13.8	14.1	14.5	15.0	15.4	15.9	16.4	16.9	17.5	18.1	18.7
81	9.7	13.1	13.4	13.8	14.2	14.7	15.1	15.6	16.2	16.7	17.3	17.9
82	9.1	12.4	12.7	13.1	13.5	13.9	14.4	14.9	15.4	15.9	16.5	17.1
83	8.6	11.7	12.1	12.4	12.8	13.2	13.7	14.2	14.7	15.2	15.7	16.3
84	8.1	11.1	11.4	11.8	12.2	12.6	13.0	13.4	13.9	14.4	15.0	15.5
85	7.6	10.5	10.8	11.1	11.5	11.9	12.3	12.8	13.2	13.7	14.3	14.8
86	7.1	9.9	10.2	10.5	10.9	11.3	11.7	12.1	12.5	13.0	13.5	14.1
87	6.7	9.4	9.6	9.9	10.3	10.6	11.0	11.4	11.9	12.4	12.9	13.4
88	6.3	8.8	9.1	9.4	9.7	10.1	10.4	10.8	11.3	11.7	12.2	12.7
89	5.9	8.3	8.6	8.9	9.2	9.5	9.9	10.2	10.6	11.1	11.5	12.0
90	5.5	7.8	8.1	8.3	8.6	9.0	9.3	9.7	10.1	10.5	10.9	11.4
91	5.2	7.4	7.6	7.9	8.1	8.4	8.8	9.1	9.5	9.9	10.3	10.8
92	4.9	7.0	7.2	7.4	7.7	8.0	8.3	8.6	9.0	9.3	9.8	10.2
93	4.6	6.6	6.8	7.0	7.2	7.5	7.8	8.1	8.5	8.8	9.2	9.6
94	4.3	6.2	6.4	6.6	6.8	7.1	7.3	7.6	8.0	8.3	8.7	9.1
95	4.1	5.8	6.0	6.2	6.4	6.7	6.9	7.2	7.5	7.8	8.2	8.6
96	3.8	5.5	5.7	5.9	6.1	6.3	6.5	6.8	7.1	7.4	7.7	8.1
97	3.6	5.2	5.3	5.5	5.7	5.9	6.1	6.4	6.6	6.9	7.3	7.6
98	3.4	4.8	5.0	5.2	5.4	5.6	5.8	6.0	6.3	6.5	6.8	7.1
99	3.1	4.5	4.7	4.9	5.0	5.2	5.4	5.6	5.9	6.1	6.4	6.7
100	2.9	4.2	4.4	4.5	4.7	4.9	5.1	5.3	5.5	5.8	6.0	6.3

FIGURE 5.2 Previously, everyone had to use these more detailed life expectancies.

Source: IRS Publication 590.

your investments to still provide income if you live longer than the average person. You should add about 25 percent more years to the life expectancy values that you get from most tables. The IRS periodically changes life expectancies by small amounts, but you can always get updated values of Figure 5.1 and the values corresponding to Figure 5.2 from Publication 590, which can be accessed at the IRS website, www.irs.gov.

Now suppose you are 65 years old and your spouse is 63. Figure 5.2 shows a 27.2-year life expectancy. If you add 25 percent of that, you get 34 years, so it is equivalent of saying that you want your money to last until you are age 65 plus 34, or your age 99. If you die first, the money would run out when your spouse was 97. Actually, if you do a new calculation each year, the money will never run out, but pickings may be pretty slim late in life if you overspent early in retirement.

Affordable Spending from Social Security

Social Security is the base source of income for a large number of retirees. What is surprising is its cavalier treatment in almost every retirement plan. There are a number of reasons for this. One reason is its peculiar income tax. Another is the difficulty accommodating rapidly escalating Medicare deductions. Still another is some discounting because it is likely to fall behind a full inflation adjustment even without the Medicare deduction problem, and finally, if you have not started getting payments yet, there is an income gap that has to be filled until payments begin.

Not all of Social Security is currently taxed. See last year's tax return to find whether 0 percent, 50 percent, 85 percent, or whatever was taxed. These percentages may well go up in the future to help fund the essentially bankrupt system now. You might want to assume that it is taxed at 100 percent rate as is likely to be the case at some point in the future.

I've developed a very simple formula that accounts for Social Security's failure to keep pace with inflation. It is implemented in the Post-Retirement Worksheet in Appendix C and evaluated in Appendix F, Post-Retirement Assumptions, which tests the assumptions we have used.

If you are not yet taking Social Security, Appendix C's Post-Retirement Worksheet helps calculate the gap costs.

By accounting for Social Security gaps, peculiar taxes, and potential failure to keep up with inflation, you are likely to get a better perspective of Social Security's contribution to your retirement.

> The most terrifying words in the English language are: I'm from the government and I'm here to help. —Ronald Reagan

Affordable Spending from Pensions and Immediate Annuities

Pensions or immediate annuities can either provide fixed payments or cost-of-living-adjusted (COLA) payments. Pension payments are just like immediate annuity payments, so you can use the same method for either a pension or a lifetime annuity that is making regular payments.

There are also immediate annuities that purport to offer better performance because payments are tied to investment performance. Most of these have so much limiting small print that the gains may be purely speculative. At any rate, these are not like conventional pensions.

COLA Pensions

Only a few people get COLA pensions, although many retirement programs mistakenly assume that all pensions have COLAs. COLA pensions are almost exclusive to government employees and include the retirement benefits for military personnel. These benefits are often capped at some maximum inflation rate. You should multiply your COLA pension quote by the amount shown in Figure 5.3 which depends on your remaining life expectancy and the cap percentage.

Severance Pensions or Annuities

If your pension is a consequence of a severance contract, remember to reduce the entry by at least 7.65 percent to reflect the deductions for Social Security and Medicare.

COLA Benefit
As a Percent of Uncapped Pensions

Life Expectancy	COLA Caps			
	3% Cap	5% Cap	10% Cap	No Cap
10	93%	97%	100%	100%
20	71%	82%	96%	100%
30	60%	75%	95%	100%

FIGURE 5.3 If future inflation is very high, a COLA cap may reduce your pension benefit significantly. These numbers are based on an historical analysis starting in the year 1965.

Fixed Pensions

Fixed pensions degrade in value with time because inflation erodes their purchasing power. I lost 30 percent of my pension's purchasing power in the first 10 years of my retirement. My father lost 80 percent of his purchasing power from the time he retired until his death. Therefore, it is necessary to save a little each year, invest the savings, and then draw down the savings later to compensate for inflation.

I developed a very simple equation for a retiree's use to determine how much a fixed pension or annuity a retiree can spend. It is simply the after-tax payments multiplied by the current age of the retiree divided by 100. We will compare this simple formula with the more complex result from more precise financial equations in Appendix F, Post-Retirement Assumptions. The simple equation, however, works just about as well and does not require speculative assumptions about returns, inflation and life expectancy.

NOTE

The rest of the after-tax fixed pension will go into savings to be drawn down later to compensate for inflation.

Pension Gaps

If you have not yet started getting your pension, then you have to account for the income gap between now and when the payments start. The Post-Retirement Worksheet in Appendix C does this for you. If you are irretrievably committed to retirement and have a large gap that you cannot fund from investments, you may have to borrow some money (ugh!) or, better, get a good part-time job in the interval.

Affordable Spending from Part-Time Work

In order to simplify the calculations in the Post-Retirement Worksheet, we are going to assume that you will deposit your take-home pay (gross pay less taxes and other deductions) to investments, even though you may subsequently withdraw some of those savings shortly to support what is otherwise affordable spending.

Some retirees get a part-time job just to pay for one or two special costly items and then quit right after they have earned enough. That is not consistent with the calculations in the Post-Retirement Worksheet, which allow you to work any length of time, but you can get the best of both worlds by simply adding the costs of those special items to the reserves and entering the after-tax compensation from part-time work to savings. That way, you will still have constant inflation-adjusted spending for everything else and still be able to buy the large purchase(s).

Alternatively, if you know that your part-time work is for something very specific and that you absolutely won't continue work after accumulating enough for that item, leave out the part-time work contribution as well as the item you will purchase. This is the easiest thing to do in that situation.

If spouses are going to retire in different calendar years, you can use part-time work entries as a means of accounting for the additional compensation between the first and second retirement. The retirement year for the plan entry is the year the first spouse retires. The part-time work contribution to savings is the after-tax income of the second spouse (less income tax and any other deductions) multiplied by the number of years between the two retirements. However, both spouses must still constrain spending to the affordable amount calculated in your plan.

Investments as a Retirement Resource

Just as there is some judgment in the size of Social Security, pensions, tax rates, and life expectancy that you use in a retirement analysis, there is some judgment required for investments. Most people think of the choice of returns and inflation as being the key uncertainties, but there are a lot more elements that we address here.

There is always the big question about whether to include the value of your home as an investment. Many people have so little savings that they may either have to get something out of their home equity or delay retirement or take on serious part-time work. Home equity is such an important and controversial subject in retirement analysis that it is addressed separately.

Reserves are another judgmental item that effect investments because these are the parts of investments that you set aside for either something specific or a general catchall for unknowns that are inevitable in anyone's future. These, too, we look at separately in the text that follows.

Our approach is to reduce investments for reserves and taxes and then divide the remainder by life expectancy. This would be correct for the situation where the after-tax growth of investments equals inflation, but does not cover cases where you want to plan on a return that is not equal to inflation. Therefore, we follow that with a simple correction for returns that I've found to work just about as accurately as more precise financial equations. I will give you some help with this in the Post-Retirement Worksheet in Appendix C and evaluate the assumptions involved in Appendix F, Post-Retirement Assumptions. You will see that they are surprisingly good.

If you want to have a more hands-on approach to your allocation assumptions, investment costs and historical returns, see *J. K. Lasser's Your Winning Retirement Plan* (Hoboken, NJ: John Wiley & Sons, 2001) or one of the retirement planning programs at www.analyzenow.com.

Your Home as an Investment

Because people have saved so little, many writers and planners are suggesting that your home should be considered an investment. I disagree

home equity

the part of your home that you own. Home equity is the current market value less the current indebtedness. If you have a mortgage, you own the equity and the lender owns the rest.

and think that, at best, only part of your *home equity* should be considered an investment. You may disagree with me.

My reasons are very basic. First, I believe that a home of one kind or another is necessary until you are resigned to a nursing home or are on the deathbed of a hospital. (I've even seen people in nursing homes who believe they will be able to return to their old home someday and insist that relatives not sell it.) Another reason is that a home can be an excellent reserve late in life. I saw that with my parents, who downsized a number of times to recover some equity to use for living expenses. A home can help support long-term care costs that may go beyond the early estimates for such care. Or it might make it possible to trade to another home in another city that is closer to a son or daughter that can help you when aged.

A home is of questionable value relative to being an investment, per se. You might quantify some incremental return by assuming some price, tax, and maintenance cost growth less the growth of rent for an apartment that would fit your lifestyle. The fact remains, however, that home values sometimes go down even though, by and large, they go up. A home is not a liquid investment, and borrowing on its value can be costly. It takes time to sell, find a replacement, and move. At best, you might add as an investment the equity you could safely recover by downsizing or one-half of your equity if you think you might later rely on a reverse mortgage.

Reserves for the Known and Unknown

Emergencies and Unknowns

Everyone should have some savings set aside for unforeseen emergencies that would not be used for normal retirement expenses. Generally, these reserves should not be less than 10 percent of existing savings in my opinion. Unfortunately, those with little savings should have a larger percentage because unforeseen expenses for elderly parents, adult children, job loss, long-term care, and uninsured health problems are not necessarily proportional to your income.

Nothing in this world is certain but death and taxes.
—Benjamin Franklin, in a 1789 letter to M. Leroy of the
French Academy of Sciences

Long-Term Care

Few simple retirement planning methods address the need for long-term care (LTC). If you are not wealthy enough to self-insure for LTC and don't want to rely on Medicaid, you might want to include a period of LTC in your reserves. For example, two years of such care in today's values might be about $140,000, but there are many ways to reduce this such as making reductions from income you will be receiving anyway or getting help from relatives or insurance. (See Smart Insurance in Chapter 6.)

If you were to subtract the costs of LTC in today's values from your investments, the theory would be that the amount you subtract would grow fast enough to equal the growth of LTC costs. If you are subtracting part or all of these reserves from a deferred tax account, you will also have to subtract the taxes that would be due, but you can do all of this in today's dollar values if you go along with our assumption that part of your investments will be growing at the same rate as long-term care inflation.

Replacement Reserves

Another category of items exists that needs reserves, but we can plan for them with some specificity. These include such things as replacing automobiles or a roof. These reserves can be very small when the item to be replaced is new, but they have to be very large when the time for replacement comes. Ideally, if the time comes to replace something like a car or roof that costs tens of thousands of dollars, you would like to be able to draw that amount from your reserve savings.

The principles of replacement reserves are simple. (We will review them in Chapter 6.) What is difficult is the implementation. Most people are going to have to change from buying large ticket items with loans to saving enough to finance the purchase themselves with existing cash. During the transition period, they will be making both debt payments on, say, an automobile, while putting aside some money to save for the next automobile. Effectively, they are providing money for two automobiles at the same time and thereby severely reducing the amount they have available for other uses.

It is almost mandatory to make this transition before you get into retirement because it makes such a big difference in your retirement income and expenses. Things that you buy with debt cost a lot more of your income. Things that you can buy with cash make interest on the cash until the money is actually used for the purchase. Said another way, if you have to pay 7 percent interest but can make 6 percent on your savings, the difference between debt financing and self-financing is 13 percent.

Reserves for Income and Medical Insurance Gaps

Then there are the reserves needed to replace employer's insurance, Social Security, and pensions from the time you quit work until you start receiving Medicare, Social Security and/or pension income. I've seen many cases where it is impossible for people to come up with the cash to support the years without Social Security or pension income. We show you some simplified computations in Appendix H, Replacement Reserve Worksheet, which help you through this.

Total Reserves

So if the total of your reserves exceeds the after-tax value of your investments, retirement is going to be very uncomfortable financially. Furthermore, if the money has to come from a qualified deferred tax savings account, and you are younger than 59½, you either have to accept an additional 10 percent tax penalty or strictly adhere to one of the few ways to avoid those penalties.

If you want to tap an IRA or other deferred tax savings plan before age 59½, contact a professional or the provider of the IRA and review your alternatives. In general, you have to start an orderly withdrawal process under some very strict rules (Section 72(t) of the Internal Revenue Code). You must take substantially equal payments over at least five years or until reaching 59½, whichever is longer, but the process is fraught with danger if you don't fully comply.

Total Affordable Retirement Spending

To get the total amount that you can afford to spend each year from your retirement resources, you add the individual contributions from Social Security, pensions, part-time work, and investments. People don't have problems with the addition, but they often have problems understanding what the numbers include or exclude.

The Post-Retirement Worksheet in Appendix C calculates affordable spending on an after-tax basis. This means that you do not have to include income taxes as a budget item within that affordable spending result. Saying it another way, we effectively subtracted the income tax before we started the analysis. If you had 100 percent withholding of taxes from your paycheck, we are really determining how much of the take-home pay that you can spend, and indirectly, how much you must save from that paycheck to compensate for inflation later on.

We also work with the after-tax value of investments. We do that by subtracting the taxes in today's dollars from the current investment values. We subtract ordinary taxes from deferred tax accounts, capital gains taxes from taxable accounts, and no income tax from tax-exempt accounts. In effect, this is equivalent to assuming that all investments are in deferred tax accounts at different tax rates. Over a long period of time, this simplifying assumption is slightly conservative compared to simplified programs assuming all investments are in taxable accounts using after-tax returns.

In addition to subtracting taxes from investments, we subtract whatever you enter for reserves. With the exception of replacement reserves, the detailed budget within the affordable spending limit should not have any provision to fund an item that is already covered by the reserve. The reserves do not have to be in separate accounts. You could envision them this way so that the remaining investments would be the source for all of your other spending requirements. For example, if you had included $20,000 for a vacation time-share in reserves, and you bought the time-share for $20,000 this year, it is apparent that the affordable spending budget would not have to include the time-share purchase because you used your $20,000 investment reserve for it. The affordable expense budget, however, would have to include all of the other ongoing costs of a time-share such as homeowner's dues, assessments, and property taxes.

There is one exception to the treatment of reserves so far reviewed, that is, for replacement reserves that will be discussed in Chapter 6, Implementing Your Plan. Unless a replacement is a one-time event and is already fully funded, the affordable spending budget has to cover the annual amount that you are paying to the replacement reserve. (See column E in Figure 6.2.) The amount of the reserve that should have already been accumulated (column F in Figure 6.2) should be subtracted from investments used to calculate affordable expenses—just as you would subtract any of the other reserves.

The total cash outflows in any year are therefore the sum of affordable spending with special purchases included as part of your reserve and income taxes. These do not add up to your retirement income in any year because part of that income goes into savings early in retirement, whereas, late in retirement, you draw on investment principal, not just interest and dividends.

Later, I discuss an alternative that exists in the Post-Retirement Worksheet to separately deal with debts depending on how you want them considered.

The Retirement Autopilot

autopilot

a device in an airplane or system that controls without human input. In an airplane, an autopilot is designed to smooth the flight in gusty air. In a planning program, it is those equations that smooth spending budgets from year to year.

When you do an analysis every year you can have large year-to-year changes in affordable spending if you have sizable investments with a significant stock allocation. It is possible to use a smoothing technique that reduces the affordable spending year-to-year changes so that it is easier to accommodate them.

The idea for this comes from my years in the aerospace industry where an *autopilot* is old hat. An airplane autopilot helps smooth the flight of an airplane through turbulent air. A retirement autopilot helps smooth the spending changes in turbulent markets. An airplane autopilot does not know in advance when or where or what size gust will hit the airplane, but it reduces the shock. The same is true of the retirement autopilot. It does not know in advance when or how big market changes will be, but it reduces the shock—which otherwise might be very difficult to accommodate (see Figure 5.4).

You can get your own image of the autopilot smoothing by engaging the Retirement Autopilot featured in *Dynamic Financial Planning Pro*, which can be downloaded from www.analyzenow.com; or you can see examples in *J. K. Lasser's Your Winning Retirement Plan*. We have incorporated a simplified add-on to the Post-Retirement Worksheet in Appendix C to let you include the autopilot in your calculations in case you hit turbulent markets.

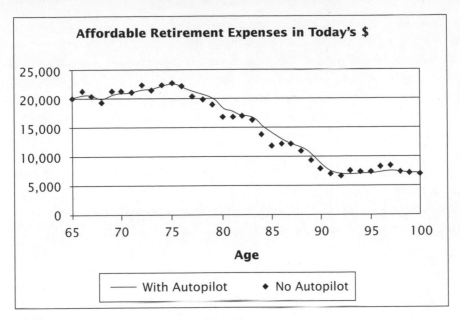

FIGURE 5.4 The autopilot reduces year-to-year changes. It will not cure the underlying fundamentals that drive long-term results.

A Spending Alternative for Debts

It would be nice to think that people are free of debts after retirement, but they often have a mortgage and payments for automobiles and other previous purchases. At the time your debt payments end, you will have a sudden jump in what you can spend for everything besides debt. If you do not plan to take on additional debt after paying off your existing debts, a more sophisticated way to account for debts and avoid the sudden disposable income change is to divide the debt by your life expectancy, adjust the result for your actual after-tax interest, and then subtract it from your total budget above. We show you how to do this in the Post-Retirement Worksheet.

This little trick is approximately equivalent to subtracting debts from investments. After all, debt is really a negative investment. If you subtract debts from investments, then it is apparent that neither the remaining investments nor other income would have to be used to pay for the debt. You could pay off the entire balance if you wanted.

The problem with subtracting debts from investments is that it does not account for the situation when the debt is bigger than your investments nor when the after-tax interest rate is different from the after-tax return on the investments. The approach used in the appendix solves those shortcomings. Another good thing about using this method is that if you want to pay off the debt completely in some future year with some of your investments, you won't find that the smaller investment level will have much effect on the affordable spending for everything except debt. So if you choose to add the debt alternative, affordable spending does not include the debt payments.

Therefore, with the optional debt method, your total cash outlays are affordable spending, income taxes, anything spent that was included in reserves—and your debt interest and principal payments. If you also pay mortgage insurance or include property tax with your debt payments, these items would have to be included in your affordable spending budget.

Implementing Your Plan

Three things are needed for the salvation of man:
To know what he ought to believe;
to know what he ought to desire;
and to know what he ought to do.
  —Thomas Aquinas, *Two Precepts of Charity*, c. 1250

I t does not do any good to have a plan if you do not execute it. Unfortunately, the lack of follow-through is all too common. People will pay thousands of dollars for professional advice and then do not use it. It takes both motivation and self-discipline.

It is not unlike people who want to lose weight. They sign up for their local exercise gym, pay their quarterly fee, go one or two times, and then let all kinds of things interrupt. By the time the next quarter fee is due, they just don't have the time for exercise. The truth is: It is just not a high enough priority yet. What drives many people to exercise is a stroke or heart attack. Of course, then it is too late to have prevented this condition, but now they are motivated and all of a sudden have the discipline to follow the therapist's orders.

Financial planning is not much different from people who say that they should be losing some weight. They start but don't follow through with the steps to be successful. Then retirement approaches, and they try to get religion only to find that all they can do is make the best of the little they have, just as those who are recovering from a stroke or heart attack. The same is true of retirees. Unless they adhere to a plan by following through on containing spending and investing appropriately, they too soon become financial cripples.

119

It is extraordinarily important to have the cooperation of your spouse and anyone else on your payroll. If they too are not motivated and disciplined, the plan is useless.

That B Word Again

The primary control for executing a plan comes down to that ugly B word: *budget*. There are many ways to implement a budget, some of which are short and simple and others very tedious. All require some degree of control and discipline. The consequences of overspending require compensating and more compelling actions to recover. Figure 6.1 illustrates how you might use a table to revise spending or savings.

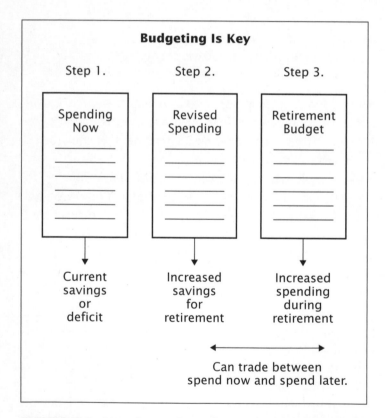

FIGURE 6.1 Your future depends on a budget that provides annual savings and has concurrence from involved family members.

The methods in this book give you bottom-line numbers, that is, the amount that you should be saving before retirement and the most you can spend after retiring. You have to figure out a way to live with those results even if your final plan does not have large savings before retiring or big spending after retiring.

Before retiring, you have to budget for everything that is left *after* you have subtracted taxes and retirement savings from your gross income. Midway through your life, you have to give serious consideration to "replacement" budgeting so that, by the time you retire, you no longer have to buy expensive items on credit. (I address this shortly.) Saving for retirement and replacements may not be comfortable, but the mechanics for retirement savings are easy if you can use automatic deductions from your paychecks. After retiring, you lose that advantage, and you must be in total control.

Once you have already set aside savings before retiring or limited investment draws after retiring, then you have to address budgeting the remainder. At some time, almost everyone has to use a sharp pencil and detail all current expenses to reconcile them with what is affordable. After that, the detail may not be necessary if you continue to add a specific amount to investments before retiring or draw no more than a specific amount after retiring.

Developing a budget that is both realizable and constrains spending starts with a list that shows where your money is going now. You can do this with a simple do-it-yourself list or use one of the commercial financial programs that automatically classify all of your current expenses into categories that you choose. After you have the list, you can develop the budget that satisfies your savings and/or spending requirements and gets the support of your family members. Without the support of all those that consume your income, the budget will fail.

Perhaps the simplest way to work on a budget is to split things into just a few categories such as:

1. Payments for things that are difficult if not impossible to control such as mortgage payments, property taxes and insurance.

2. Utilities over which you have limited control of their usage.

3. Replacements, transportation, and food where you have some more control.

4. Totally discretionary items such as electronics, clothes, entertainment, vacations, and so forth.

> ### Saving Takes Hard Decisions
>
> Sometimes you have to think outside the normal budget box.
> - Get a second job.
> - Reduce number of wheels.
> - Share quarters/rent out a room.
> - Downsize or relocate.
> - Take a family member off your payroll.
> - Work longer.

When you first try to squeeze everything into the bottom-line numbers, even category 1 is up for grabs. At that point, you might realize that you cannot afford your current home.

There is more control of utility bills than most people admit. Your home is an important element in determining these; but the modern family now has significant utility expenses that are largely unrelated to home size or location. Phone, cable, and Internet costs are completely out of hand for many people.

Nevertheless, once you reach the point of getting to acceptable values of the first three categories, the problem resolves to controlling the truly discretionary items. There are many ways to budget and/or control such spending. At one extreme, some people put cash in envelopes every week. At the other extreme, some people simply have a minimum target value in their checking account that, if too low, requires cutting back the following month. Some people use a credit card that categorizes expenses in the monthly bill and try to compensate the following month to reduce overrunning areas. Some people try to make regular deposits to a savings account for entertainment and/or vacations and those savings are their relief valve as well as a motivational element.

Replacement Budgeting

There are key items in budgeting that need to be addressed and are generally ignored. These are items that wear out and need replacing such as automobiles or a roof.

Replacing worn out or obsolete items can be painful for anyone, especially retirees. Unfortunately, conventional retirement planning programs do not provide much help with expenses that are irregular or may occur at uncertain times. The best way to cope with these is to set aside a reserve for replacements and budget an annual wear-and-tear contribution to that reserve. Then you will have the cash in your savings to buy large value items outright instead of having to borrow. With the possible exception of real estate, retirees should never buy anything on credit that requires interest or may have a penalty.

In order to do this, you need to make an estimate of the number of years the expensive things around your home will last. When the time comes to replace something, its cost and trade-in value will be somewhat different than your assumptions—as will the amount of time it lasted. However, in the long-run, you will be much better off than all of those people who do not understand how to do replacement cost budgeting. You will be paying yourself the interest instead of paying someone else the interest! The difference is huge.

If you could invest the money that you would save for replacement items at a return that keeps up with inflation, it is easy to calculate how much you need to save each year and how big your reserves should be at this time. For example, consider that you expect to replace your automobile every five years and that you would have to pay $20,000 (at today's value) after trading in your old vehicle. This means that the vehicle capital cost (not its operating costs) will be $20,000 divided by five years, or $4,000 a year for a wear-and-tear contribution to your reserve. Every year you would make a new calculation and make a new deposit. By making a new calculation each year, you address the inflation issue because your replacement cost will be higher and so your annual contribution to savings will go up a little, too.

The total of the annual wear-and-tear contributions can be alarming—but probably not as much as what the size of your replacement reserve should be today. Suppose that your automobile is two years old. That means your reserve should already be 2 × $4,000 = $8,000. Very young people consider this kind of computation to be absurd. By the time they add up all of the items requiring replacement reserves, they have nothing left in their savings for anything else, much less retirement. If you are a retiree in this situation, you are already in real financial trouble because the replacement reserve cannot be used as the part of your investments that contribute to your normal living expenses. Your bad situation is exacerbated further because your normal living expenses have to cover the annual wear-and-tear deposits to a replacement savings account.

Items you should consider for replacement cost budgeting are things such as your automobile, roof, furnace, water heater, carpets, exterior painting, interior painting, and electronics such as computers or a large-screen televisions (see Figure 6.2).

If you belong to a homeowner's association that does not have a replacement reserve and an annual budget for wear-and-tear savings, you will very likely have large assessments in the future. You will have to include your share of this omission as part of your own reserves because those assessments will be inevitable. Competent homeowner's associations have very detailed replacement cost analysis and significant reserves.

It is a good idea to keep replacement reserves in an account that is liquid, not something like a stock fund or real estate that might be difficult to sell and get as much as you want when you need it. Alternatively, this account can be a theoretical part of the rest of your liquid investments as long as you remember to subtract this theoretical amount from the investments used to determine how much you can otherwise spend for normal retirement expenses. In addition, your normal retirement expenses budget should include the wear-and-tear deposit to savings even though you may not spend any of it in this coming year. When the time does come to replace an item, the funds will come from the reserve.

Unless you are older than age 59½, replacement reserves should not be in a deferred tax account. That is because you will then pay a 10 percent penalty plus income tax on withdrawal if in an IRA or encounter severe payback restrictions if borrowing from a 401(k) or equivalent. If you are over 59½, the IRA penalty goes away, but the taxes do not. Therefore a reserve in any deferred tax account must be larger than you would otherwise calculate. For example, if you needed $24,000 for an automobile replacement and your ordinary income tax rate was 20 percent, the deferred tax reserve would have to be

$$\$24,000 \,/\, (1 - 20\%) = \$24,000 \,/\, 0.80 = \$30,000$$

A	B	C	D	E	F
Description	Cost to Replace	Normal Service Life	Years in Use Now	Annual Savings B / C	Reserve Size Now D x E
Car - Trade	$20,000	5	2	$4,000	$8,000
Roof	$20,000	20	4	$1,000	$4,000
Furnace	$2,000	10	4	$200	$800
Water heater	$1,000	10	4	$100	$400
Carpets	$10,000	10	4	$1,000	$4,000
Painting	$5,000	10	4	$500	$2,000
Electronics	$5,000	5	2	$1,000	$2,000
			Totals	$7,800	$21,200

FIGURE 6.2 It is simple to calculate how much of your budget should go to savings each year to replace expensive items (Column E) as well as the amount you should have saved already (Column F), but it is hard to face these realities in planning.

Curb Family Consumption

It takes either a parent with obvious control of the family and/or both parents speaking in unison to keep children from spending too much. Parents also have to set a good example or their sons and daughters will not follow.

There was an article in a recent *Seattle Times* that reported about an adult couple with two children of driving age. The parents decided they could do without automobiles, a truly remarkable decision considering that they lived in Issaquah, a very upscale urban community where life without a car is difficult. So the parents set the example. No cars. The husband rides a bike to work over 30 miles. That is impressive, not only

> ### Possible "No" Candidates
>
> It is a lot easier to find ways to get your family to reduce spending when you realize that you won't be able to spend anything in retirement. You might say "No" to:
> - Anything that comes into your house on a wire or with radiation.
> - Anything that has a battery, chips, or motor.
> - Anything that has fur or feathers.
> - Anything with a prominent label.
> - Anything that is on a CD or DVD.
> - Anything you can borrow instead.
> - Anything that requires credit.

because of Seattle's heavy traffic, but also Seattle is not known for the driest and sunniest of days.

On the average, to meet their planned objectives, people have to make considerable reductions in discretionary spending—as well as to recognize that many things are really discretionary even though you or members of your family have not felt that way in the past. Look particularly at your home, automobiles, and everything that uses electricity or power. Look at your utility bills. Maybe you really don't need an expensive cable TV alternative or all the communication devices that you have. Consider how much you spend for food at restaurants. Maybe you cannot afford that cute puppy that costs thousands of dollars over its life.

Stop Buying on Credit

The alternative to replacement budgeting is to buy things on credit and hope that you can pay for them in the next few years. If you are forced to buy by incurring debt, you are not saving. You are living beyond your income. If you cannot completely pay your credit card bills every month, tear up the cards and start paying down the debt immediately. Few people realize the cost of credit until too late in their lives. For example, paying for a $1,000 item over five years really costs almost $1,800 if the credit card rate is 12 percent. If you miss a payment, your interest rate may go to 21 percent and you have to stretch the payments over ten years, that $1,000 item really costs $6,700.

> **TIP**
>
> Credit cards provide great profit to the lenders and equally great increased costs to the card users. Tear them up if you cannot pay the balance every month.

It is much better to start saving the money needed for your future purchases and then make the purchase only after you have saved the required sum. It may take a while for you to get into this position, but it is one of the real secrets to making money. If you can make 8 percent on your investments, that $1,000 item will only cost you about $850 if you just put away $170 a year for five years because the interest you earn will bring the total to $1,000.

Paying only $850 instead of $1,800 means that you would have over $4,000 more to spend in retirement in 20 years or $20,000 in 40 years with an 8 percent pre-retirement return. You can extend this philosophy if you look ahead and consider that many of the things you have will wear out and need cash for their replacement. Start building some reserves for things such as auto, appliance and roof replacement. You don't want to have to pay for these with future credit.

In addition, don't be misled by "No Money Down" and "No Interest Till Next Year" signs. You will pay even more for such purchases because you are effectively borrowing more. So pay with cash. Cash purchasers often get a discount, especially with large value items such as automobiles, so the savings are even greater buying with cash than buying with credit.

The object is to get yourself to the point where you can do "replacement budgeting." That is a big step in the direction towards making real money.

Downsize Your Home Now

Downsizing means replacing a larger more expensive home with a smaller, less expensive one. If you know you need to get money from your home to support your retirement, it is better to downsize now than to wait until later, especially with the current $500,000 capital gains tax exemption. Tycoon Bernard Baruch was once asked how he got so rich.

He answered that he always sold too early. That advice applies here as well. If you start investing the money you save from downsizing and the lower maintenance and other costs, you very likely will be much further ahead by taking immediate action. It normally would take years of extraordinary house appreciation to benefit from delayed downsizing.

Larger homes have larger property taxes and cost more to maintain. Roughly, costs go up faster than the square footage, so a 3,000-square-foot home can have maintenance and property tax costs more than twice that of a 1,500-square-foot home.

Larger houses also tend to beg for more furnishings and things to fill closets and shelves. It is not just that larger homes require more carpet: they require more furniture and provide space for things that otherwise might cause people to ask where they would put the new item. The larger viewing distances mean larger television screens and more lighting. People tend to buy many more clothes when they have a walk-in closets and more food and kitchen appliances when there is a large pantry. Decorating a large wall is more expensive than decorating a small one.

In spite of government support, the reverse mortgage alternative to downsizing has not been popular. Not only does it not solve the larger maintenance and furnishing problems of a larger home, but the fees associated with such loans are painfully large. Also, consider that if you are forced to live away from your home for 12 consecutive months, you have to repay the reverse mortgage, and your payments will end. Reverse mortgages are really meant to be a last resort short of having to go on welfare rolls. To learn more about reverse mortgages, the AARP has a website devoted to the topic at www.aarp.org/money/revmort.

One caution: Be sure to invest, not spend, the gain that you recognize from the sale less the purchase of the smaller home. Furthermore, to really capture the gains, invest the incremental savings from reduced maintenance costs and property taxes.

Are you considering buying a vacation home or time-share after retiring? Think through this very carefully because it is the opposite of downsizing and increases all of the previously mentioned problems. Furthermore, debt on such an investment requires a total tax analysis of the alternatives, particularly if extra funds must be drawn from deferred-tax accounts and would put you in a higher tax bracket or trigger a higher Social Security tax bracket.

> **TIP**
>
> Downsizing your home as soon as possible can provide large tax-free retirement gains. Buying a second home in retirement is seldom a good investment and increases furnishing, maintenance, and utility costs.

Don't Forget Your Health

One of the most important things you can do is not financial and requires no speculation. That is to do the things that keep you healthy. You won't be able to give up your medical insurance, but your uninsured expenses will be lower, you will feel better, and you will live longer. Being in good shape in retirement is a real blessing, while living in pain is an extraordinary burden. Not only should you want to be active during most of your retirement, you don't want to be confined to a wheelchair if it is at all possible.

Perhaps the thing that should be the first priority is to exercise regularly. One-half hour of walking almost every day is the minimum for most people. The next priority should be eating vegetables, fruits, fish, and a modest amount of meat while minimizing fatty foods, pastries, and sweets.

Finally, treat your eyes, ears, and teeth kindly. These things naturally get to be problem areas as you age and often are not insured. Impaired vision can be debilitating, hearing aids can cost thousands of dollars, and expenses to save teeth can cost tens of thousands. You don't want to be forced to use false teeth and face all of their problems if you can avoid it.

So start being health conscious now. If you are married, get your spouse and children on regular exercise routines as well as on healthy diets. Don't let your children install high-volume speakers in their cars or go around all day with iPod audio buds stuffed in their ears playing loud music. The iPods can reach 120 db, which is equivalent to standing next to a jet airplane at deafening takeoff power. Everyone should have some UV protection from the sun to prevent skin cancer and eye damage. As children, we were never told that the eye's lens, unlike skin, continues to tan throughout our lives thereby reducing our ability to see under dim light conditions when we are older. And surely follow the advice to brush and floss teeth twice a day.

Health problems? See a doctor, but first you may find some interesting information at the following health awareness websites:

- Agency for Healthcare Research and Quality, www.ahrq.gov/consumer
- WebMD, www.webmd.com
- Healthline, www.healthline.com

Smart Insurance

Without knowing it, you can be underinsured or overinsured. Being underinsured may cost you dearly in a catastrophe as many have learned, Being overinsured entails large premiums that may leave you destitute in retirement. So it is wise to reach a compromise. Nevertheless, there are some kinds of insurance that you likely will need all of your life such as medical, homeowners, and auto liability insurance. Early in life you may need life insurance and late in life long-term care insurance.

Medical Insurance

Medical insurance is the most expensive and most necessary insurance as you get older. Your employer may provide a policy during your working years and offer a lower-cost policy for retirement. In most cases, however, you will have to find your own economical source after you retire. For this, you want to thoroughly investigate a number of alternatives and determine the cost of your options.

After age 65, Medicare helps immensely. You are automatically enrolled in Part A for hospital coverage, but you will most likely want to sign up for Medicare's Part B for doctor expenses and/or consider either a health maintenance organization (HMO), a preferred provider organization (PPO) or a Medigap health policy and, perhaps, Medicare's Part D for drug coverage. If you are still working at 65 or over and have an employer's group policy, you can delay starting Part B until the month after you retire. There is a lot of information about Medicare at the Social Security Administration's website, www.ssa.gov, or you can call 1-800-633-4227.

If you retired before age 65, you have much more exposure and should carefully weigh the merits of your alternatives. The government requires that companies with more than 20 employees offer laid-off or early retirees COBRA insurance. This bears the initials of the Consolidated Omnibus Budget Reconciliation Act of 1986. This means that those people can continue the employer's medical insurance for 18 months (or 36 months in some cases), but now the former employees, not the employer, must pay the premiums. The group rate for these premiums is likely to be lower than you can find elsewhere for the same coverage. However, there are no pat answers because there are so many variables that depend on your own judgments and the alternatives available. You can find more about COBRA at www.cobrainsurance.net.

Long-Term Care

After medical insurance, the next most daunting question facing those looking at retirement is whether they should buy a long-term care (LTC) policy. There are two kinds of retirees who absolutely do not need it: (1) those who will live on so little in retirement that their medical costs will be covered by Medicaid; and (2) those who have enough wealth that they can afford to pay the costs at the time.

The vast majority of people that are in between these two cases should either have relatives or support networks that are willing to provide the care and/or LTC insurance. Although the annual costs for LTC insurance may be lower long before you retire, you may make the best decision sometime between age 50 and 60 when you can better assess your own situation and have to worry a little less whether your insurer will still be around and whether the insurer will increase the annual costs despite protests to the contrary. Most often, there are loopholes that afford the insurer some escape, so you have to read the fine print very carefully. Also, it is important to consider only insurers rated A or better by A. M. Best and "strong" by Standard & Poor's and Moody's because you want your insurer to outlive you.

LTC insurance does not have to be large enough to cover the total bill, which averages over $75,000 per year per person now and is going up every year. For that reason, no matter how much you choose to insure should have some inflation protection.

So how much LTC coverage should you have? To answer this, you need to estimate the length of care (perhaps a year or two) and how much of the care can be covered by relatives, Social Security, pension, savings withdrawals, and either sale of your home or proceeds from a reverse mortgage. For example, suppose that LTC is $75,000 per person, and the normal annual expense you can support is $50,000 for both you and your spouse. Further suppose that one spouse can live on $30,000 of that leaving $20,000 to offset the other spouse's LTC expenses. That brings the $75,000 annual insurance bill down to $55,000 ($75,000 less $20,000) per year for one of you.

The odds are that both spouses will not need LTC, so you might opt for a *joint* $55,000 per year policy to cover the first spouse to need the care instead of two separate policies totaling $100,000 per year (2 × $75,000 less the $50,000 that you can afford to pay directly). You may be able to reduce the costs further if you consider a care provider in your home instead of an institution. Remember, too, that payments to you in excess of $250 per day are taxable as income—and $250 is a 2006 value, an amount that will likely increase in the future.

Insurance companies try to get you to buy three years worth of care and get inflation protection. The latter is certainly desirable, but you probably don't need the money for three years care if you have some reasonable equity left in your home.

In that situation, you can get some cash for LTC either by selling, renting, or refinancing your home. Any one of these can reduce the necessary coverage even more and may possibly eliminate the need for LTC insurance altogether. That is the principal reason I don't like to see people include the value of their home as an asset when calculating how much they can afford to spend for normal expenses during retirement. Also, it is a good reason to pay off a mortgage before or not too long after retiring. If home prices hold, many people could get enough from their home equity to cover several years of LTC care—and that is likely to be enough.

You might want to look into a number of alternatives. One source that gives you three quotes is Care Quote at 1-800-587-3279 or Long Term Care Quote at www.longtermcarequote.com. Another is New Retirement's site at www.newretirement.com. An outstanding LTC reference site is *www.longtermcare.gov.*

Life Insurance

When you have a young family, you will also want life insurance, but term insurance is usually the best buy. Five times your current income

may be sufficient. You probably don't need life insurance later in life if
you have sufficient resources to support a long period of retirement. If
you are very wealthy, you might consider life insurance in a trust so that
heirs will have money to pay estate taxes.

But suppose you already have a life insurance policy other than
term insurance. You might want to consider selling the policy rather than
continuing payments or letting the policy lapse. There is a lot of information on this on the Web. Just search with the keywords "viatical life
insurance." You will find such websites as InsBuyer at www.insbuyer.
com/viatical.htm and others that are helpful.

Invest More Prudently Than Ever

No one knows the best investments for your savings because no one
knows what will happen in the future to the economic environment
much less any particular investment. The theorists tell you that they
can match an investment allocation to your risk tolerance, but all of
this is based on history that is not likely to repeat itself, particularly in
the recent economic environment that has been, and will continue, to
develop.

During the bull market of the 1990s, you could invest in almost
anything and make money. Technology stocks and dot-coms were especially attractive and had huge gains. But after 2000, they lost most of
their gains very quickly as did the majority of stock investments. Bond
funds were not immune from problems either. Bonds lose their value
when interest rates increase. So the large returns from bond funds are
gradually disappearing as the Fed continues to raise interest rates. In the
last few years, we have seen more humble forecasters and less planning
examples based on 10 percent or more returns.

Another lesson people learned from Enron and other disasters is not
to have a large part of your own company's stock in your retirement plan.
If you are ready to transfer your savings plan to an IRA, consider taking
the stock out separately. If done properly, you can pay capital gains rates
rather than ordinary income taxes.

It is best not to try and chase the market by buying things that have
gone up and selling those securities that have fallen. You are more likely
to buy near market highs and sell near market lows, just the opposite of
that which is needed for growth. The average person does far worse than

allocate
to specify the percentage distribution of different kinds of investments.

rebalance
to redistribute the amount invested in different kinds of investments so as to be in accordance with specified allocations.

the market averages both because of this poor buy/sell pattern as well as because the average person incurs appreciable transaction costs and invests in accounts and securities that have high internal costs.

In spite of the ups and downs of various kinds of securities, you can reduce the volatility and increase the long-term growth by using allocation rules to set how much money you will keep in stocks, bonds, or other retirement assets. In fact, good allocation rules help you sell securities that are pricy and buy securities at low values. You can further reduce the volatility and increase long-term growth by diversifying within these allocation categories. I will show you some painless ways to *allocate*, diversify, and *rebalance* in the chapters that follow.

Need for Professional Help

If you can understand the discussion on investments in the next chapter, you may not need professional assistance. If you don't understand, make a one-time visit to a professional planner. Chapter 10 can help you select a professional.

If you are interested in more self-help, you can find detailed information on investment management at www.analyzenow.com and my book, *J. K. Lasser's Your Winning Retirement Plan*. It is produced by the same editing team as the *Books for Dummies* series and is easy to follow—and was recommended by *BusinessWeek* as one of the two best books on retirement planning and the most practical. *J. K. Lasser's Your Winning Retirement Plan* has also been reviewed and cited television and radio financial programs and in many publications including the *Wall Street Journal, Smart Money, Financial Planning, Kiplinger's, Money, AARP Bulletin*, and the like.

Chapter 7

Investing the Simple Way

t is said that the simplest way is often the best way. It certainly makes a big difference in the time that you have for other pursuits.

There is no magic about investing. The steps are simple:

1. *Save*: preferably with regular savings deposits.
2. *Invest*: Select the "home" or "homes" for your investments to reside such as an employer's savings plan, an IRA, a Roth, taxable investments, or tax-exempt investments.
3. *Allocate*: Set the percentages that should go into the primary allocation categories of (a) fixed income investments like bond funds and certificates of deposits and (b) equities such as real estate and stock funds. Increase the allocation to fixed income investments slightly each year as you age to reduce volatility.
4. *Diversify*: Choose diversified securities (e.g., mutual funds) within each allocation category.
5. *Rebalance*: Review the balances each year and switch money between categories if necessary to meet the allocation percentages in step 3.

Most people do not need a professional to invest their savings. In fact, many employers offer automatic payroll deductions for savings and provide a savings plan with a number of investment choices. You don't want to miss investing at least as much as the employer matches because those matching funds are free money and equivalent to 100 percent return in the first year. Most people should save the maximum amount permissible under the employer's plan and even supplement this with additional regular savings contributions.

Homes to House Investments

required minimum distributions (RMDs)

after age 70½, retirees are required to start distributions from deferred tax accounts that have to equal or exceed the RMD specified for their age in IRS Publication 590. The "divisors" used to calculate RMDs originally were life expectancies but now imply longer lives (see Figure 5.1).

You must select the homes for your savings deposits. These homes are not houses, they are particular places that have their own tax peculiarities. We break these down into tax-deferred, taxable, and tax-exempt accounts. More technically, deferred tax accounts are "qualified" as plans by the IRS and include employer's savings plans (401(k), 403(b), and the like, as well as IRAs, Roths, and annuities. Qualified plans defer taxes, so they are taxed at ordinary (your maximum) rate when withdrawals are made. Other investments often have different and lower tax rates. Qualified plans also have penalties for early withdrawals, usually before age 59½, and most have penalties for failing to meet the *required minimum distributions* (RMDs) after age 70½.

NOTE

Homes for investments have different tax rules although you often find similar fund opportunities in different homes.

Contacts for Several Lost-Cost Mutual Funds

- Vanguard, www.vanguard.com or 800-997-2798
- Fidelity Investments, www.fidelity.com or 800-343-3548
- TIAA-CREF, www.tiaa-cref.org or 800-842-2252
- T. Rowe Price, www.troweprice.com or 800-225-5132

Employer Savings Plans

The choices of homes for investments are often more a matter of convenience than tax considerations. When employer's matching funds are available, there is no contest. You would almost always choose the matching fund alternative. Also, the most convenient homes for the majority of people are employer sponsored savings plans including the new Roth 401(k). Employer plans offer automatic payroll deductions, often have employer matching funds, and usually a wide variety of investment choices. Those are big pluses.

IRAs

The next best choice is usually an IRA, preferably a Roth IRA if you qualify. IRAs and Roth IRAs are administered by mutual fund companies such as Vanguard, Fidelity Investments, TIAA-CREF, and T. Rowe Price to name a few. These offer a wide selection of investments within each category and are usually eager to help you with information.

Roth IRAs The primary advantage of a Roth IRA is that there are no income taxes on the earnings nor on the withdrawals if you have held the Roth IRA for at least five years and are then over age 59½. The disadvantage is that there is no tax deduction for any savings contributions. For this reason, many planners say that there is no after-tax income difference between a tax-deductible IRA and a Roth if you would have the same tax rate in retirement as when working and could get the same *returns* from the investments in each one. In fact, there is a difference

returns

short for return on investment. The return from bonds is interest and sometimes capital gains or losses. The return from real estate is rent and capital gain or loss. The return from stocks is dividends and growth reflected in either unrealized capital gain if you have not sold yet or actual capital gains (or losses) from the sale. Return is the sum of annual principal growth (or loss) plus dividends, interest and/or rent. It is most often expressed as a percentage growth over a one-year period.

because the tax savings from a deductible IRA would have to grow in a taxable account at the same after-tax return as the before-tax return in the IRA and Roth. Therefore, the Roth IRA may have the advantage over a deductible IRA even with the same pre- and post-retirement tax rate and return.

The chances of the Roth outperforming a deductible IRA improve greatly when the tax rate in retirement will be higher than when working but will likely underperform when the tax rates in retirement will be lower. A Roth would definitely look better than an IRA built from after-tax deposits. Roth IRAs also offer the advantage that you don't have to start taking out money at a specified minimum rate when you pass age 70½ and are likely to be better for heirs.

Annuities

With the exception of immediate annuities, annuities are almost always high cost and sometimes overly complex homes for investments, so you should not even consider them as a home for your funds except in unusual circumstances. Insurance companies are fond of selling variable annuities, usually one of the highest cost investment homes. Be especially careful to ask about and evaluate the costs of a variable annuity within a deferred tax savings plan. These are often sold to unsuspecting organizations by greedy fund administrators who take large fees in the process at the expense of the savers.

Immediate Annuities   The ultimate home for your investments when elderly may be immediate annuities that you can buy from mutual fund or insurance companies. You invest a certain amount and in exchange get payments for the rest of your life and your spouse's life if you so select. These payments are usually fixed and paid in monthly, quarterly, or annual amounts. More recently, however, there are some inflation-adjusted immediate annuities that offer attractive benefits for those who do not want to manage a stock portfolio, individual government inflation-adjusted bonds, or real estate to offset inflation. The initial payments are lower than for a fixed payment annuity; but the long-term benefits may be much better, particularly in a high inflation environment.

Investment Real Estate

Investment real estate can be an attractive home for investments. However, it is not for the timid or those adverse to lots of bookkeeping and hands-on work. You can avoid the hands-on part by joining partnerships, which are often fraught with perils. And partnerships are a tax reporting headache. Or you can buy *real estate investment trusts* (REITs). REITs are sold by brokers just like stock. Your deferred-tax provider may offer them as well.

Taxable or Tax-Exempt Investment Homes Except for retirees already drawing from deferred-tax homes, taxable or tax-exempt homes are the better choice for emergency or replacement reserves. They are also important for supplementing retirement funds.

If you have already saved the most you can each year in a deferred tax plan like those above, then additional savings should go into taxable or tax-exempt accounts. You can maintain such accounts in a mutual fund company or with an investment broker. Then your investment choices are virtually unlimited. However, it is usually better for most people to stick with low-cost stock index funds, low-cost bond funds, and money markets with competitive returns and checking privileges. A broader range of alternatives might include individual stocks, investment real estate, certificates of deposit (CDs), corporate bonds, tax-exempt municipal bonds, treasury bonds and bills, *Treasury inflation-protected securities* (TIPS), savings bonds, guaranteed income funds, and so forth.

real estate investment trusts (REITs) this represents ownership in a company that may own and operate income producing real estate or finance mortgages. The REIT may have a very specialized kind of real estate ownership or be diversified. There are REIT funds that have stock in numerous REITs. Unlike dividends, returns from REITs are taxable at ordinary income rates.

Treasury inflation-protected securities (TIPS) these are bonds issued by the Federal government with principal adjusted for inflation. The adjustment is taxable every year as ordinary income, so TIPS are better investments for deferred tax accounts than taxable accounts.

Tax Considerations

After considering matching funds and convenience, tax effects are usually the next consideration in choosing a home for investments. You have to make assumptions about tax rates in the future in an environment where tax laws change almost every year and with each new administration. Furthermore, what might otherwise be federal or state income tax may migrate into many other forms of tax including sales tax, property tax, gas tax, utility tax, and the like.

A good way to illustrate the power of income tax on the major investment homes is shown in Figure 7.1, where we compare deferred tax accounts with taxable accounts and Roths. Comparing taxable and tax-exempt accounts with deferred tax accounts is tricky because you would like to keep them on the same basis. To do that, you have to account for the additional savings you can make because you get a tax deduction when making deferred tax account deposits. These savings would likely be deposited to a taxable account, hence the "extra" adjustment shown in Figure 7.1. Alternatively, if you were still below the maximum allowable contribution to the deductible deferred tax account, you could make an additional contribution in an amount equal to the tax savings and approach the same results as with the Roth.

The Roth is the clear winner providing that you qualify, that is, if your income is less than whatever limits are set. Your investment advisor, employer, or mutual fund provider can help you with this. In addition, you may be able to convert a regular IRA to a Roth or an employer's savings plan to an IRA and then to a Roth (see Chapter 4).

The next best is usually a deductible deferred tax account such as a 401(k), 403(b), deductible IRA, and the like—providing that you get the extra savings by investing the tax deduction (shown as "Extra" on Figure 7.1) that you get from such accounts. That is followed by an IRA made with after-tax income deposits and then taxable accounts that are even more subject to the whim of the congress.

Figure 7.1 shows several kinds of taxable accounts. The first represents a taxable account that benefits from lower tax rates on capital gains and dividends. The next represents what would happen if congress did not give such tax breaks or the situation where a person has high turnover funds that cannot take advantage of long-term holding benefits. The third taxable account is labeled "Tax managed," where the stocks are taxed at the lower rates while the municipal bonds are tax-exempt. Obviously, the tax benefits help those in the high-tax brackets, but, even then, their losses to taxes are very high.

If you can save more than you are allowed to save in deferred tax accounts and are in one of the highest tax brackets, you may want to keep your stock funds out of the deferred tax category because this category is taxed at ordinary income rates. The tax breaks for capital gains, dividends, and tax-exempt municipal bonds are likely to provide better performance than in a home for deferred tax investments. Also, there is the extra value if you leave any significant sums to heirs because the tax basis in non deferred tax funds is marked up to the value on your death or six months after your death.

After-Tax Post-retirement Income in Today's Dollar Values

$1,000 plus inflation added each year before retiring
20 years of deposits, 30 years of draws, 3% inflation
All accounts have 50% stock before retiring and 35% after.

Home for investments (a)	Income Tax Rate				
	10%	**15%**	**30%**	**40%**	**50%**
Deductible deferred-tax	1,435	1,356	1,116	957	797
Extra from tax savings (b)	143	191	340	403	448
Net: Deductible + Extra	1,578	1,546	1,456	1,360	1,245
Non deductible IRA	1,514	1,474	1,352	1,271	1,191
Taxable funds (c)	1,425	1,272	1,133	1,008	895
Above w/o tax breaks (d)	1,369	1,172	1,002	854	727
Tax managed (e)	1,255	1,205	1,156	1,110	1,066
Roth (0 tax)	1,595	1,595	1,595	1,595	1,595

(a) Returns reflect investment costs and reverse dollar-cost-averaging
    Pre-retirement returns: 7.25% all except "tax managed" at 6.5%
    Post-retirement returns: 6.38% all except "tax managed" at 5.4%

(b) Tax savings from deductions invested in taxable account.

(c) Full tax on interest, ½ tax on stocks.

(d) Scenario with no tax breaks for dividends, interest and capital gains.

(e) Stocks taxed at ½ income tax rate. Muni bonds not taxed.

FIGURE 7.1 The chart compares the inflation-adjusted retirement income you would theoretically get each year of retirement from saving $1,000 (plus an inflation adjustment) for 20 years.

High-income people now sometimes opt for "separate accounts" or "client managed accounts" when they have enough money so that an asset manager can tailor individual stock and bond purchases to the person's "needs." These usually involve large fees that severely reduce returns to the point that they generally fall behind index funds. Another expensive investment is a hedge fund. If you are interested in one of these, I suggest that you first read Roger Lowenstein's *When Genius Failed* (New York: Random House, 2000). That will sober you fast.

Also, if you are vulnerable to high taxes, consider tax-managed funds. These try to select investments with low dividend payments and rely, instead, on capital growth. When they must sell stocks for a capital gain they select the particular purchase dates and issues that have the least gains and often are able to offset the gains by also selling stocks that were in a losing position.

We will talk about investment selection later. It is important to first select the home(s) for your investments and then select an allocation rule. So let's talk about allocations next. Investment selection comes after you have selected the investment home and allocation rules.

Allocation Rules Rule

Many studies have shown that the way in which you allocate (divide up) your investments in categories is more important than the particular selection of investments within a category. At the highest level, you would determine what percentage of investments should go into equities (stocks, stock funds, and investment real estate) versus the remaining percentage that should go in fixed income investments like CDs, bonds, or bond funds. If you are not using a lifecycle fund that does all of this automatically, you have to decide on an allocation rule to guide you. You will also need a rule if supplementing a life-cycle fund with other investments.

TIP

It is generally a good practice to keep track of allocations in more detail than just fixed income and equities.

The allocation rule I use is considered to be too conservative by many modern planners. It has served me well, however, and I would recommend it to anyone with significant, though not outrageously large, investments. The rule is to keep the percentage of equities (stocks and investment real estate equity) below 110 minus my age but not to let it go less than 100 minus my age. So, when I was 40 years old and started using this rule, the percentage of my equities was kept below 110 − 40 = 70 percent and above 100 − 40 = 60 percent. Since the remainder of my investments was in fixed income securities (bonds, CDs, and money markets), I subtract the percentage of equities from 100 percent to get the limits for fixed income investments. This means that at age 40 I kept the fixed income allocation between 30 percent and 40 percent. When the stocks got outside of these limits, I would rebalance toward the center, that is, close to 65 percent stocks. My experience has been that I usually don't have to rebalance but about every other year (see Figure 7.2).

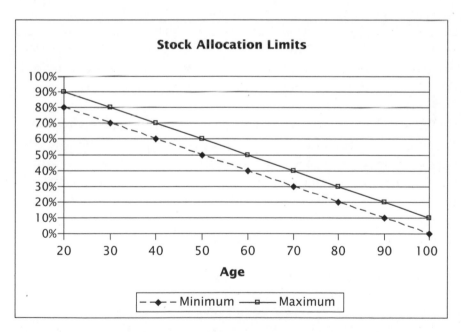

FIGURE 7.2 I keep the total of my stocks within the limits of this chart depending on my age. Before retirement, this helped me decide where to deposit my new savings. Now in retirement, it helps me determine where I should take my withdrawals.

Financial managers, fund managers, and individuals who are sticklers for allocation control also use some percentage rule within each category, say, a certain fraction of the stocks, should be in large capitalization (cap) stocks, small-cap stocks, value stocks, and international stocks. The smaller the subdivision of assets, the more you have to mind allocation changes. Some funds are made up of funds within many categories and effectively rebalance daily.

Generally, I only look at my investment allocation quarterly, perhaps because I'm lazy or because, long ago when I bought individual stocks and bonds, I found that I had sometimes switched some stock to bonds and then had to reverse the procedure a couple of months later. Only the broker benefited from the additional stirring.

Rebalancing Simplification

Rebalancing is simple within deferred tax accounts because there is no tax impact. However, there is a practice you can use for taxable (nondeferred tax) accounts that has helped me a lot. Within my taxable accounts, I have all dividends, capital gains distributions, and interest automatically deposited to a money market account. This provides a ready source of cash to help with rebalancing and makes it easy to know the cost basis for tax computations when I withdraw principal.

My own practice is to pay attention to the major split between equities and fixed income, and only redistribute elements between lower-level categories when one of the lower-level categories gets disproportionately large or small. If I were a real allocation stickler and wanted to control all elements within the same ±5 percent tolerance that I use at the top level, I would have to deal with some relatively small numbers. For example, if I targeted my small-cap stocks at 10 percent of my investments, I would have to watch for changes at ±0.5 percent of my portfolio.

Rather than do that, I wait until my stock/bond/real estate allocation gets outside the limits and then rebalance using the subcategories that have brought about the major reason for the unbalance.

Diversifying the Easy Way

Because the future is uncertain, it is very important to hold a portfolio that is widely diversified. That is, you should divide your investments into different kinds of securities so that you might have some money in large company stocks, small company stocks, international stocks, real estate, bonds, and other fixed income investments. History has shown that each of these categories is a better investment than the others in various years, but that no one category is consistently the top investment category.

Investment *hybrids* are securities that can reduce your investment management work immensely. The allocation rules and rebalancing are left to financial firms. All you have to do is sit back and enjoy the growth or income.

> **hybrids**
> a mix of different kinds of investments in one fund. Hybrids have a specified distribution of stocks and bonds that are rebalanced frequently to preserve stated distributions.

The traditional hybrids were equity-income funds and balanced funds. Equity-income funds invest in both stocks and bonds, usually with a lot of latitude from an allocation standpoint and reliance on the fund manager's judgment. Balanced funds are an older concept but with a relatively constant allocation of stocks and bonds. You can get balanced funds that are 60 percent stocks and 40 percent bonds that are good for working people. Alternatively, you can get balanced funds that are 40 percent stocks and 60 percent bonds. These are good for retired people. And you can get 50/50 balanced funds that are 50 percent stocks and 50 percent bonds. These are good for almost any age person, but they should be supplemented with stock funds when young and bond funds when retired.

You can also get balanced funds that are "tax-managed." These are good for higher-income people because the bonds are tax exempt, and they manage the stocks to reduce taxes from ordinary income.

Some of the major low-cost mutual fund families are now offering "target retirement" or "life-cycle" diversified funds that are designed to reduce the investment risk as you get closer to retirement. These are hybrids that mix stocks and bonds and reduce the stock allocations as you age. That simplifies investments because you really only need a money market fund and a life-cycle fund. I would go for this approach if I were still working and just let the money ride.

I don't know what the future holds any better than anyone else. My feelings are that as long as consumerism and deficit spending rage on, I would have more than half of my investments still in the stock market if I were working. If a life-cycle or balanced fund would not have enough fixed income or equities to satisfy my allocation rule I would supplement it with whatever was lacking—for example, a bond fund or a mix of large, small and international index funds (see Figure 7.3).

Later in life, you may choose to convert part of your investments to an inflation-adjusted immediate annuity. Here an insurance company manages a mix of stocks and bonds. In return for a lump sum of principal, they give back monthly, quarterly or annual payments for life that are adjusted upward for inflation in each period. These are well suited for older people who want a relatively constant stream of income that is inflation compensated. It is wise to invest in these over a period of years so that, for example, you might invest 10 percent of your funds in year one, another 10 percent in year two, a third 10 percent in year three, etc., until you reach the point where you still have funds for emergencies or large ticket items. Once you purchase an immediate annuity, you cannot get the principal back, and your heirs will get nothing, except your spouse if you so specify.

Allocation Alternatives

in order of complexity:
Keep it simple with a life-cycle fund
OR
Supplement balanced funds with equities/bonds
OR
Balance your own selection of index funds
OR
Diversify and rebalance yourself considering:

Fixed Income	**Equities**
Long-term bonds	Large company stocks
Intermediate-term bonds	Midsize company stocks
Short-term bonds	Small company stocks
Government TIPS	International stocks
Savings I Bonds	Value stocks (L, M, or S)
CDs	Growth stocks (L, M, or S)
Money Markets	Investment real estate
etc.	etc.

FIGURE 7.3 Life-cycle funds are easier than do-it-yourself mixes where you have to select diversified securities and do the rebalancing yourself.

If you want to make a rough comparison of an inflation-adjusted annuity to a fixed payment annuity, you should multiply the payments from a fixed payment annuity times your age divided by 100 and then compare that with the initial payment of the inflation-adjusted annuity. This is because you must save part of a fixed payment annuity to compensate for inflation later on.

There are some financial planners that like to include Social Security, pensions and payments from immediate annuities in an allocation analysis. They do this by assuming a death date and calculating the present value of all future payments. I don't believe in controlling allocations this way because it almost always leads to recommending too much of your savings be invested in stock accounts. This is great for the planner who may get a kickback on your mutual fund investments, but yields an allocation that is too much investment risk for most people. On the other hand, including the present value of future payments from pensions or annuities does give you a better overall perspective of risk, particularly if you think that your pension trust may go belly up. It is still a puzzle to me why any analyst would want to add the present value of Social Security to an allocation analysis.

If you use hybrid investments before retiring and transfer a part of those hybrids to immediate annuities later in retirement, you don't have to pay much attention to the following chapters on diversifying equities and fixed income investments. The chances are good that your performance will be better with low-cost hybrids than immersing yourself in the temptations of the broad marketplace.

Investing When Retired

There are some major differences between appropriate investments for working people and those who are retired.

The *seriousness* of financial failure is the first major difference. It is much harder to go back to work to get additional income after retiring, whereas the working person can delay retirement and continue to earn. There is nothing that is financially sadder than a retiree who watched investments fall precipitously and consequently spent savings too early. The difficulties of finding and performing work as an elderly person can be enormous.

Reverse-Dollar Cost Averaging

The second major difference is that retirees generally make regular, systematic withdrawals from their investments. This is the opposite of working people who make regular deposits and benefit from dollar cost averaging—that is, the gains from buying more shares of stocks when the prices are low and fewer shares of stocks when the prices are high. The retiree does just the opposite: When the stock prices are high, the retiree sells fewer shares than when the stock prices are low. This is called *reverse-dollar cost averaging*. Unfortunately, most simple retirement planning programs do not account for what can be a very painful penalty.

Simplifying Investments

Just like working folks, retirees now can simplify their investments by buying life-cycle funds or balanced funds with a fixed allocation of stocks and bonds. As a retired person with perhaps half of my retirement life behind me, I have large unrealized capital gains in taxable accounts. So I have decided not to switch to life-cycle funds. Doing that would create a significant tax burden.

I do have a low-cost, tax-managed balanced fund that I've had for a number of decades. Tax-managed funds are another interesting wrinkle in the field of mutual funds. These are managed to utilize tax-exempt securities when possible, minimize turnover to reduce ordinary income taxes, and sell losing positions to offset recognized capital gains.

With the exception of my wife's account, I don't buy individual stocks. (My wife likes to tell her friends about the stocks she has that go up—but she is very quiet about the ones that go down.) I like to keep stock investments simple and invest the largest share in a tax-managed total market index from a low-cost mutual fund. In addition to my tax-managed total market and balanced funds, I have a value fund and some other tax-managed index funds including large-cap and small-cap stocks. My efforts would be simpler if I had just a life-cycle fund.

My fixed income investments are largely in municipal bonds. These I hold to maturity so that I don't have broker's fees on the selling end—and I try to buy "original issue" bonds because their fees are set by the issuer. My former company has a great stable value fund in its 401(k), so I've stuck with it for several decades and not transferred the money to an IRA as recommended by many financial planners. I've also been accumulating

Savings I Bonds, which are my ultimate security in case the whole financial world falls apart.

Inflation-Protected Investments

I could be wrong about what will happen to inflation. Nevertheless, I do like inflation-protected government Savings I bonds that you can buy either at a bank or on the Web. Another alternative is TIPS that you can buy at a government auction or through a mutual fund. TIPS are better for deferred tax accounts (IRA, 401(k), etc.), while I bonds are not because in the difference in the way they are taxed. Also, I'm getting to like the new inflation-adjusted immediate annuities.

Immediate Annuities

If you are retired and considering buying an immediate annuity, look into some of the new offerings with inflation-adjusted payments. These are especially attractive to older widows, widowers, or those in some kind of assisted care who do not really want to have anything to do with investments but would like to have a regular, well-defined income until death. The initial payments from an inflation-adjusted immediate annuity will be less than from a fixed payment immediate annuity. However, if inflation turns out to be higher than normal, most people do much better with the inflation adjustment in the long run.

You buy immediate annuities from a mutual fund or insurance company and get monthly, quarterly, or annual checks until you die—or your spouse dies if you choose a last survivor option. Each year payments from an inflation-adjusted annuity go up (or down in a depression), perhaps up to a maximum, which might be 10 percent inflation in any year. But these never fall below your initial investment in a depression. A large part of those payments are "excluded" from income taxes until you get all of your original investment back. Just don't put all of your investments in an immediate annuity or you won't have any flexibility because, once invested, you are locked into a certain payment schedule. The best thing to do with annuities is to buy them in increments over a period of years so that you have the most flexibility when you are younger and the most certainty of income when you are older.

laddering

time-wise diversification. This is the intentional staggering of maturity dates for bonds or CDs so that approximately the same amount of principal comes back every year over a period of years. You can also ladder immediate annuities by purchasing approximately equal amounts each year over a period of years thereby getting larger payments as you age.

You can compare immediate annuity offers with your own self-administered savings plan using a free immediate annuity calculator on www. analyzenow.com. This will help improve your perspective and choice.

Laddered Bonds

Laddering means that you buy bonds that mature in different years as shown in Figure 7.4. Then, when they mature, your principal comes back to you more or less evenly over your foreseeable lifetime. In the meantime, you get the interest every year until the individual bonds mature. My laddered bonds are tax-exempt municipal bonds because of my income bracket and because I buy them outside of my tax-deferred accounts. If I were in a lower tax bracket and if I were buying them in an IRA, I would probably either buy very highly rated corporate bonds from a broker or a low-cost mutual bond fund based on a balanced bond index.

Laddering Bonds

Bond	Matures
ABC Municipal Bond	2007
DEF Municipal Bond	2009
GHI Municipal Bond	2011
KLM Municipal Bond	2013
NOP Municipal Bond	2015
QRS Municipal Bond	2017
TUV Municipal Bond	2019
XYZ Municipal Bond	2021

FIGURE 7.4 Stagger maturity dates over a number of years with bonds or CDs and diversify bonds using different entities, that is, not all from ABC.

Laddering works with certificates of deposits (CDs) as well. Using an example, suppose that you buy five CDs, one at 3 percent that matures in one year, another at 3.5 percent which matures in two years, and so on, with the last CD at 5 percent maturing in five years. The net first-year return is 4 percent. As each CD matures, replace it with a five-year CD. After four years, you will have all 5 percent CDs, which is a gain of 1 percent from the first-year ladder.

Rebalancing

Rebalancing means restoring your allocations to your target values when one component either grows too much or falls too much. An interesting fallout of rebalancing is that it can enhance returns because you are selling securities that have gone up in value or buying ones that have gone down in value—just like you are supposed to do theoretically. That is, buy low, sell high.

Rebalancing is easy and is unlikely to be necessary except every other year or so if you have a minimum and maximum allocation rule like I use. In fact, it may hardly be necessary at all if you use lifecycle funds.

If you are working and saving regularly—and paying attention to what is happening to your allocations—you can assist rebalancing by focusing your deposits from new savings on the sector that is falling behind your allocation target. You are buying securities when their value is relatively low.

The same is true if you are retired and making regular withdrawals from investments. Simply favor withdrawals from the accounts with the greatest growth. This also means selling when securities are high, even though you are not buying when they are low.

I prefer to have all of my interest, dividends, and capital gains distributions from taxable and tax-exempt accounts deposited to a money market fund. This has proved to be an adequate source, together with my selective withdrawals and stock gifting, to rebalance without having to sell my stock funds.

Figure 7.5 and the blank Rebalancing Worksheet in Appendix G show the method I use for rebalancing. It is easy to do with a hand calculator and even easier if you know how to use Microsoft Excel.

You would need a program on Excel if you were going to do rebalancing within major sectors. For example, if an international stock fund was supposed to be 10 percent of your portfolio, and your limits were plus or minus 5 percent, you would have to control that fund allocation to within plus or minus 0.5 percent of your total portfolio. This is too fine for me and requires more attention than I want to give. So I am a little lax about rebalancing at lower levels, but life-cycle funds do this all automatically.

Rebalancing to Allocation Targets

Letters in parentheses refer to entries, e.g., (A) is entry in cell A

Total Investments	Fixed Income	Equities	Instructions
A $100,000	B $40,000	C $60,000	Break total investments into 2 parts: Fixed income & Equities
	D 40	% Fixed Income 100 x (B) / (A)	
	E 35	My age now. This is the upper % limit for fixed income. See Chpt. 7, Rebalancing.	
	F 25	(E) – 10 This is the lower percent limit for my fixed income. See Chpt. 7, Rebalancing.	
	G 5	Too much fixed income: If (D) greater than (E), enter (D) – (E), else enter 0.	
	H 0	Too little fixed income: If (D) is less than (F), enter (F) – (D), else enter 0.	
	J 10	Percent to get to target allocation (G) + (H) + 5	
	K $10,000	If (G) is greater than zero, sell this much fixed income and buy equities: (A) x (J) / 100	
	L $0	If (H) is greater than zero, sell this much equities and buy fixed income: (A) x (J) / 100	

FIGURE 7.5 This figure shows how I determine how much I need to move from bonds to stocks or vice versa. I include stocks, stock mutual funds, and investment real estate equity in (C).

Refinement: If you are in one of the highest tax brackets, consider using after-tax values of investments in A, B, and C, but this means that if you are using a deferred tax account to rebalance, you should multiply the amount in K or L by $1 / (1 - \text{Tax rate})$. For example, if you are rebalancing in an after-tax deferred tax account and K is $10,000 and your tax rate is 20 percent, then the amount you should use for the actual rebalancing is

$$\$10,000 / (1 - 0.20) = \$10,000 / 0.80 = \$12,500$$

Annuities

There are lots of different kinds of annuities, but not many that you should own. For the most part, annuities are a big money maker for insurance companies and do not provide you with results that you could get several other ways. The more complex the annuity, the more you should be suspicious.

There are two exceptions to avoiding annuities. The first is a simple variable annuity under very limited conditions. The second is an immediate annuity, also under limited conditions. I will explain in the following sections.

Variable Annuities

These are deferred tax vehicles that defer the income taxes on the underlying funds until you start to make withdrawals, usually permitted only after age 59½. The reason that they are seldom attractive is that they generally have very high costs and, to make things worse, may offer only high-cost funds within, them thereby hitting the investor with a double whammy.

Nevertheless, when my children were young, I bought them each a low-cost variable annuity. This is one of the exceptions to annuity investments. I had maxed out on other deferred tax alternatives and wanted a place in which I could put some savings that would take the money out of my estate and would be available when the children retired. In this case, the funds could grow for a very long time without taxes and without any bookkeeping on either my or the children's part.

Vanguard is one of the few firms that offers lost-cost variable annuity opportunities. Even then, if you want a deferred tax vehicle, you should first make sure that you have taken full advantage of your employer's savings plan, a Roth if you are eligible, your own IRA, or if you are capable, laddered bonds.

If you are in a high-cost variable annuity, you can call the mutual fund that offers a more attractive variety, and they will arrange for the transfer in a 1035 tax-free exchange. They do all of the paperwork for you. However, your variable annuity may have a provision that has a penalty to try and thwart a transfer, so you would have to consider that as well.

Unfortunately, one of the worst places for a variable annuity is within an employer's plan. Some employers are swayed by fast-talking salespeople who sell them a package for their employees, often school teachers who are investing in a 403(b).

Immediate Annuities

These are very simple investments that have a special place in some people's portfolios. You plunk down a sum of money with a mutual fund or insurance company and start getting payments immediately. These payments may be monthly, quarterly, or annually and last for a specific period or until you die—or until your spouse or other designated person dies if you chose a survivor option. The payments are greater if you buy when older and, in some cases, if you can show you have a medical condition that will likely shorten your life.

This type of investment is attractive for older people who do not want to be bothered with managing their money and simply want a monthly check that they can count on. (Buy only from a highly rated company to ensure that the payments will last as long as you do.) The major downside is that immediate annuities remove all flexibility. Once you have invested, you can no longer get your principal back if you decided you wanted the money for something else.

Because they are so inflexible, it is usually better to ladder the immediate annuities—that is, buy a little each year over a long period before being heavily committed. In general, each successive purchase will provide higher payments because your life expectancy is shorter. Therefore, the insurer knows that the payments will not last as long.

There are a number of varieties of immediate annuities. The oldest and simplest form is the one that makes fixed payments. There are immediate annuities that make payments dependent on stock market prices (usually excluding any growth from dividends). These, however, may have such high costs and exceptions that they are unlikely to do better than a fixed annuity except in a period of a very prolonged bull market.

A more recent offering of an interesting immediate annuity alternative is one where payments are adjusted each year to account for inflation. The initial payments are lower than a fixed payment annuity, but will exceed the fixed payments if inflation continues to grow and you live long enough. I think that these may be one of the better investments to help protect from high inflation rates, but again, once invested, you can not go back and get your principal.

Immediate annuities have a very unusual tax treatment unless they are in a deferred tax account. Part of your payments is "excluded" from income taxes because it is a return of principal. In addition to the payment quote, you get a mysterious number called the *exclusion percentage*. This is the percent of the payment that is excluded from income tax. But beware! Years later, the exclusion will suddenly disappear when you finally have recovered all of your original investment. Then the entire payment is taxed.

Theoretically, you should get back your original investment by the time you reach your life expectancy. So, in the simplest of cases, if you wanted to invest $100,000 and the combined life expectancy was 20 years, each year you would exclude $5,000 from income tax (i.e., $100,000 divided by 20). The amount of the payment in excess of $5,000 is taxed at your ordinary income tax rate until the total of your exclusions exceeds your original investment. Then the entire payment is taxed.

Inflation-protected annuities may have a different kind of exclusion. Only the growth of the payments may be taxed until your exclusions exceed your original investment. This is likely to be near the year of your life expectancy at the time of the purchase. But what happens if you live longer than this? The answer is that the full amount of each payment is taxable. Late in life that might not be a welcome reduction of your income.

On the other hand, if you die young with an immediate annuity in a nonqualified account, either your survivor or heirs will experience another problem. This is when the survivor or heirs try to get some money back from the IRS because the full exclusion amount was not used or will unlikely be used by the survivor. Accountant fees to produce the miracle of getting money back from the IRS are likely to be more than the refund.

People who die young with immediate annuities leave money on the table that the insurance company picks up. The IRS gets more than its fair share. People who live longer than average beat the insurance companies bet on life expectancies, but the IRS never loses. The IRS only bets on sure things.

More Complex Annuities

My advice is to be very cautious about annuities with complex features because the added features are likely to give you little gain compared to other investment alternatives while providing the annuity issuer a substantial profit and the salesperson a fat commission. For example, an annuity might be based in part on the value of a certain set of stocks. You would "participate" in a certain percentage of the gains or have certain caps. The contract may permit the insurance company to change the rules unilaterally or maybe sometimes with the permission of a state insurance commission. All of these things are designed to help the insurer sell the product and make more money from your money. I've seen contracts—that don't surface until you are virtually committed—having a dozen pages of small print, some of which is ambiguous. Be careful! Get a review from someone not associated with the salesperson or insurer.

Rollovers

If you are in a high cost or otherwise unfavorable annuity, you may be able to get out of it with a 1035 exchange. Insurance companies try to make that unpalatable by inserting clauses for early withdrawals or the like. Some insurers try to get your business by converting a competitor's annuity into one of their own also using a 1035 exchange. You can take advantage of this by asking a low-cost annuity insurance company or mutual fund to give you a quote and evaluate any penalties from rolling over your money into one of their annuities. The receiving company does the rollover for you if you decide to go ahead.

Seeking Larger Returns

Returns on investments are the annual growth percentage. So an investment that started the year with $10,000 and ended the year with $11,000 grew $1,000. $1,000 divided by the initial $10,000 is 0.10 or 10 percent. Of course, if part of the reason it grew to $11,000 was because you added money, the return would have been smaller. If you had withdrawn some money and still ended up with $11,000, the return would actually have been bigger than 10 percent.

A good approximation for return on investment is A divided by B where

$$A = \text{Ending balance} - \text{Beginning balance} - \text{Deposits} + \text{Draws}$$

and

$$B = \text{Beginning balance} + 0.5 \times \text{Deposits} - 0.5 \times \text{Draws}$$

This is a before-tax return. Some financial journalists have used a similar formula and said that if your draws were to pay the taxes, you would get an after-tax return. Not so! The equation does not care about the reason you withdrew your money.

The search for larger returns on investment is important for both working people and retirees. Working people benefit from greater investment growth and retirees benefit from larger current income, often in the form of interest and dividends. The return on a stock is the sum of the increase in price of the stock plus the dividends. For that reason, the growth of a stock market index understates the total return because it ignores the stock dividends unless specifically called total return.

Few people recognize the volatility of stocks. Figure 7.6 represents the year-to-year variation in total returns, that is, the sum of dividends and growth or decline of the price itself. The illustration is for the Standard & Poor's 500 index, which essentially represents the largest 500 capitalization stocks on the market. Smaller stocks are even more volatile.

Some people think that bonds remain at constant values. They don't. That is because interest rates change all of the time. When interest rates go up, the value of a bond goes down. This hits bond mutual funds very hard. The way to avoid this is to buy bonds yourself from a broker

Stock Returns
Are Far from Constant Values

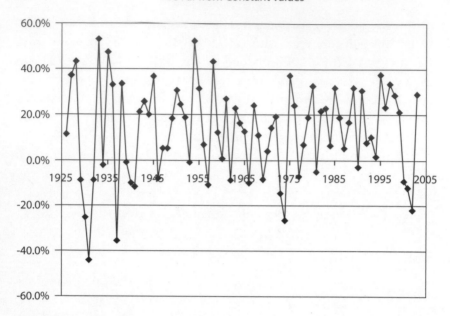

FIGURE 7.6   Stock returns fluctuate—sometimes wildly even though they may represent large stable companies as for these S&P 500 stocks.
Source: Global Financial Data.

or the government—and then hold them to maturity when you will get your full principal back. Figure 7.7 shows how much interest rate can vary over a period of years.

High returns almost always equate to high risk; and low returns should equate to low risk but do not always. That is because fees and costs can produce low returns even though the underlying securities have high risk. It is hard to overstate the penalties of high fees and costs. Some people think that a fee or cost of 1 percent or even 2 percent is a small number. However, this small number is a large percentage of the underlying security return.

For example, suppose that a stock index grows at 10 percent a year, but that the combination of loads, costs and fees total 2 percent, which is not uncommon. That 2 percent is 20 percent of what you will make from the investment. If you also engaged a professional to manage your money for you, and he charges 1 percent of your assets every year, you have lost 3 percent of your 10 percent or the equivalent to 30 percent of your return. Some people lose 50 percent of their return and even more after taxes. Over a 20-year period, a $10,000 investment would grow to over $62,000 at 10 percent return, just under $39,000 at 7 percent, but only $26,500 at 5 percent. In other words, the high fees in the latter case took away $35,500 from your account and gave it to the fund, brokers, and agents.

Let's look at some examples of the importance just 1 percent can make to a retiree over a long period. We do this by using a very simple case of a person who starts with no investments and has the capability of saving 15 percent of his wages every year for 25 years before retiring. We assume his wages grow with inflation and that he invests this in a portfolio of 50 percent stocks, 40 percent bonds and 10 percent money markets, all with typical investment costs. Figure 7.8 tells us that he can get 26 percent of his current wages for retirement income for 15 percent savings rate over 25 years. Now, if we can adjust the investments so that he can get just 1 percent more return, either by reducing costs and/or with a larger stock allocation, then he can get 34 percent of his current wages as retirement income. That is a large gain in retirement compensation.

**Interest Rates
AAA Corporate Bonds**

FIGURE 7.7 Bond interest rates change all of the time, but much more slowly than stocks.

Source: Global Financial Data.

Figure 7.8 also shows that to get retirement income close to 34 percent of his current working wages with the lower return investments, he would have to save 20 percent of his income. So, by just getting 1 percent more return, he gets almost the same retirement income as he would by saving 5 percent more of his current working wages. That is a lot of leverage.

Figure 7.8 also shows what can happen if he loses 1 percent of his return. It is not hard to lose 1 percent of what should be your return. You can do that or more just by buying high-cost funds, generating large brokerage fees with excessive trading, adding the fees of a professional financial manager, or you can do it by reducing your stock allocation by about 20 percent. If you are young and switch to a lower stock allocation right after a market decline, you may get hurt at least twice as bad.

The major way most people get larger growth is to have a larger allocation of stocks as compared to bonds or other fixed income investments. This is the classic trade of growth and risk. On a long-term basis, stocks have better returns than fixed income investments. They are, however, much more volatile. If you happen to retire after a market crash, you have a very large problem. That is why life-cycle funds and financial managers gradually shift from stocks into a larger percentage of fixed income investments as people age.

**Retirement Income
As a % of Current Wages***

Annual Savings	Years till Retire	Return on Investment		
		Less 1%	Nominal	Plus 1%
	15	7%	8%	10%
10%	25	14%	18%	23%
	35	23%	31%	43%
	15	10%	13%	15%
15%	25	20%	26%	34%
	35	34%	47%	65%
	15	14%	17%	20%
20%	25	27%	35%	45%
	35	45%	62%	86%

* Assuming nothing saved before starting deposits.

FIGURE 7.8 A 1 percent change, either up or down has profound effects on retirement income. For example, with 35 years to retire, someone who can get 1 percent more return than nominal will get almost twice as much retirement income as someone who gets 1 percent less than nominal.

Although there is no guarantee that the future will be like the past, historically, small-cap stocks have done a little better than large-cap stocks. The S&P 500 is often the choice index for those who are more conservative stock investors. The Russell 2000 is one of the indexes that represents smaller capitalization stocks since, out of the largest 3,000 companies, it covers the 2,000 smallest companies. It can outperform the S&P 500 often, but not always. The Wilshire 5000 index essentially represents the entire stock market and, over the long haul, has returns between the large- and small-cap indexes.

You can also get higher returns with fixed income investments if you ladder bonds, that is buy a group individual bonds, each of which matures in a different year. The longer-term bonds generate a higher interest rate. When the shorter-term bonds mature, you can replace them with longer-term bonds to extend your horizon. Eventually, you will have a portfolio of mostly long-term bonds, some of which will be maturing in the near term.

Review your securities to see if you could take some simple steps to get better returns. You can check your actual progress by using the return calculator in Appendix D, Return-on-Investment Worksheet.

Investment Costs

We have already seen the devastating effects that costs have on returns. The finance industry has over $300 billion overhead costs each year. We pay for this overhead whenever we make a financial transaction.

Mutual fund companies now have to provide information on many, but not all, of their costs. There is now more visibility on so-called 12b-1 costs that are the kickbacks to the one that sold you the product. However, there still is little visibility on transaction costs when the mutual funds buy or sell securities. This is the spread between the buy and sell values that the security trader takes home.

There are many firms that sell Class A, B, and C shares. These have costs that are in addition to any internal costs that they may have. Class A shares have a commission that is levied when you purchase them. These front end loads can be as much as 5 percent and sometimes even higher. That is a lot of money, but the shares also have small 12b-1 fees of perhaps 0.25 percent to compensate the brokers.

Class B shares have larger 12b-1 fees, perhaps 1 percent, and charge a redemption fee that declines each year you own them. After a while they convert to Class A shares. Class C shares have even larger 12b-1 fees together with a 1 percent redemption fee. Unlike Class B, they don't ever convert to Class A shares. If your only choice is to buy a mutual fund that sold as a Class A, B, or C, then many advisors say to buy the Class A shares since they ultimately will cost you less.

Try to unravel the cost differences by going to the NASD's Mutual Fund Expense Analyzer at www.nasd.com/InvestorInformation/InvestmentChoices/MutualFunds/index.htm. Even it may not capture all costs, such as sale charges (loads) on reinvested dividends, exchange fees, or account maintenance fees. See the warning on the site. Comparing several alternative investment opportunities is enlightening.

Investment costs are confusing, but the one thing that is sure is that your investments will not grow as fast as the reports on their individual constituents that you read in the newspapers.

If you choose to have someone manage your money for you, the manager usually charges between 1 and 2 percent of your assets each year. There are also money managers who will charge a fraction of this. Furthermore, the manager may make the charge at the beginning of the year which may hurt even more. These charges are in addition to the costs that you pay for the individual securities in your portfolio. The best reason to use a money manager is that you feel strongly that the manager will do better than you would.

It is very difficult for a money manager to do better than the market average because the manager has to select securities that do 1 to 2 percent better than the market average. Every year a small percentage of managers do this, but they seldom repeat their performance in succeeding years. When you get a report on your portfolio performance, make sure that it accounts for the manager's cost. There are many employee savings plans with costs in excess of 3 percent, which may be more than half of your return much of the time. Costs are often difficult if not impossible to find in financial reports.

You can make your own performance check by using Appendix D, Return-on-Investment Worksheet or the more accurate return calculator at www.analyzenow.com.

Probably the greatest cost is that the average person buys when the market is high and sells when it is low. Thus, the actual returns of individuals are less than the market average not just because of costs but because of poor disciplines. They read about an investment that has done well and then buy it *after* its good performance is nearly finished. Or they own a security that has lost substantial value and *then* decide to sell it. If they would simply buy low-cost index funds and stick with them, they would do much better.

The Best Investment When Approaching 62

I'm often asked to recommend investments for those interested in early retirement and what they should do about Social Security. For those with sufficient savings, I believe that the best answer often is to maximize the amount that they can get from Social Security providing they have significant investment reserves for future large purchases and emergencies.

Let's look at an example of a relatively high wage earner with a non-working spouse. Lower-wage earners would not have to save as much and do better proportionately.

Suppose we have a married couple of equal ages approaching age 62 with $290,000 invested conservatively in a retirement account with returns at least equal to inflation. (The example also works if they have a little less in a taxable account depending on their tax rate.) Then the primary wage earner can delay the start of Social Security until age 70 and a low-income spouse can delay Social Security until age 66. It does not do any good for a low-income spouse to delay any longer than the full retirement age.

Now let's further suppose that the primary wage earner's Social Security report shows the following:

$1,350 per month at 62
$1,860 per month at 66 (full-retirement age)
$2,540 per month at 70

With $290,000 available, the couple would have enough to support themselves for eight years with an annual income of $41,640 adjusted upward for inflation each year accounting for the low-income spouse's contribution of $930 per month starting at age 66. After the eight years, their combined Social Security would equal $41,640 per year for their life until one died at which point the survivor would get $30,480 per year, all inflation-adjusted.

$41,640 is $19,365 more per year than they could get if both started Social Security at age 62. Effectively, that $290,000 of savings bought a lifetime immediate annuity that pays $19,365 per year with an unlimited inflation adjustment and is theoretically guaranteed by the government. I say "theoretically" because who knows what will happen to Social Security in the future. Nevertheless, congress will telegraph its actions long before a person would have to change directions and people would most likely still be better off.

So what kind of inflation-protected immediate annuity could you buy on the market for $290,000? The best I could find was Vanguard's which would pay close to $11,900 per year. That is only a little over 60 percent of the extra value you would get by delaying Social Security. Also, its terms were not as good because Vanguard's inflation adjustment was then capped at 10 percent per year, its death benefits were less, and it did not have government backing.

The example here is for a couple in a situation that requires the maximum savings. Whether single or married, however, delaying Social Security can be one heck of an investment and may be even better than the example. Try Appendix B, Age to Start Social Security, or the free Social Security at 62, 66 or 70 calculator at AnalyzeNow.com to see how you would fare—and also look at Figure 7.9.

Annual Income

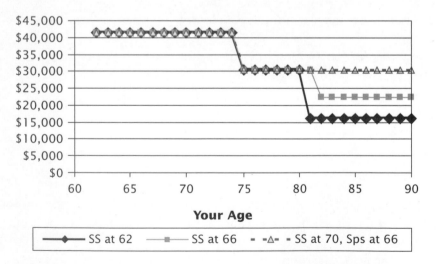

FIGURE 7.9 This chart depicts annual income in today's dollar values for the couple when one dies at 75 and the other lives on. The gains later in life are very significant and important.

Source: www.analyzenow.com.

More Investment Involvement

Many people want to get involved in the management of their own stocks, bonds, and real estate without getting into mutual funds. In this chapter, we take a step up in complexity compared to buying lifecycle funds, balanced funds, or managing your own small set of stock and bond index funds. Be forewarned! Each step in complexity takes more work and does not ensure getting better results. My brother-in-law takes it a step further in complexity and uses real-time signals for stock trading. He spends almost full time in front of his computers and sometimes does a little better and some times a little worse than I do. I chide him that I don't have to do all of this work and pay attention to daily, weekly, or even monthly changes in stock values or interest rates. I would rather ski, golf, help people plan, assist journalists, and write.

There are also very wealthy people that get into client-managed accounts, where professionals take over their money and invest in numerous things to try and reduce the volatility and risk while raising the return. They may augment the client's investments with hedge funds that may involve lots of leverage, make short bets, get into commodity trading, use money arbitrage, and other techniques that are beyond the scope of this book as well as being controversial and sometimes judged to be illegal. If you are interested in this, I suggest that you read three of my favorite financial books:

1. John Bogle, *John Bogle on Investing* (New York: McGraw Hill, 2001).
2. Larry E. Swedroe, *What Wall Street Doesn't Want You to Know* (New York: St. Martin's Press, 2001).
3. Roger Lowenstein, *When Genius Failed* (New York: Random House, 2000).

Diversifying Stocks

> Stocks have reached what looks like a permanently high plateau.
> —Irving Fisher, Yale Professor of Economics, October 17, 1929,
> just before the Stock Market Crash of the Great Depression

Stocks are a form of equities. Equities represent ownership as opposed to bonds that represent the debt of an institution. When you buy a stock, you are a part owner in a company and get a return that varies each year. When you buy a bond, you are lending money to a business or community and get fixed income in return. Stock equity is the current market value of the stock or stock fund. Real estate equity is the current market value less the remaining debt on the property. Equities vary much more in price than the value of fixed income investments so they are more risky.

Let's talk about stocks first. The simplest low-cost way to get diversity with stocks is to buy a total stock market index fund. For example, Vanguard, which pioneered index funds, offers a Total Stock Market Index Fund based on an index which essentially represents the vast majority of U.S. companies.

It is possible to reduce the variation in stock market portfolios as well as to enhance long-term growth by diversifying into somewhat dissimilar groups of equities such as real estate, large company stocks, small company stocks, growth stocks, value stocks, and similar categories for international stocks. Good hybrids do a lot of this for you. However, if you go to a professional manager to invest your money, you will more likely get a number of specific funds (possibly with high loads) that represent many of these categories. Or, if you have enough money, a book full of individual investments.

If you go to a stockbroker, your risk is much higher because you will get a very small number of stocks in each category. This does not offer the same degree of diversification, and brokers are famous for getting you to trade stocks. This often earns more for the broker than for you. Each trade represents some additional broker income, both going in and out of the market.

A former broker told me that he had to earn 2 percent in fees in order to get a bonus from his employer. Since the firm charged 1 percent for every trade, he had to get his clients to turn over their investments once a year so that he could get 1 percent on the sale and another 1 percent on the purchase of a new security. Of course, his clients thought the reason for the sell/buy advice was to improve their performance, not the performance of the broker. I believe that both he and the firm strived to help their clients. But when the recommendations turn out badly, you sometimes wonder. There also were times when he was asked to unload some of the firm's inventory of certain stocks or bonds by advising clients to buy them. That is even shakier.

Stock traders get glued to *CNBC* television, *Investor's Business Daily*, the *Wall Street Journal*, or their own favorite or even customized websites. These sources are fueled by the most recent report on economic indexes, which various forecasters identify as leading or lagging indicators. My view is that these are part of history and should be viewed in perspective, not used for hair-trigger responses.

Fuel for Financial Forecasters

- Consumer sentiment, consumer confidence.
- Construction spending, farm prices, CPI, inflation.
- Motor vehicle sales, chain store sales, commodities.
- Housing starts, new home sales, home sales.
- Jobless claims, help wanted index, wage growth.
- Wholesale trade, durable goods orders, metal prices.
- Petroleum status report, import/export prices.
- Money supply, gross domestic product, Fed rate.
- Business inventories, industrial production.
- Manufacturing index, nonmanufacturing survey.
- Corporate profits, personal income, and outlays.
- Stock and bond indexes, interest, market volume
- And so on, and so on, and so on.

Numerous studies have shown that people do much better investing in a group of low-cost index funds rather than investing in specialized funds or individual stocks. That is also true of professional money managers. I once rode on an airplane from Seattle to New York with the chairman of one of the Fortune 500 companies. He was on his way to fire his money managers because they had not done as well in the previous five years as the major indexes. He figured that he could save a lot of money by just buying index funds and get better performance.

Major mutual fund companies offer an extensive array of index funds from which you can choose. Instead of buying index funds from a mutual company, you can buy exchange traded funds (ETFs) from brokers or the major mutual fund companies that also trade stocks for you.

Some of the most common ETFs are Diamonds (representing the Dow Jones Industrials), SPDRs (representing the S&P 500), QQQs (representing the largest cap stocks on NASDAQ exchange), and a large array of iShares, Vipers, and Spiders that represent many index segments. Use the Internet to search and examine the variety of iShares, Vanguard Vipers, and S&P Spiders.

There is not much difference between an index fund and an ETF that represents the same category except that the ETF can be sold at any time of the day while funds are sold at the closing price of the equities on the day of the sale. ETFs also incur brokerage costs both in buying and selling but may have lower internal costs.

> October is one of the singularly most dangerous months to speculate in stocks. Others are November, December, January, February, March, April, May, June, July, August, and September.
> —Mark Twain

CAUTION

I think it is wise to avoid complex things that may get you into trouble: hedge funds, convertible arbitrage, market-neutral funds, commodities, drilling ventures, and investments with contracts. It is better to keep things simple.

Diversifying Fixed Income

There are many kinds of fixed income investments including CDs, savings bonds, bond funds, treasuries, corporate bonds, municipal bonds, and so forth. All of these represent lending money in exchange for getting interest on the loan periodically and the principal back at the end of a specified period. In general, the interest is higher with longer periods. Sometimes longer term bonds pay less interest, which usually signals some form of economic trouble coming. Also, the interest rate is higher when the underlying firm is in trouble and has a poorer loan rating. So called "junk" bonds represent the highest interest rate on the spectrum, while the most stable bonds and lowest interest rate bonds are government issues.

Fixed income securities offer more stable values than equities; but in many cases their values vary as well. This may be due to a reevaluation of the underlying value of the security. More often it is simply a change in the current interest rate compared to the investment's stated rate. For example, when interest rates go down, bond values go up. When interest rates go up, bond values go down. You won't notice this if you buy money markets, savings bonds, CDs, or hold bonds until they mature. You can easily detect the shift in underlying values in mutual funds that invest primarily in bonds.

There are three primary ways to diversify fixed income securities:

1. Buy a diversified bond fund which is by far the easiest.
2. Buy bonds that represent different underlying entities.
3. Buy bonds that mature in different years.

For example, you might buy some bonds issued by municipalities in different parts of the country or corporate bonds from different industries. You might also buy issues of these that mature in different years, perhaps an equal amount that would mature in each year of a 10- or 20-year period. This is called *laddering*, a concept introduced in Chapter 7.

Laddering has a great advantage other than offering time-wise diversification. Each year a bond matures, you can replace it with a bond that matures one year later than the oldest maturity in your bond portfolio.

Suppose you had a set of 10 bonds where one matured in each of the next 10 years. When the first bond matures in the first year, you replace it with one that will mature in 10 years. Now you have two 10-year bonds. The next year you replace the two-year bond with another 10-year bond. Now you have three 10-year bonds. After nine years, you will have all 10-year bonds, which give your bond portfolio a higher return than the initial portfolio that averaged five years maturity.

I buy several kinds of fixed income investments that work well with my high-tax bracket, including tax-exempt municipal bonds (munis), a guaranteed income fund in my 401(k), and government bonds. The latter ones are government I savings bonds, which are suitable for almost anyone. In a sense, I bonds are not true fixed income investments because they have an inflation adjustment. I consider them to be much better than the ultimate conservatives who buried gold to be used in case of a very serious economic emergency. I bonds have several pluses:

1. They are very secure.
2. They are a deferred tax security.
3. They benefit from inflation—something that I feel is inevitable.

I also buy some for my children because they can use them as they see fit including a potential tax-free source for my grandchildren's education. However, if education is the primary objective, 529 funds are likely to be a better all-around choice.

Diversifying Real Estate

First, let me emphasize that I do not feel that people should consider their home as an investment for retirement planning purposes. If they are near retirement and plan on downsizing, the residual cash from the downsizing can be considered as a retirement resource providing that the money will be invested and not used to buy a timeshare, automobiles, or other noninvestments. The remaining equity in a home is an ultimate reserve than can help cover financial uncertainties very late in life either by acquiring more debt, such as through a reverse mortgage, or by outright sale pending subsequent life in a retirement home, low-cost rented apartment, or with a relative.

Small investors have trouble diversifying if they get involved with investment real estate. Ideally you would like to have a mix of real estate in different categories such as residences, apartments, commercial, industrial, government buildings, and the like, as well as some of each in quite different locations. This would have been impractical advice for most investors, even those who invest mostly in real estate, but the development of real estate investment trusts (REITs) and mutual funds built around these make such diversification possible.

REITs are really a proxy for real estate. The underlying investments are real estate, and they are obliged to provide REIT owners the net cash flows. These trade like stocks. You can also get REIT funds that specialize in certain reality areas or ones that are broadly diversified. REIT funds are by far the easiest way to invest in the real estate market and get some diversification. However, if you have lots of money or want to really get involved, you can probably do better with direct ownership because REITs have high internal costs and do not have the usual tax breaks. For more information on particular REITs, consult the National Association of Real Estate Investment Trusts website at www.nareit.com and Value Line's at www.valueline.com.

Those who do best in real estate are often those who make it their primary business such as a developer or a general partner in a firm that holds many properties. Nevertheless, a lot of people have purchased real estate partnerships including myself. There is a joke about partnerships that I have found to ring true: A partnership starts with a general partner who has all of the knowledge and limited partners that have all of the money. In the end, their positions are reversed. The general partner has all of the money and the limited partners have all of the knowledge. (You might not laugh at this until you have been in a losing partnership.)

Let me illustrate the potential growth and risk in investment real estate with examples from two close associates, although I could give similar results from my own experiences.

The first case is a friend who, very early in life, started buying old houses, fixed them up, and then rented them. He seldom sold except in an occasional 1031 tax-free exchange. Using depreciation and interest costs to offset his rental income, he paid very little income tax over his entire life. Ultimately, he owned over 50 houses and living units simultaneously. For retirement, he sold all of the residences using the tax-free 1031 exchanges and bought a number of U.S. Post Office buildings. He now receives handsome cash flows and will avoid capital gains taxes on his death because of the tax basis markup.

The other case is quite different. A wealthy business associate invested heavily in apartments in Seattle and elsewhere. He was highly leveraged with mortgages on the property and used accelerated depreciation to reduce his income taxes. Then came the real estate crash of 1987. The market value of the apartments fell to values less than the mortgages so he could not get any cash from the sale. He abandoned the investments. Because he had taken so much depreciation, he incurred subsequent income taxes that were beyond his capability to pay. He is no longer wealthy.

I believe that to be successful with hands-on real estate, you need a tough, business-oriented personality. It is often said that you have to be willing to evict your mother if she fails to make the rent payments. There is an element of truth in that statement. What is more important is having an eye for situations in which you can get unusual capital appreciation and financially capable renters that provide a positive and sustained cash flow. This requires a genuine understanding of TUMMI costs, that is, taxes, utilities, maintenance, management, and insurance.

Chapter 9

Before You Die

Of course, we never know when we are going to die. Nevertheless, the preparation for death goes hand in hand with retirement planning. I am going to cover several subjects that I believe are the most important things that you can do to help your survivors after you die. Taking precedence, of course, is to make a projection of the resources available for your surviving spouse if you are married or the amount you might be leaving your children. This is an essential part of the retirement planning process that we have just reviewed and is quite visible on the planning programs at.www.analyzenow.com.

In this chapter, we look at three specific things to do before you die. The first of these is developing an estate plan. This is the process where you create a will, power of attorney, and other documents that are appropriate for your situation. It may also require positioning of your assets to minimize estate and income taxes both at state and federal levels. Almost all of these require professional assistance; but you have to decide what you want to pass through a will and what you want to bypass the will.

The next thing we cover is how you can reduce the workload for your *executor*, who can often be a family member. You should do this

executor
the person identi-
fied in a will to
see that the terms
of the will are
fulfilled. This may
require assistance
from profession-
als in investing,
taxation, law, and
accounting as
well as former
employers and
the Social Security
Administration.

whether rich or poor. Settling an estate is not easy, particularly if you have to search all over for records of various kinds.

The final thing we look at is gifting. If you can afford it, there is great personal pleasure in giving money away. Only the IRS will be unhappy because you have reduced the size of your taxable estate. The recipients will be very grateful.

Estate Plan

One output of the planning process is an estimate of the size of your estate and some thought of survivor benefits. Helping beneficiaries to get estate proceeds is not easy—unless you die a pauper or default to your state's plan for those who die without a will. The executor bears most of the work needed to complete the requirements specified in a will (see Figure 9.1).

An executor is a very busy person, generally for about a year. Some of the things an executor does include:

- Enumerate and value the assets.
- Pay claims including funeral bills, taxes and fees.
- Maintain the properties.
- Represent the estate if there are claim actions.
- See that legal obligations are fulfilled.
- Distribute assets to beneficiaries.

Executors often find that they may also have to develop strategy to minimize taxes, determine which investments go where and invest funds—all carefully recorded. The tasks can be so daunting that executors also can get significant remuneration, often as prescribed by the state. Many executors engage a professional to help.

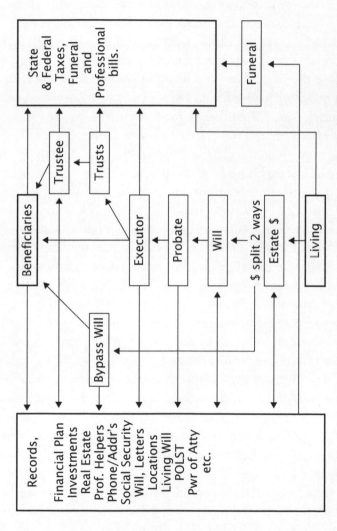

FIGURE 9.1 The executor of a will is right in the middle of a large number of things that have to be done. You can help reduce that burden before you die.

Your will may create trusts for minors, a marital trust to reduce estate taxes, a qualified terminal interest property trust to help the surviving spouse but still get the remainder to your designated heirs, a generation skipping trust, or trusts for other purposes. Putting IRAs into a trust is really tricky and another area where you should get help from a professional. Trusts require trustees, may involve arguments about interpretations of intent, and can last many years. Trustees follow the instructions in the trust, invest the funds, distribute the income, perform as a gate for principal dispersal, prepare tax returns, pay taxes, report status, and finally close the trust. They can be compensated for their efforts.

You can make both your life and the lives of your survivors, executor, and trustee much easier if you keep good records, have necessary documents and information at hand. These things can include: a will; durable power of attorney; living will or other health care directives; income sources; financial status; home tasks needing service; instructions for complex tasks; and, tremendously important, key contacts and orderly files.

Having a list of key contacts handy is useful both before and after a death. Some of the contacts could be those for medical assistance; relatives; church; best friends; closest neighbors; computer help; lawyer; accountant; insuring companies; employee or retirement benefits office; financial advisor; broker; bank; mutual funds; and, if you are really thinking ahead, the Social Security Administration, funeral home, newspapers for obituary, and the Veteran's Affairs Office.

Orderly files may take some time to organize, but the work goes quickly if you buy a couple of boxes of hanging files and a cabinet to hold them. Files should contain bills due and paid, home maintenance log; computer usernames and passwords; Social Security information; investments; income, taxes; financial ledger; insurance (auto, home, liability, life, medical and long-term care); medical care log; drugs; trip plans (confirmation numbers, airline. and hotel phone numbers); award program point status; and copies or list of items in your safe deposit box.

In my view, every family should have a safe deposit box. Loss of some information in a home fire or some other tragedy can be extraordinarily difficult to replace. Things you should consider for safe deposit storage are computer backups, usernames, and passwords; investment securities; mortgage, trusts; financial summaries; and broker and mutual fund information; wedding license; birth certificates; Social Security card; military discharge papers; several copies of death certificates if there is a deceased spouse; property and auto titles; cemetery deed if you purchased a gravesite; insurance policies; photos of home interiors; copy of wills; powers of attorney; living will; gift tax returns; home purchase data; photocopies of credit cards and drivers licenses; insurance policies; and photos of valuables.

All of these things are do-it-yourself, rainy-day projects that you can do in several weekends. However, there are some things that require the help of a professional. These are creation of wills, trusts, power of attorney to act in financial matters on your behalf, and durable health care power of attorney (or health care advance directive or living will). Some states have forms for the latter. In the state of Washington, it is a POLST, that is, a Physician's Order for Life-Sustaining Treatment, which you and your physician sign. There is also some red tape involved—due to the Health Insurance Portability and Accountability Act (HIPAA) privacy law—that restricts access to medical information. For that reason, you may need a HIPAA waiver to get doctors' help.

People who have been executors say that the biggest help of all is to have a location list that tells them where to find the things that they will need. A location list should include the locations of wills; durable power of attorney; health care directive or equivalent; safe deposit and list of its contents; investment files; titles; insurance policies; tax returns; checkbook(s); computer usernames and passwords; jewelry; stashed cash; keys; and lock combinations.

Finally, if you are very thoughtful and considerate of your survivors, you should have a plan for financial actions after your death. This plan should include provisions for survivors' welfare and letters with major messages for your spouse, children, and grandchildren, executor, and trustees. Consider leaving some instructions relating to priorities, things to do, things to destroy, things to save, obituary, funeral and burial instructions, and—this is the fun part—a legacy of photographs and accomplishments.

Here lies W. C. Fields. I would rather be living in Philadelphia.
—W. C. Fields, proposal for the wording of his epitaph

Help for Your Survivors

There are things other than money to leave your survivors. High on that list are some instructions concerning your care if severely disabled and a set of records that help your executor. I set out to do this for my wife—and ended up with a one-inch thick, three-ring binder—with tabbed separators—full of material. While the details are peculiar to my life and family, the subjects I address may serve as a blueprint for your own document. Here are some of the key things:

- *Very personal.* The first section contains a letter to my wife expressing my feelings and the major things that I would like for our children and grandchildren.

- *Home maintenance.* I have a series of tabs in the binder for nonfinancial items that were my responsibilities at home such as maintenance schedules and contacts as well as how to cope with the idiosyncrasies of our home such as the sprinkler operation, emergency power, and the like.

- *Funeral arrangements.* There is also a funeral tab that states a few of my wishes and people whom I would like to be informed on my death.

- *Financial summary.* Then there are numerous financial tabs, beginning with a financial overview that gives some sense to when financial reports and actions have to be finished.

- *Key references.* I keep a list of the professionals who can help with financial matters. I also record the location of birth certificates, marriage license, financial records and passwords and usernames.

- *Investments.* I have a table that includes each security's name, owner's name, its current value, purchase date and price, beneficiary if any, tax status (taxable, exempt, deferred) and whether its stock, cash, bonds, real estate, partnership or something else. You should also list whether it is a joint or separate account. (A joint account may bypass your will.) I use Microsoft Excel and update the current values quarterly and rebalance annually if necessary. My wife is not an Excel user, so she will either have to learn Excel or do the calculations by hand.

- *Bond ladders.* Staggering bonds over a period of years has several benefits including diversification and spread cash receipts. I have a list with the first to mature at the top and the last at the bottom. I include essential data such as purchase price, purchase date, interest, and the like.

- *Social Security.* My Social Security tab has information about how to contact the Social Security Administration when I die and the residual Social Security income that my wife will get.

- *Pension.* This has a very similar format to the Social Security tab with key names and hard to get phone numbers. It took me a while to find the information, but in my case it is Boeing's Deceased Affairs Office.

- *Estimated income tax.* It is important to have a rough estimate to see that the withholding is higher than the safe harbor amounts.

- *Insurance.* This tab includes information about my life insurance, and other insurance such as medical, automobile, liability, homeowners. and death benefits from my previous employer as well as some advice about changes after my death.

- *Wills.* Here I have a list of contacts who could help set up the specified trusts and do the necessary tax work. It also has a full copy of our current wills.

- *Durable power of attorney.* This has the notarized document that gives my spouse the power to act in my behalf if I am unable.

- *Medical information.* Here are copies of my medical history, the drugs I take, doctors phone numbers, health care proxy for someone to make medical decisions if I am unable, and a medical advance directive that has my wishes in the event that I do not respond due to injury or dementia.

This binder is an ever-changing document as I add more details and update the financial information. While your financial records and legal documents may not be as extensive as mine, it is important to leave a clear list of key names and phone numbers, policy numbers, and the whereabouts of essential legal documents that allow your spouse and heirs to claim their legacy and proceed in your absence.

Take Advantage of Gifting

Gifts to Children

I feel that the best time to give monetary gifts to benefit children is either when your children are very young or you are in retirement. Do not give money to children, even for their college, if you cannot afford it. So the first thing to do is to make a conservative plan with help from this book or with the help of a suitable computer program or a competent professional fee-only planner. The plan will tell you how much you should be saving if working, or, if retired, how much you can afford to spend in retirement. If you can live below the amount you can afford fairly comfortably, then you can afford to make gifts to children so that the total of what you spend on yourself this year plus that for children's gifts is not above the plan's value.

If the amount that you can gift is below $12,000 per child each year if you are single or $24,000 per child each year if you are married, then you don't have to file a gift tax return. (These amounts are adjusted upward periodically for inflation.) Say you have two married children. Then you and your spouse can give $24,000 total annually to each child and their spouses—so you are up to $96,000 annually. If you have four grandchildren, you could give away another $96,000. Few people should have to file a gift tax return. Even if you do, you don't have to pay gift taxes unless the amounts in gift tax returns that exceed the $12,000 limits total to over $1 million from you and another $1 million from your spouse with current tax rules. Otherwise, the gift tax returns simply reduce the amount of tax credit for inheritance taxes

I like the idea of giving money so that it may be hard for the children to spend until years have passed. Legally, you have to tell children that you have gifted the money to them, but if you put it into savings bonds in their name or a low-cost variable annuity, you can keep the paperwork at your home, not theirs. Another possibility is to set up a charitable remainder trust with the assistance of a charity. You can have a certain percent of the principal paid to the children each year until they die, after which the charity gets what is left.

WARNING

Exercise caution: Once the money is donated to a gift fund, you cannot get it back. Also, there are minimum amounts to start the funds as well as for the cash transfers to individual charities.

Charitable Gifts

There are many people who tithe or give significant sums to charities. There are some ways to gift that leave you and the charity with more money and the government with less.

The first thing to consider is giving appreciated securities. If you have stocks that have large gains from their growth, you can save capital gains taxes by gifting the stocks directly to the charity. This is much better than selling the stocks and then giving cash to the charity. You have to pay capital gains taxes if you first sell the stock. You don't pay the taxes with a direct transfer of the stock to a qualified charity or charitable fund.

Even better, you can donate the securities directly to a "donor-advised" gift fund such as Vanguard's Charitable Endowment Program or Fidelity's Charitable Gift Fund and get a charitable deduction. Then, at a later time, you can ask the fund to give cash to the charity in any amount up to the total balance. If you donate the securities early, the balance grows tax free in a portfolio of your choice, thereby amplifying the amount you can give to charities. In addition, you get an earlier charitable tax deduction, thereby keeping some more of your money for its own subsequent growth. Those

phase-out of deductions
an effective tax increase because high-income people cannot take the full deductions from income. Their deductions are "phased out" as their income increases. Most wealthy people are allowed only the standard deduction in spite of what might otherwise be substantial deductions—especially for charitable contributions.

subject to the *phase-out of deductions* get a still further benefit if they make larger but less frequent donations to the gift fund. To learn more about the two example gift funds, consult the following:

- Fidelity Charitable Gift Fund, www.charitablegift.org or 1-800-952-4438.
- Vanguard Charitable Endowment Program, www .vanguardcharitable.org or 1-888-383-4483.

Tax-Free Contributions from an IRA

Normally, any withdrawal from an IRA would be taxed at ordinary income rates based on both your normal income plus whatever you withdrew from the IRA. But if you are age 70½ or older, you may be able to make a contribution directly from your IRA to a charity up to $100,000 without having to pay income tax. This may be an easy way either to provide a larger contribution to the charity or to give less expensively because, after 70½, you have to make withdrawals anyway. Check with your tax preparer or the IRS at www.IRS.gov to see that this provision is still in effect. It is currently set to expire after the end of 2007.

A Critical Review

Whether you do your financial planning by yourself, with assistance, or totally delegate the responsibility to someone else, it is important to take a critical look after the effort is done. If you are married, make sure that your spouse understands the contents and is committed to support the actions needed to implement it. Depending on the age of your children, they too may be involved, particularly if you are elderly and have adult children.

Besides commitment, you should try to get a perspective that answers important questions. Is the plan conservative? Is it consistent with your view of what may happen to your family and the economy? Does it have some room for error? Retirees tell me that their biggest financial surprises were family-related—elderly parents needed financial assistance, a divorced daughter with children now living under the same roof.

It is also good to look at your past financial performance. If you did as well as the market average, you did better than the average investor because the average investor loses so much to the financial industry.

I would like to start off with some of the things that many people have found out the hard way so that you don't have to repeat the same mistakes. Then I discuss whether you need professional help and how to get it.

Hard-Learned Lessons

> From fortune to misfortune is but a step; from misfortune to fortune is a long way. —Yiddish proverb

You may have to learn things the hard way as did I, or you can take advantage of the lessons of others. Here are some important caveats to consider that may help you immensely.

Look hard for low costs and taxes   You often can improve your investment growth as much or more by paying attention to the costs and tax consequences of different kinds of investments.

Don't invest in anything that eats, floats, drills, or is appraised with a magnifying glass or scale   This was the advice my father gave me. I learned it myself when I invested in oil drilling. I not only lost money, I had a horrendous bookkeeping job for tax returns. However, I remembered my father's advice when a friend tried to get me into a sure-fire catfish farm business. My father's advice was a great save.

Avoid partnerships and tax gimmicks   A partnership reduces you to a humble observer who has little if any control. A neighbor of mine could not sell a partnership when he wanted to retire and even had real trouble giving it away. The appraisal costs were awful. And avoid tax gimmicks: They usually help the promoter much more than you.

Be wary of someone who wants to manage your money.   You can easily find someone who wants control over your investments when you go to look for professional help. You may be in a position where money management is what you need, but be careful. The professional may come out far better than you do and has no downside risk. You should thoroughly understand the costs and the professional's means of compensation.

NOTE

Better the devil you know than the devil you don't.

You've heard of someone who has a foolproof method   Don't believe it. He would not be selling the method and its associated seminars, books, tapes, and the like if he could make that much money for himself. Barnum said there was a fool born every minute—and that's enough.

Don't buy individual stocks and don't try to "time" the market   More likely you will end up buying at the top and selling at the bottom. Market timers are disappearing rapidly.

In addition to all of the foregoing, which were some of my lessons, I think that there are a number of other very practical things that deserve emphasis.

Keep good records   When you make a new investment, set up a folder for it. If it is not apparent from the normal paperwork you get, include a sheet with whatever is the basic information about the investment as well as phone numbers where you or your executor can reach someone who can provide more information. Save periodic financial reports. But you usually don't need to keep an out-of-date annual report or prospectus. If you start a small business on the side, your record keeping increases enormously.

Save your income tax returns   It is best to save your income tax data and returns for seven years. If you had to file gift tax returns, you need to save these until both you and your spouse die. At that time, they will be used to calculate your estate tax.

Keep a file for heirs or your executor   At the minimum, this should include a letter to your spouse or children that tells where to find your investments, insurance policies, will, living will, power of attorney, and so on. Include a list of people who will be key in handling your affairs when you die or are disabled. There should be information about your insurance policies and a list of your investments with their current values as well as a list of the sources of your income now and your survivors' income sources and amounts.

Rent a safe deposit box at a bank   Think about what will happen if your house burns down or you lose all of your information in a catastrophe of some kind. Use a safe deposit box for original copies of your most vital documents and a backup copy of key computer files.

Investments Review your investment status at least annually. Calculate your percentage of fixed income versus equity investments and rebalance if necessary to a rule that you establish. (See Appendix G.) This is the most practical way that I know to buy when prices are low and sell when they are high as well as to gradually move to a more conservative position as you age. Check to see that you are getting the investment returns you should by using Appendix D.

> Investor: One who bought stocks that went up. —Malcolm
> Forbes

Reserves Set up a reserve to replace expensive items that wear out so that you don't have to pay for these with credit. (See Appendix H.) Also, set aside some money for unforeseen emergencies so that you do not budget all of your financial resources for everyday living expenses. Think about a reserve for long-term care (LTC) as an alternative to LTC insurance.

Taxable investments You need a checking account to pay all of your current bills, but you should also have a higher-interest money market fund with checking. Use the money market for your investment proceeds. That is, have all of your taxable and tax-exempt returns (dividends, interest, return of principal) and required minimum distributions from deferred tax accounts deposited to the money market—automatically if possible. One of the pluses for deposits of returns is that it makes it easier to know your tax basis for capital gains reporting when you start to make withdrawals. It makes it easier to rebalance investments as well in order to meet your allocation targets. You can then use the money market as the source of funds for whatever is the part of the allocation that is short. You don't need a money market fund within a deferred tax account because there is no tax consequence from rebalancing.

For retirees only Take your required minimum distributions from deferred tax accounts near the end of the year. That way you can adjust the withholding so that you don't give the government more money than required to meet the "safe harbor" requirements for withholding. The safe harbor varies and depends on income level. In general, it is an instruction to withhold whichever is the smaller: 90 percent of this year's required tax or 100 percent or more of last year's tax depending on your taxable income. So, after estimating your taxes for the current year, estimate your withholding. Make up any shortcoming with an end-of-the-year IRA payment. This is much better than paying the tax all along, which lets the government make interest on your money rather than you and restricts your tax paying flexibility.

Always live within your means   It is impossible to stress this too much. If you are still working and are not saving, you are living beyond your means. If you are retired and are drawing money too fast from your investments, you are living beyond your means. Establish your spending and savings anchor points with plans such as those in Appendix A for pre-retirees or Appendix C for post-retirees.

Consider delayed Social Security   The best investment you might be able to make is to delay the start of Social Security. Consider age 70 as a starting year for the primary wage earner in your family and the full retirement age (65 to 67) for a low-income spouse that will get benefits dependent on the primary wage earner's Social Security benefits.

Get professional help   When you are over your head in a subject, pay for some help. If you do your homework before hand and come equipped with the information that the professional needs, you will reduce the time and cost for the assistance. Hopefully, you require only a one-time appointment instead of continued nurturing of your investments. The costs may be comparable to going to a doctor for treatment while the costs of continued nurturing may be closer to the costs of an extensive stay in a hospital.

Finally, pay attention to your health   Exercise; good diet; and care of ears, eyes, and teeth not only save you money, it keeps you feeling young and active. Nevertheless, the most important kind of insurance for you is likely to be a good medical policy.

Financial Reports May Deceive

> It is difficult to get a man to understand something when his salary depends on his not understanding it. —Upton Sinclair, *Main Street*

It is hard not to know about the numerous cases in the news and courts involving companies that deceived their shareholders with misleading oral statements and financial reports. Then there are those cases that get little publicity. For example, one major insurance company showed the growth of the S&P 500 and implied that this index represented their mutual fund performance which was, in fact, much lower than the S&P 500. Incredibly, when taken to court, the insurance company won because in a small print footnote it did say that the chart represented the S&P 500 performance. Several major insurance companies advertise the before-tax return of their variable annuities and compare it with a taxable account's after-tax return.

It is very common for financial firms to "invent" a portfolio using the best-performing securities over a certain past period. Of course, hindsight does produce a better-than-average portfolio to represent that part of history. Thus the firms' advertisements and advisors may imply that this portfolio represents their past performance capability, even though they did not actually own or recommend that portfolio previously. The fact is that only a fraction of financial firms and advisors had their clients in portfolios that truly beat the market averages after considering fees and costs.

A women's investment club in the small Illinois community of Beardstown was so proud of its performance that its members—"the Beardstown Ladies"—published a book to show how easy it was to beat the market. It was a bestseller and inspired many more investment clubs. Then an accountant checked their records and found that their 23.4 percent return was really 9.1 percent and less than the S&P 500's 14.9 percent. The ladies were counting their new monthly contributions as part of their earnings. Professional advisors are unlikely to do that, but there are things they might.

For a number of years, I attended financial seminars put on by both major firms and individual professionals. I found it was very common to illustrate examples with unrealistic returns and other inputs. Often presenters would report the performance of the underlying securities without including the effects of fees and costs that can destroy returns on investments for their clients.

It is not hard to check results and see how your actual securities performed over a one-year period and then compare the results with the average security performance in that year—or even to compare it with the performance your advisory service may have told you that you had. Try the Return-on-Investment Worksheet in Appendix D and see if you are doing as well as you were led to believe. You can also use the more detailed Free Return Calculator that you can download as a Microsoft Excel file at www.analyzenow.com.

There are a number of more sophisticated tests for security performance than return on investment for a one-year period. These include measures relative to the market such as the statistical parameters alpha, beta, standard deviation, capture ratio, Sharpe ratio, tracking error, correlation coefficient, and R-squared. In the final analysis, however, it boils down to how close you came to the market indexes that provide the reference yard sticks over a period of a number of years. The Return-on-Investment Worksheet can also help you with that.

In What Areas Do I Need Help?

I believe that the average person who takes the time to try and understand the material in this book will need little professional help in the planning and financial aspects. However, there are those who would rather have their free time—and have the financial means—can turn this responsibility over to someone else. There are also people who have reached the point where they may no longer have the capacity to handle these matters competently. In this case, they should seek professional help anywhere from consultation up to full financial responsibility for their affairs.

You might want to specifically consider how you stand in the following areas:

- Forecasting how much you must save before retiring or how much you can spend after retiring.
- Determining whether you should save in deferred tax accounts, Roths, or taxable or tax-exempt investment vehicles.

- Allocating, diversifying, and selecting investments.
- Selecting medical, life, home, liability, medical, drug, long-term care, or other insurance products.
- Estate planning including wills, power of attorney, living trusts, living wills, and the like.

Of course, there are some areas here where few people can use a self-help guide successfully without some degree of help, especially for wills, durable power of attorney, and other legal documents.

Finding Professional Help

> No man is wise enough by himself. —Titus Maccius Plautus, c. 204 BCE

There are people who do not need the help of a financial professional; many who could use infrequent help; and some who would have great difficulty without a lot of professional handholding. If you understand what is in this book, are doing well in relation to the forecasts, and are able to invest with returns not too far below the market, you could get along quite well without any significant professional help except for wills and powers of attorney. If you are not quite that confident, then you could use some help from one or more visits to a certified financial planner (CFP). Try consulting the website of the Certified Financial Planner Board of Standards at www.cfp.com. Alternatively, you might use a certified public accountant with a personal financial specialist degree (CPA/PFS). Consider consulting the American Institute of Certified Public Accountant's Personal Financial Specialists (AICPA), which has a website for its Personal Financial Planning (PFP) Center at http://pfp.aicpa.org.

If you are within 10 years of retiring and, though successful thus far, would prefer confirmation that you are on the right path, you could benefit from a visit to a fee-only planner or a professional who charges by the hour. If you are totally incapable of managing investments, or are wealthy enough that you can afford to pay what would be equivalent to an executive financial secretary (so that you can have more time on the golf course), then go to a CFP who manages your financial affairs for you. Just realize that this professional can get paid quite handsomely in

Need a pro?
Calibrate yourself to see if you need professional help. Perhaps not if:
• You can make a plan yourself.
• Your annual savings are enough.
• Your investments are growing satisfactorily.
• Your investments are diversified.
But a pro's help may be advisable if:
• You have serious credit problems.
• You need legal assistance.
• You are contemplating a complex investment.
• You are committing to retirement in the near term.

the process if you don't keep tabs on how he or she is compensated. Watch out for hidden fees for those recommended funds.

There are other times when you are well served to use a professional. You may want advice before going to a lawyer to develop a will. You might want help developing a plan for your children's education. Or you could need help with debt problems or an investment proposal for which you could use a second opinion. Expect to pay well over $150 an hour—and carefully prepare the material that the professional needs to help with the decision making. You can save yourself a second appointment.

Understand that any professional has to make a living and will view you as a source of revenue. If the professional can go so far as to get you to turn over your money to him, he has his greatest income opportunities. Excluding the totally unscrupulous, there are many who still take what I think are obscene fees, get kickbacks, and make earnings on your investments whether you do or not. If an advisor wants more than 1 percent fee to manage your account and wants you to convert many of your existing investments to high-cost mutual funds or a set of stocks that he recommends, opt out.

Remember that if you give a professional financial management responsibilities, most will not only get commissions from the products they sell, they may well get an extra bonus from their company for selling high-cost products or earning fees above a certain threshold based on a percentage of the assets under their management. Stand alone private practitioners may get an award from their spouse!

There are several general ways that planners get compensated. You want to make sure that you fully understand the alternatives available to you. Take into account the various pay methods listed below as well as the internal costs of the mutual funds or exchange traded funds that comprise your account. Pay for each hour of service or an annual retainer fee.

- *Fee-only planners.* These get a fixed percentage of the assets that you put under their control. If the planner gets 1 percent of your assets and you expect to get 8 percent return on those assets, the planner will be one-eighth of your gains.

- *Fee-based planners.* These planners receive a mix of commissions and fees—and compensation from the funds as well as from the fees. The total can be 3 percent or higher. If the underlying investments return 8 percent, the planner gets 3 percent and you get 5 percent. You might be better off buying CDs.

- *Commission-only agents.* They are paid from a certain percentage per trade. If you don't do much trading and pick invest ments yourself, this could cost less than fee-only or fee-based professionals.

If you need more than a couple of hours of financial consulting, on a scale of best to worst, professionals who are fee-only CFPs are best. You can find one in your area by consulting the website of the National Association of Personal Financial Advisors at www.napfa.org. These would be followed by a certified professional accountant (CPA) who also has a personal financial specialist degree (PFS). To find one of these, consult AICPA's Personal Financial Planning Center website at http://pfp.aicpa.org.

In the middle category are chartered financial consultants (ChFC) or chartered financial analysts (CFA). You can find information at the websites of the American College (www.theamericancollege.edu) and the CFA Institute (www.cfainstitute.org).

TIP

If you are going to use a professional to control your investments, make sure that they will accept "fiduciary" responsibilities. This legal term defined in the Employee Retirement Income Security Act (ERISA) means that they are obliged to act in your best interest, not theirs.

At the other end of the scale are insurance salespersons and stock-brokers who can have a string of degrees such as a certified retirement financial advisor (CRFA) or certified senior advisor (CSA) after their names. To find out what these various credentials mean, the NASD features a Professional Designation tool on its Investor Information page at www.nasd.com. Of course, within the top categories, there can still be some bad actors and some good ones in the lower rated categories. You will have to determine for yourself and the references you get.

Many of the younger planners trying to build a client base give free seminars on planning. It does not hurt to go to these. But be cautious about buying any personal help until you have heard a number of different similar seminars and done some research about the presenters and their firms. I wrote an article for *Kiplinger's Retirement Report* (December 2003) on this subject. It caused a minor uproar from those who pick up clients from what I called "trolling," a fishing term used to describe dragging bait behind the boat until a fish finally grabs it. There are both notoriously evil trollers selling get rich schemes and a number that I know personally who really give helpful seminars whether or not you later buy their services.

Before committing to a financial advisor or manager, do some thorough checking. This is as important as the search for a new family doctor. Therefore, you have to invest some time, especially if you are going for a financial manager. First check to see that the advisor is registered by getting source information from the North American Securities Administrators Association at www.nasaa.org. Ask if there are any complaints about him or her. Then check with the Financial Planning Association at www.fpanet.org or 1-800-282-7526. Seek out personal references, too. The Securities and Exchange Commission (SEC) has an Investment Adviser Search engine, which uses a national data base for licensed professional planners (www .adviserinfo.sec.gov/IAPD/Content/Search/iapd_OrgSearch.aspx).

It is very important to know about problems that an advisor had in the past. Look for criminal charges, legal judgments, bankruptcies, and complaints. Be wary of those who make their money selling get-rich books, instructional seminars, how-to tapes, and so on. You might get some more information by entering the professional's name or firm by searching for it on the Web and reading what you find.

Finally, make a free face-to-face interview, preferably with two or three candidates. Ask the advisors to describe their education, work experience, typical client wealth, what they will do for you, how they charge, the family of funds or securities they often recommend, and the contents of the plan that you would get. There is an excellent list of questions that you can use—from the Financial Planning Association—to evaluate each candidate on at www.fpanet.org/public/tools/tenquestionschecklist.cfm.

You might want to challenge the candidates to describe the confidence that they have in projections they make for their clients. It is best if you hear words such as

> It is a reasonable projection **if** we live no longer than planned and **if** the statistics of future returns, inflation and taxes are similar to historical values, and **if** we select investments and allocations that moderate risk, and, importantly, **if** there are not any surprise financial events in your life.

Ask for references, including current clients. Go on to ask candidate advisors what they do about investment selection, insurance planning, and estate planning. It is likely that they work with a lawyer for the latter—and that should involve another face-to-face meeting with questions about what you will get and the costs.

When you get home, check out references, do some Web research and give the information you find the smell test. If the proposition promises extraordinary returns, sounds very risky, or would involve costs that look like a leech sucking on your investments until you die, avoid it like the plague. Try another candidate. Also, avoid any involvement you don't thoroughly understand, is overly complex or you cannot get in written form to review later.

Expect to pay several thousand dollars for a complete plan or several hundred dollars an hour or so of help. A less expensive alternative to seeking out your own professional is to use the fixed price (or sometimes free) advisory services of the major low-cost mutual fund companies like Vanguard, Fidelity Investments or T. Rowe Price. But be cautious about using brokerage firms or credit card companies for general advice. The mutual fund companies require that you fill out a questionnaire that they will analyze and provide you with a report based on their findings that, though not entirely customized, will most likely serve you well. They will try to get you to transfer some of your assets to their own mutual funds, which may be a good thing in many instances. You can then do all they recommend, be selective, or do a little now, some later and some much later. You cannot go too far wrong if uncertain by standing pat with one-half of your investments and investing the other half as recommended.

You can probably get by with little professional help for planning and investing. Nevertheless, it is really important to get some professional legal help for a will, power of attorney, and a health care directive such as a living will. The National Association of Estate Planners & Councils (NAEPC) can suggest such experts—consult its website at www.naepc.org. Just as it is important to be well prepared when you go to a professional for planning help, it is important to do the same for the legal help. Lawyers can cost more on an hourly basis. Know what you want to leave to whom and remember to ask for guidance on designating beneficiaries. Also, remember that joint accounts, employee savings plans, IRAs, and trusts may bypass your will.

Selecting a professional

- Investigate candidates very carefully and consider several:
  - National Association of Personal Financial Advisors, www. napfa.org
  - AICPA's Personal Financial Planning Center, http://pfp.aicpa. org
  - Financial Planning Association, www.fpanet.org
  - Certified Financial Planner Board of Standards, www.cfp.com
  - Your mutual fund, www.[Your mutual fund].com
  - Research credentials.
  - North American Securities Administrators Association, www. nasaa.org
  - NASD, www.nasd.com
  - SEC's Investment Adviser Public Disclosure site, www.adviserinfo. sec.gov/IAPD/Content/IapdMain/iapd_SiteMap.aspx
- Meet face to face.
- Check references.
- Understand what you get and what it costs.

Reprise

You can't escape the responsibility of tomorrow by evading it today.

—Abraham Lincoln

A

Pre-Retirement Worksheet

It is very hard for someone who is not retired to know how much money will be needed for retirement. You can find many references of anywhere from 60 percent of your current wages to over 100 percent. If you are currently using about 20 percent of your income to support children and another 20 percent for retirement savings, you might go for 60 percent. If you don't have children and are not putting away much for retirement, 100 percent might be more appropriate. The purpose of this appendix is to show you how much you might get in retirement as a percent of your current wages. You have to relate that to what you believe you will need in retirement versus what you are spending now. This projection is in terms of today's dollar values so that you don't have to try and estimate what future dollars may be worth today.

Use the worksheet that follows for your analysis. Since it is a good idea to make projections in each future year on about the same date, you should make a new copy of this appendix each year for that year's entries and results. Each year should be in the dollar values of the year you make the projection. It is interesting to look back at some of your older projections and see how things have changed.

The first component of your retirement income is the Social Security payments for you and your spouse. Every U.S. worker gets an estimate each year from the Social Security Administration (SSA). A nonworking spouse gets about 50 percent of the working spouse's full retirement age value at about age 66 and significantly less at age 62. You can find information about this other conditions in the *Mysteries of Social Security* in Chapter 3 and/or contact the SSA at 1-800-772-1213 or visit its website at www.ssa.gov for more information and possible changes in the rules.

Each step in the process is illustrated by an example in the material that follows. Enter your own numbers above the example and follow the instructions including the operations that show adding, multiplying or dividing numbers from previous steps. Also, it is a good idea to review the material in Chapter 3 as you proceed.

In the worksheet that begins with Figure A.1, "you" should preferably be the primary wage earner. The worksheet helps you estimate retirement before-tax income as a percent of your current wages.

The numbers in parentheses refer to numbered steps in the worksheet shown in the figures. For example, (5) refers to the $1,700 in the fifth step of Figure A.1.

Before completing the pension part of the worksheet (see Figure A.2), you may want to go back and review Chapter 3. It is important to distinguish between a COLA pension (which few people get) and a fixed pension as well as whether the pension quote is in today's dollar values or future dollar values.

The investment contribution calculation is shown in Figure A.3. It is wise to review the material on *reserves* and *savings contributions* in Chapter 3 before making step 17 and 18 entries.

Social Security Contribution(s)

#	Value	Description
1	a 50 b 48	Ages now: a = you, b = spouse. If no spouse, enter your age in b too
2	50	Age you plan to retire. Retirement is when current wages end, and part-time wages, if any, begin.
3	70	Your age to start social security, but not less than your retirement age
4	66	Your spouse's age to start social security, but not less than spouse's age at time you retire
5	$1,700	Monthly social security forecast from annual SSA report or your own calculation from www.ssa.gov.
6	$600	Spouse's own monthly social security or part of yours if larger. (See Mysteries of SS, Chpt. 3.)
7	$2,300	Total of your and your spouse's social security forecast, (5) + (6)
8	$5,000	Current gross monthly wages for you and your spouse
9	46	Social security as a percent of your wages, 100 x (7) / (8)

FIGURE A.1   Social security contributions.

Before completing the pension part of the worksheet you may want to go back and review Chapter 3. It is important to distinguish between a COLA pension (which few people get) and a fixed pension as well as whether the pension quote is in today's dollar values or future dollar values.

Cost-of-Living-Adjusted (COLA) Pension(s)

	You	Spouse	
	You	Spouse	
10	a 66	b 66	Age to start COLA pension, but not less than age at your retirement.
11	a $500	b $100	Monthly COLA pension. If inflation adjustment capped, see Figure 3.2.
12	a 10	b 2	COLA pension as percent of wages, 100 x (11a) / (8), 100 x (11b) / (8)

Fixed Pension Contribution(s)

	You	Spouse	
	You	Spouse	
13	a 66	b 66	Age to start fixed pension, but not less than age at your retirement
14	a 50	b 48	Age (13) if quote in today's $. If quote is in future dollars, enter age now (1).
15	a $2,000	b 500	Monthly pension. If severance pay, reduce by 7.65% for FICA and MC
16	a* 20	b* 5	Fixed pension % contribution* (14a) x (15a) / (8), (14b) x (15b) / (8)

* Calculation accounts for need to save part of a fixed pension for future inflation compensation.

FIGURE A.2   Pension contributions.

The steps in Figures A.3 and A.4 determine the contributions from your savings to date. Then we calculate the contributions from additional annual savings until you retire using Figure A.5 with the help of Figure A.6.

The calculation for part-time work in Figure A.7 assumes that you are going to invest the after-tax wages to be drawn down over your remaining retirement as opposed to saving for a particular expense. If the latter, do not make any entries here.

Contribution of Savings Accumulated To Date

17	$200,000	Balance of current savings
18	$50,000	Reserves for emergencies, (e.g., 10% of balance), replacements and other needs*
19	$150,000	Net savings for retirement spending, (17) - (18)
20	12	Years till retire.** (Retirement is when your current wages stop.), (2) - (1a)
21	6.1	Factor from Figure A.4. Use closest value to your case and value of (20).
22	15	% existing savings contribution, (19)x(21) divided by <u>annual wages</u> = [(19) x (21)] / [12 x (8)]

* If you plan to retire before being able to get Medicare, include the cost of medical insurance from retirement to age 65.
** If you retire before starting social security or pensions, you need to complete the adjustment at the end of the worksheet.

FIGURE A.3 Past savings contribution.

Existing Investments Growth Factors

Years till Retire	Portfolio Return on Investment		
	Conservative	Nominal	Aggressive
1	3.7	4.3	4.9
3	3.9	4.6	5.3
6	4.2	5.1	6.0
9	4.5	5.6	6.8
12	4.8	6.1	7.8
15	5.2	6.8	8.8
20	5.8	8.0	10.8
25	6.5	9.4	13.4
30	7.3	11.0	16.5
35	8.2	13.0	20.3

FIGURE A.4 Existing investments growth factors.

Contribution of Future Annual Savings

23	10	Percent of your future wages (8) that you will be saving, e.g., 10 for 10% per year
24	0.63	Factor from Figure A.6. Use closest value to your investment choice and years till retire (20)
25	6	% new savings contribution, (23) x (24). Note, can round to nearest whole number.

FIGURE A.5   Future savings contribution.

New Savings Deposits Growth Factors

Years till Retire	Portfolio return on investment is:		
	Conservative	Nominal	Aggressive
1	0.04	0.04	0.05
3	0.11	0.13	0.15
6	0.24	0.28	0.32
9	0.37	0.44	0.52
12	0.52	0.63	0.75
15	0.69	0.84	1.02
20	1.00	1.25	1.56
25	1.36	1.76	2.26
30	1.78	2.37	3.16
35	2.27	3.12	4.30

FIGURE A.6   New savings deposit growth factors.

Step 38 in Figure A.8, which shows total retirement income, tells the story. You have to decide whether that percent of your current wages sounds like enough for your retirement. I like young people to shoot for 100 percent.

In order to provide supplementary support after you retire but before you start a pension or Social Security, you need to complete Figure A.9.

Contribution of Part-Time Work

26	*** 20	Part-time retirement wages as a percent of current wages (8), e.g., 20 for 20 percent
27	4	Years you will work
28	30	Years you (and spouse) will live in retirement. Probably conservative to add years to Figure 5.2.
29	3	% part-time work contribution, (26) x (27) / (28)

*** This can also be used to represent work of non-retired spouse

FIGURE A.7 Part-time work contribution.

Total retirement income as % of current wages

30	46	% from social security, (9)
31	12	% from COLA pensions, (12a) + (12b)
32	25	% from fixed pensions, (16a) + (16b)
33	15	% from retirement savings to date, (22)
34	6	% from new retirement savings, (25)
35	3	% from part-time work, (29)
36	107	Total as a percent of your current gross wages, (30) + (31) + (32) + (33) + (34) + (35)
37	20	% result from calculation (54) below if you plan to retire before starting social security or a pension
38	87	Net retirement income as % of current wages (36) - (37)

Step 38 tells the story. You'll have to decide whether that percent of your current wages sounds like enough for your retirement. I like young people to shoot for 100%.

FIGURE A.8 Total retirement income.

If you retire before social security or pensions start, you need to adjust the total above.

39	8	Your years from retirement to your social security, (3) − (2)
40	$163,000	(39) times your <u>annual</u> social security, (39) × (5) × 12
41	48	Spouse's age now, (1b)
42	**** 6	Years from your rtmt to spouse's social security, (4) − (2) + (1a) − (1b), but not less than zero
43	$43,200	(42) times spouse's <u>annual</u> social security (42) × (6) × 12
44	**** 4	Years from your rtmt to your COLA pension, your (10a) − (2).
45	$24,000	(44) times your <u>annual</u> COLA pension, (44) × your (11a) × 12
46	**** 6	Years from your rtmt to spouse's COLA pension, = (10b) − (1b) + (1a) − (2), but not less than 0
47	$7,200	(46) times spouse's <u>annual</u> COLA pension, (46) × (11b) × 12
48	**** 4	Years from rtmt to your fixed pension, your (13a) − (2) but not less than 0
49	$48,000	(48) × your <u>annual</u> fixed pension × Age / 100, (48) × (15a) × 12 × (14a) / 100
50	**** 6	Years from your rtmt to spouse's fixed pension, = (13b) − (1b) + (1a) − (2) but not less than 0
51	$17,280	(50) × spouse's <u>annual</u> fixed pension × Age / 100, (50) × (15b) × 12 × (14a) / 100
52	$302,880	Total investments to support gaps, (40) + (43) + (45) + (47) + (49) + (51)
53	25	Years the surviving spouse will live in retirement (Adding extra years here is NOT conservative.)
54	20	% reduction in retirement income to support gaps as a % of wages, [100 × (52)] / [(53) × (8) × 12]

**** Enter zero if result is minus number

FIGURE A.9 Final steps for early retirees.

For a more refined estimate that is bettered tailored for the kind of expenses, debt, part-time work, investment details, etc., use one of the programs at www.analyzenow.com discussed throughout the book. If you have Microsoft's Excel, you can download one of these programs and determine if the extra detail is warranted in your case.

You may want to seek the help of a professional planner in addition to analyzing your own results. It is often worthwhile getting a different perspective, particularly as you get within 10 years of that important retirement decision or believe that you may have serious difficulties meeting your goals. See Chapter 10 for some tips to assist in selecting competent and unbiased assistance.

B Appendix

Age to Start Social Security

Usually, but not always, it is easy to determine whether it is better to start Social Security at age 62 or later. Review the *Mysteries of Social Security* in Chapter 3 and *When to Start Social Security* in Chapter 4 before using the worksheets that follow. It is very important to note that if you believe that you may have to work full time between the ages of 62 and 66, it is unlikely that you would want to start Social Security during that interval. That is because any income over $12,480 (in 2006 dollar values) reduces Social Security payments by $1 for every $2 of wages over most of that period. Check www.ssa.gov or 1-800-772-1213 for current limits.

The worksheets help you determine whether you have sufficient savings to consider delaying Social Security and the best age to start Social Security. Other considerations can be important too. If there is a very high probability that you will not live past age 80 and retire before or at age 62, then the best choice is usually to start Social Security at 62. That may also be the best thing to do if you believe there is a high probability that the government will make an appreciable reduction in benefits part way through your retirement—or that you can make more than 8 percent after-tax return throughout your retirement years.

We are going to work with pretax values of Social Security. The worksheets that follow, however, imply that your benefits will continue to increase with inflation and that you can earn income on your investments that is at least equal to inflation but less than 8 percent return. Then the best solutions are those that give the highest lifetime pretax Social Security payments.

For a broader look, including your choice of returns, tax rates, income needs for single people and married couples, and to view what happens when savings are exhausted, use the Free Social Security Calculator that you can download at www.analyzenow.com.

Note that this appendix does not specifically cover a possible shortfall in medical insurance until you and your spouse each reach the Medicare age of 65. To account for this, add the extra cost of additional insurance to the reserves that you need; that is,

$$\text{Monthly medical insurance costs} \times \text{Months required}$$

You should try some different cases in Figure B.1. Then the better result is usually the one with the larger lifetime income in step 8.

The numbers in parentheses refer to numbered steps in the worksheet shown in the figures.

You could use a separate copy of Figure B.1 for each spouse if you are married. But it is not sufficient to look at the benefits for each spouse on a standalone basis if one of the spouse's earned Social Security benefits are significantly lower. This is almost always the case for a spouse who has worked only a few years or had very low income. In such situations, you should do a survivor's benefit analysis by using the worksheets on Figure B.2 and B.3.

The low-income spouse is entitled to the larger of (1) the low-income spouse's own Social Security, or (2) 50 percent of the full retirement age benefit of the higher-income spouse providing the low-income spouse waits until the low-income spouse's full retirement age to start Social Security. For more information see the section Mysteries of Social Security in Chapter 3 and www.ssa.gov.

After death of the high-income spouse, the low-income spouse is entitled to get 100 percent of the Social Security benefit of the high-income spouse instead of up to 50 percent of the full retirement age amount when both spouses are still living. Unlike the case when both spouses were still living, there is no reduction in the survivor's benefit if the low-income spouse started benefits before the low-income spouse's own full retirement age.

Age to Get Most Social Security for Primary Wage Earner or Single Person

	Case 1	Case 2	
1	60	60	Your age at retirement
2	62	66	Age to start Social Security
3	2	6	Years without Social Security (2) – (1)
4	1,500	2,000	Monthly Social Security
5	36,000	144,000	Savings used before Social Security starts, (3) × (4) × 12

If you haven't saved at least this much in Case 1 or 2, that case won't work for you without sufficient pension income.

	Case 1	Case 2	
6	85	85	Age of death
7	23	19	Years of Social Security (6) – (12)
8	414,000	456,000	Primary wage earner's lifetime Social Security: (4) × (7) × 12

You may want to try different ages in step (6) to see how that affects the larger total payments in step (8).

FIGURE B.1 Determine the better age to start Social Security by entering a different age for each case in step 2.

For many couples with sufficient savings and good health, the best choice may well be for the high-income spouse to delay Social Security until age 70 and the low-income spouse to delay taking benefits until the full retirement age, that is, 65 to 67, depending on the low-income spouse's birth year. This is dependent on the government's continued support of existing benefits which is probably more likely than support for benefits of future generations when the government may reduce promises of future benefits.

It is not necessary to assume that cases 3 and 4 on Figure B.2 correspond to cases 1 and 2, respectively, on Figure B.1. You can base the case 3 and 4 alternatives both on either case 1 or 2 in Figure B.1 if you choose. The surviving spouse is trying to find the case that gives the largest lifetime payments in step 25. But first the couple has to confirm whether it has sufficient savings in step 16 to delay the start of Social Security.

If you are retiring before age 59½ and need savings to support the gap between retirement and starting Social Security that are largely in a deferred tax plan like an IRA, you should contact your deferred tax plan provider or a professional to discuss the requirements and implications imposed by section 72(t) of the Internal Revenue Code which requires that you take substantially equal payments for at least five years or until age 59½, whichever is longer.

**Family Savings Needed Considering
Lower Income Spouse's Social Security.**

	Case 3	Case 4	
9	62	66	Lower income spouse's age to start Social Security
10	58	58	Lower income spouse's age at retirement of higher income spouse
11	4	8	Years without Social Security (9) – (10)
12	750	1,000	Lower income spouse's Social Security. See text.
13	36,000	96,000	Savings used before Social Security starts, (11) × (12) × 12
14	Case 2	Case 2	Select either Case 1 or 2 for the better primary wage earner case.
15	144,000	144,000	Savings needed for primary wage earner: Enter (5) for case above.
16	180,000	240,000	Total savings required: (13) + (15)

If you haven't saved at least this much in Case 3 or 4, that case won't work for you without sufficient pension income.

FIGURE B.2 Use this table to determine whether your family has saved enough to consider delaying the start of Social Security.

If your savings are sufficient to cover the requirement in step 16 plus any amount needed for replacement or emergency reserves and medical insurance until you reach age 65 when you can get Medicare, then you can go on to pick the best age for the survivor to start Social Security (see Figure B.3).

The case with the larger value in step 24 is usually the better choice if Social Security payments continue to increase with inflation, tax rates remain relatively constant and your returns are below 8 percent. You can do a more comprehensive analysis with the free program to help decide whether to start Social Security at 62, 66 or 70 that you can download at www.analyzenow.com and the other retirement planning programs available at that site.

Age to Get Most Social Security for Surviving Lower Income Spouse.

17	83	83	Lower income spouse's age at primary earner's death*
18	21	17	Years of Social Security till age in step (17): (17) – (9)
19	189,000	204,000	Social Security payments before other spouse dies, (18) × (12) × 12
20	95	95	Lower income spouse's death age
21	12	12	Years between deaths of both spouses: (20) – (17)
22	2,000	2,000	Survivor's monthly Social Security after primary's death. See text.
23	288,000	288,000	Social Security payments after primary's death. (21) × (22) × 12
24	477,000	492,000	Total Social Security payments of survivor. (19) + (23)

* You can try different ages in step (17). They do not have to correspond to the age you selected in step (6).

FIGURE B.3 See which alternatives give you the most lifetime income.

Another thing to consider is the source of your reserves. If they are in a deferred tax account such as an IRA or a 401(k), you have to exercise caution, particularly if you want to make withdrawals before age 59½. Unless you follow the Internal Revenue 72(t) rules exactly, you will get a 10 percent penalty in addition to the income tax you have to pay on the withdrawals. So, if your withdrawals for the Social Security gap must come from a deferred tax plan, you likely will want to do two things: (1) Run an analysis on Dynamic Financial Planning Pro from www.analyze now.com; or (2) get the assistance of a professional financial planner.

Post-Retirement Worksheet

H ere is a sensible way to determine how much you can spend each year assuming that you are retired and possibly have a part-time job. There are more steps than in the typical simplified Web program or magazine retirement planners, but the additional work will get you a more realistic result considering your assumptions. We have to get into more detail because this analysis is so vital to your future. This is especially true if you would overestimate how much you could spend in retirement and consume your savings prematurely.

Your objective is to find the amount that you can spend, increase spending with inflation and have your investments last until you die. The final result is in step 83 (or step 96 if you use the refinements) in the worksheet that follows. Most people can skip many of the steps and still get results that are more realistic than the majority of computer programs.

Each year you establish a new annual budget based on the sum of:

1. Your annual after-tax Social Security.
2. Your annual after-tax COLA pension.

3. Your annual after-tax fixed pension times your age divided by 100.

4. Your after-tax, *return-adjusted* investments divided by the number of years you expect to live.

Investment component (4) is more refined than the method that the IRS uses to compute the required minimum distributions from an IRA or employee's savings plan. Remember that your plan should use a conservative (longer) number of years you expect to live. Life expectancy tables represent only the average age to die, and you may well live longer than average.

Since you should continue to make projections in each future year on about the same date, you want to record the entries for this and future years on separate pieces of paper. So, before you begin, make a copy of the Post-Retirement Worksheet for your entries.

Each step in the process is illustrated by an example in the material that follows. Write in your own numbers above the example and follow the instructions—including the operations that show adding, multiplying, or dividing numbers from previous steps.

It is a good idea to review the points made in Chapter 5 as you go along because it can improve your perspective. The steps below parallel the headings in Chapter 5.

Let's get started.

In the worksheet that begins with Figure C.1, "you" are the primary Social Security recipient. The numbers in parentheses refer to numbered steps in the worksheet. For example, (3) refers to the $6,400 in step 3 of Figure C.1.

We begin with an analysis to estimate the average tax rate you may encounter over the majority of retirement years. Obviously you cannot do this with precision. However, before entering your judgmental value in step 7, consider whether last year's taxes were representative; review the sections Estimate a Future Tax Rate in Chapter 5 and Significantly Higher Taxes in Chapter 2.

Tax rates

1	$50,000	Last year's Adjusted Gross Income (AGI from tax return)
2	$12,000	Last year's deductions
3	$6,400	Last year's exemptions
4	$31,600	Last year's taxable income: (1) − (2) − (3). If this is abnormal, consider using another year as a reference.
5	$5,000	Last year's state & federal income tax
6	0.10	Last year's income tax rate: (5) / (1) Based on Adjusted Gross Income
7	0.11	Future rate: Add a little to (6) to be conservative. If last year not representative of future, recalculate Tax / AGI

Life expectancy

8	65	Your age now
9	27.2	Life expectancy from livingto100.com or Figure 5.2
10	6.8	Extra years in case you live longer: Perhaps 25% of (9)
11	34.0	Years investment should last: (9) + (10)

FIGURE C.1 Tax rates and life expectancy.

If you have not yet started your Social Security benefits, you may want to review the Social Security sections in Chapters 3, 4, and 5 before completing the Social Security worksheet in Figure C.2.

Social security

12	$18,000	Your <u>annual</u> payments (before deductions)
13	$9,000	Spouse's <u>annual</u> payments (before deductions)
14	$27,000	Total: (12) + (13)
15	5.0	Years till you start social security (0 if started)
16	2.0	Years till spouse starts social security (0 if started)
17	$90,000	Gap you must fill from savings: (12) x (15)
18	$18,000	Gap spouse must fill from savings: (13) x (16)
19	$108,000	Total soc. sec. gap to come from savings: (17) + (18)
20	100%	Percent of social security to be taxed*
21	$2,970	Income tax on total social security: (7) x (14) x (20)
22	$24,030	After-tax annual value of total social security: (14) – (21)

* Get this from tax return by dividing taxable social security by gross social security. Future rates may be higher. 100% may be likely.

Social security adjustment to keep up with inflation

23	1%	It's likely that social security will increase less than inflation. Enter estimate of the shortfall. Could be 1%.
24	0.14	0.4 x life expectancy x inflation shortfall: 0.4 x (11) x (23)
25	0.86	1.00 – (24)
26	$20,666	Affordable spending from social security: (22) x (25)

FIGURE C.2 Social Security.

Let us next look at Cost-of-Living-Adjusted (COLA) pensions in Figure C.3. If your COLA pension has an inflation adjustment cap, you should consider multiplying the quote by a factor from Figure 5.3 in Chapter 5 before continuing with the worksheet.

Fixed pensions or annuities are much more common than COLA pensions or annuities. Use Figure C.4 to calculate their contribution.

**Cost-of-Living-Adjusted (COLA) pensions
or COLA lifetime immediate annuities**

27	$3,600	Annual COLA pension #1 before-tax
28	5.0	Years till start COLA pension #1 (0 if started)
29	$18,000	Gap from late start of COLA pension #1 to be filled with draws from savings: (27) x (28)
30	0	Annual COLA pension #2 before-tax
31	0	Years till start COLA pension #2 (0 if started)
32	0	Gap from late start of COLA pension #2 to be filled with draws from savings: (30) x (31)
33	$3,600	Total annual COLA pensions: (27) + (30)

If either (27) or (30) are severance payments, remember to deduct at least 7.65% for social security and Medicare taxes.

FIGURE C.3 COLA pension benefit.

Fixed pensions
or fixed payment lifetime immediate annuties

34	$12,000	<u>Annual</u> fixed pension #1 before-tax
35	$7,800	<u>Annual</u> pension #1 times Age / 100: (34) x (8) / 100
36	2.0	Years till start fixed pension #1 (0 if started)
37	$15,600	Gap from late start of fixed pension #1 to be filled with draws from savings: (35) x (36)
38	$0	<u>Annual</u> fixed pension #2 before-tax
39	$0	Annual pension #2 times Age / 100: (38) x (8) / 100
40	0	Years till start fixed pension #2 (0 if started)
41	$0	Gap from late start of fixed pension #2 to be filled with draws from savings: (39) x (40)
42	$7,800	Total <u>annual</u> fixed pensions times Age / 100: (35) + (39)

If either (34) or (38) are severance payments, remember to deduct at least 7.65% for social security and Medicare taxes.

FIGURE C.4   Fixed pensions or annuities contribution.

Now total the pension or annuity contributions in Figure C.5.

Total of pensions and/or immediate annuities

43	$396	Tax on COLA pensions: (33) x (7)
44	$858	Tax on affordable part of fixed pensions (42) x (7)
45	$10,146	After-tax affordable spending from pensions: (33) + (42) − (43) − (44)
46	$33,600	Total pension gaps to be filled from savings: (29) + (32) + (37) + (41)

FIGURE C.5   Total pension and/or annuity contributions.

You can reflect future part-time work with your entries in Figure C.6.

Part-time work in retirement

47	$10,000	Annual gross wages
48	$765	Social security and Medicare tax on wages: (47) x 0.0765 or higher rate to be conservative
49	$1,100	Income tax on wages: (7) x (47)
50	$500	Other <u>annual</u> deductions, e.g., union dues, insurance
51	$7,635	Annual wages less taxes and deductions: (47) – (48) – (49) – (50)
52	5.0	Years or part-time work
53	$38,175	Savings from part-time work: (51) x (52)
54	$1,123	Affordable spending from part-time wages: (53) / (11)

FIGURE C.6 Part-time work.

Do not neglect to account for reserves in Figure C.7.

Reserves

55	$50,000	Emergency reserves (perhaps 10% of investments)
56	$20,000	Replacement reserves (for high value items)
57	$70,000	Reserves for medical insurance until Medicare at 65 plus reserves for long-term-care if not fully insured
58	$0	Other known obligations
59	$108,000	Reserves for social security gaps: (17) + (18)
60	$33,600	Reserves for pension gaps: (46)
61	$281,600	Total reserves: (55) + (56) + (57) + (58) + (59) + (60)

FIGURE C.7 Reserves.

Next are the key steps for investments in Figure C.8.

Investments

62	$100,000	Tax-Exempt Investments, e.g., Roth IRA, Muni bonds
63	$300,000	Deferred-Tax Investments, e.g., 401(k), 403(b), IRA
64	$100,000	Taxable Investments, i.e., all other investments
65	$500,000	Total Investments: (62) + (63) + (64)
66	$50,000	Capital gains if sold all taxable investments today (if uncertain, 50% of (64) probably conservative)
67	$5,500	Tax on unrealized capital gains: (7) x (66)
68	$33,000	Tax on deferred-tax investments: (7) x (63)
69	$38,500	Total taxes: (67) + (68)
70	$461,500	Effective after-tax investment balance: (65) – (69)
71	$30,000	Part of home equity you consider an investment*
72	$491,500	Total Investments after-taxes: (70) + (71)
73	$281,600	Reserves: (61)
74	$209,900	Net (Investments less reserves and taxes): (72) – (73)
75	$6,174	Net divided by life expectancy: (74) / (11)
76	1.0%	Real Return**. Entry of 0% is generally conservative, 1% is typical for retiree, and 2% is aggressive.
77	1.17	1.00 + 0.5 x real return x life expectancy: 1.00 + 0.5 x (76) x (11)
78	$7,223	Affordable spending from net investments: (75) x (77)

* Might include future cash from downsizing or line-of-credit from reverse mortgage.
** Real Return = Return – Investment costs – Inflation – RDCA losses. Reverse-Dollar-Cost-Averaging (RDCA) losses often 1%.

FIGURE C.8 Investments.

Now we total the contributions in Figure C.9.

Total affordable spending this year

79	$20,666	From social security: (26)
80	$10,146	From pensions: (45)
81	$1,123	From part-time work: (54)
82	$7,223	From investments: (78)
83	$39,158	Total = this year's affordable spending: (79) + (80) + (81) + (82)

Repeat entire calculation each year.
Affordable spending (83) includes all of your normal expenses and debt payments but does not include income tax or any item included in reserves. You can also afford to pay taxes and reserve items because we subtracted those during the analysis.

FIGURE C.9 Total affordable spending this year.

If you are wisely using the replacement reserve concept from Chapter 6 and its Replacement Reserves Worksheet in Appendix H, it is important to understand how to integrate this into the analysis. You should include the replacement *reserve size now* (Column F of Figure 6.2) in step 56. However, the *annual savings* for replacements (column E of Figure 6.2) is part of the affordable spending in step 83. If you would have to make the replacement before enough had accumulated in the reserve, or the replacement cost more than the reserves you had assigned for replacement, you would overspend this year and have a negative impact on the amount that you could spend for normal expenses throughout the rest of your retirement.

The calculations that went into step 83 are more sophisticated than the majority of retirement planning programs. There are two more steps that you may want to take that are shown in the additional calculations that follow.

The first addition is an autopilot technique shown in Figure C.10 to smooth out what can otherwise be severe year-to-year variations in affordable spending caused by volatile stock or bond markets. However, this will not be very important if most of your retirement funds come from Social Security and/or a pension or immediate annuity. In that case you can skip the retirement autopilot calculation.

The second optional additional calculation relates to debts and is shown in Figure C.11. When you include debt payments as part of affordable spending there is a problem when the debt payments stop. Let's illustrate this with an example: If you calculated an affordable expense of, say, $50,000 and were making mortgage payments of $20,000 a year, you would have $30,000 left to spend for everything except the mortgage. However, after the last debt payment you suddenly have $20,000 more to spend for everything else. You can use the following alternative calculation that will keep the funds for everything else the same value both before and after the last debt payment.

Again, if you are using the replacement reserve concept from Chapter 6 and its Replacement Reserves Worksheet in Appendix H, the affordable spending budget in step 96 has to include the annual contributions to savings for the replacements in column E of Figure 6.2 or its equivalent in Figure H.1.

Retirement autopilot (Reduces abrupt year-to-year spending spending changes, but need to have used same method last year.)

84	$38,000	Last year's adjusted affordable spending (Needed to complete same calculation last year.)
85	0.042 = 4.2%	Last year's inflation: Can estimate from change in social security: [This year's SS / Last year's SS.] – 1.00
86	$1,596	Inflation x last year's affordable spending: (84) x (85)
87	$39,596	Last year's affordable spending + inflation amount: (84) + (86)
88	$78,754	Sum of this year's and last year's inflation adjusted affordable spending: (83) + (87)
89	$39,377	This year's adjusted affordable spending: 0.5 x (88)

Affordable spending (89) includes all of your normal expenses and debt payments but does not include income tax or any item included in reserves. You can also afford to pay taxes and reserve items because we subtracted those during the analysis.

FIGURE C.10   Retirement autopilot adjustment.

Optional debt adjustment (This eliminates large spending changes for non-debt items before and after last debt payment made)
Stop at (89) if going to get additional debt after paying current debts.

90	$35,000	Current balance of debts
91	$1,029	Current balance of debts divided by life expectancy: (90) / (11)
92	3.0%	Interest rate − [(7) x Interest rate] − Inflation. If loan interest not deductible: Interest rate − inflation.
93	1.51	Adjustment factor: 1.00 + 0.5 x (92) x (11)
94	$39,377	This year's adjustable affordable spending: (89) if used retirement autopilot, otherwise (83)
95	$1,554	Debt adjustment: (91) x (93)

Adjusted affordable spending for this year

96	$37,823	This year's adjusted affordable spending after the debt adjustment: (94) − (95)

This affordable spending (96) covers all of your normal expenses but excludes income tax and any item covered by reserves and debt payments (even all the way up to paying the entire debt). You can also afford to pay income tax and any item that was included as part of your reserve <u>and</u> this year's debt payment even though the debt payment is larger that the debt adjustment. Your total cash outflow this year will equal (96) + [Actual income tax] + [Cost of any items bought from reserves] + [Debt payments]. If you opt to use (83) or (89), the total cash outflows are (83) or (89) plus [Actual income tax] + [Cost of any items bought from reserves].

FIGURE C.11 Debt adjustment.

You can learn more about planning from *J. K. Lasser's Your Winning Retirement Plan* and from the many articles and programs at www .analyzenow.com. The programs on the website can help you analyze more complex retirement situations than the method above and can help you scope your estate planning. If you have Microsoft's Excel, you can download one of these programs and determine if the extra detail is warranted in your case.

Affordable Spending Budgets

Items included in "affordable spending" from Appendix C:
- Food and restaurants
- Home maintenance or rent
- Utilities, property taxes
- Insurance, uninsured medical
- Transportation
- Charities, gifts
- Support of relatives or pets
- Entertainment and travel
- Clothes, miscellaneous
- Annual replacement savings (Column E of Figure 6.2.)
- Debt payments if stop at step 83

Items that you also can afford, but are not part of "affordable spending" from step 83 or 96 in the Post-Retirement Worksheet include:
- Federal and state income taxes at step 7 rate.
- Items covered by reserves included in step 61.
- Debt payments if affordable spending from step 96.

Professional Review

It may be wise to seek a professional advisor's help for at least a one-time assessment that can provide additional perspective concerning the things we have covered in this book as well as to explore other important financial aspects such as insurance and estate planning. See Chapter 10 for some tips to help in selecting competent and unbiased assistance.

Appendix D

Analyze Investment Performance

If you are paying someone to manage your investments, it is important to check results to ensure that your portfolio is doing at least as well as the market. If it is not, you will want to either choose to manage the investments yourself or get a new manager. Further, it is possible your investment manager or your savings plan administrator is making more money than you on your investments. First you need to know your own return, and then you need to compare that performance with a composite index.

Calculate Your Own Return

You can always download and use the Free Return Calculator at www .analyzenow.com. But here is a simple way to approximate your actual return for a single year. It always gives the *before-tax* return even if some of your withdrawals (i.e., draws) were used to pay taxes. Your annual return is A divided by B where

$$A = \text{Ending balance} - \text{Beginning balance} - \text{Deposits} + \text{Draws}$$

and

$$B = \text{Beginning balance} + 0.5 \times \text{Deposits} - 0.5 \times \text{Draws}$$

If you don't like equations, here is a step by step process. The numbers in parentheses refer to results in previous steps shown in the following worksheet.

Let us begin with Figure D.1 by calculating the growth without deposits and draws.

1	110,000	End of year balance
2	100,000	Beginning of year balance
3	10,000	Growth: (1) – (2)

FIGURE D.1   Investment growth without deposits and draws.

Now we make the adjustments for deposits and draws and get the final return in Figure D.2.

4	4,000	Sum of annual deposits
5	1,000	Sum of annual withdrawals
6	3,000	Net deposits minus withdrawals: (4) – (5) If this is a minus number, keep the minus sign.
7	7,000	Growth minus net deposits: (3) – (6)

If (7) is a minus number, keep the minus sign, and remember that minus a minus means a plus. If you have trouble with minus numbers, do the calculations on a hand-held calculator. It knows how to deal with minus numbers.

8	1,500	One-half of (6)
9	101,500	Beginning balance plus (8): (2) + (8)
10	0.069	(7) / (9)
11	6.9	% return on investment: 100 x (10)

FIGURE D.2   Return after adjustments for deposits and draws.

This is a good approximation of the annual *before-tax* return of your investments even if you paid tax on it. You can do this for the total of your investments or for an individual investment.

Remember that this equation is only valid for one year. It does not work if you try to use it for two or more years. If you want the performance over a longer period, then you have to calculate the performance of each individual year first. Then compute an average and compare it with the average of the market.

Compare Your Results with the Average of the Market

You can compare your return with your advisor's results and tell if the advisor was misleading you. Or you can compare it with how the security markets fared by calculating a weighted average of the indexes that approximate your investment allocations. To do this, you would multiply the percentage allocation of your portfolio for a given investment, say bonds, times the return for the index for similar bonds. Do this for all of the categories in your portfolio until you have covered 100 percent of your allocations. Then add up all of the results. I simplify this for my own case by doing the following:

My percent fixed income investments × Total bond market index

and then add that to

My percent equities × Total stock market index

This sum is the market performance of bonds and stocks if proportioned as in my allocation. I use Vanguard's index funds in the previous equations. Vanguard's index funds closely follow the markets they represent and have very low costs. The average funds probably had performance at least 1 percent less.

Evaluating Long-Term Performance

When there are deposits and withdrawals, you should make the evaluation one year at a time using the approach above. However, you may have some accounts where you invested a lump sum and had all interest, dividends, and capital gains distributions reinvested automatically. If so, you can use Figure D.3 to determine your performance. For example, if your investments had doubled after 10 years, the figure shows you had a 7.2 percent compound return over those years.

That particular example illustrates a magic number in financial compounding. The number is 72. If you divide 72 by the number of years it takes to double your investment, you get the return. So 72 divided by 10 requires 7.2 percent return. Alternatively, you can use the number another way. Divide 72 by the return percentage and determine

Percent Return on Investment
with Single Initial Deposit
and No Subsequent Withdrawals

Years Owned	Ending Balance divided by Beginning Balance									
	1.25	1.50	1.75	2.00	2.25	2.50	3.00	3.50	4.00	5.00
1	25.0	50.0	75.0	100.0	125.0	150.0	200.0	250.0	300.0	400.0
2	11.8	22.5	32.3	41.4	50.0	58.1	73.2	87.1	100.0	123.6
3	7.7	14.5	20.5	26.0	31.0	35.7	44.2	51.8	58.7	71.0
4	5.7	10.7	15.0	18.9	22.5	25.7	31.6	36.8	41.4	49.5
5	4.6	8.4	11.8	14.9	17.6	20.1	24.6	28.5	32.0	38.0
6	3.8	7.0	9.8	12.2	14.5	16.5	20.1	23.2	26.0	30.8
7	3.2	6.0	8.3	10.4	12.3	14.0	17.0	19.6	21.9	25.8
8	2.8	5.2	7.2	9.1	10.7	12.1	14.7	17.0	18.9	22.3
9	2.5	4.6	6.4	8.0	9.4	10.7	13.0	14.9	16.7	19.6
10	2.3	4.1	5.8	7.2	8.4	9.6	11.6	13.3	14.9	17.5
11	2.0	3.8	5.2	6.5	7.7	8.7	10.5	12.1	13.4	15.8
12	1.9	3.4	4.8	5.9	7.0	7.9	9.6	11.0	12.2	14.4
13	1.7	3.2	4.4	5.5	6.4	7.3	8.8	10.1	11.3	13.2
14	1.6	2.9	4.1	5.1	6.0	6.8	8.2	9.4	10.4	12.2
15	1.5	2.7	3.8	4.7	5.6	6.3	7.6	8.7	9.7	11.3
16	1.4	2.6	3.6	4.4	5.2	5.9	7.1	8.1	9.1	10.6
17	1.3	2.4	3.3	4.2	4.9	5.5	6.7	7.6	8.5	9.9
18	1.2	2.3	3.2	3.9	4.6	5.2	6.3	7.2	8.0	9.4
19	1.2	2.2	3.0	3.7	4.4	4.9	6.0	6.8	7.6	8.8
20	1.1	2.0	2.8	3.5	4.1	4.7	5.6	6.5	7.2	8.4

FIGURE D.3 Evaluate your long-term performance for investments without additional deposits or any withdrawals.

how long it will take to double your investment. So 72 divided by 7.2 equals 10 years. If you would earn 6 percent, the rule of 72 says it would take 12 years to double. It also applies to real returns. That is, actual returns less inflation. So if you earned 3 percent real return, it would take 24 years to double the money in today's dollar values.

By doing the one-year and long-term evaluations, you can better understand your own performance. If it is too low, and you think you would do better with professional management, you could either try a lifecycle fund or go to a certified financial professional. If you already have a professional manager, and your performance has been consistently poor per Figure D.3, also consider a life-cycle fund—or a new manager.

Pre-Retirement Assumptions

Social Security

We assume that Social Security increases with inflation. This may be optimistic considering the federal funding problems, so you might want to enter a slightly lower value. One way to do this is to assume that Social Security will not be fully adjusted for inflation—which, in fact, is already true in terms of the net that you get after deducting Part B for hospital coverage.

To do this, we estimate an adjustment shortfall. So, if inflation was 4 percent, but Social Security was adjusted upwards by only 3 percent, there would be a 1 percent shortfall. The simplified equation to adjust Social Security is

$$(1 - (0.4 \times \text{Life expectancy when retired} \times \text{Inflation shortfall})) \times \text{Social Security}$$

If your life expectancy at retirement was 26.2 years (See Figure 5.2.), and Social Security payments were \$2,000, a shortfall of 1 percent would change the Social Security entry to

$$(1 - (0.4 \times 26.2 \times 1\%)) \times \$2,000 = (1 - 0.1048) \times \$2,000$$

which equals \$1,790.

This adjustment is incorporated into Appendix C but not into Appendix A so as to keep Appendix A easy to use. Nevertheless, you could make the same adjustment for Appendix A if you wish to refine the analysis. See Appendix F for an analysis of its accuracy.

Cost-of-Living-Adjusted (COLA) Pensions

COLA pensions are assumed to increase with inflation as well, so you might want to use the same adjustment as for Social Security.

There are more powerful reductions if the pensions have an inflation cap or the trust making the payment defaults to the Pension Benefit Guarantee Corporation. The factors suggested to use for COLA caps from Figure 3.2 in Chapter 3 are based on a history of someone who retired in 1965. If you are a highly compensated person, and you expect that your pension trust may default to the Pension Benefit Guarantee Corporation, you want to investigate the amount of coverage you will get.

Fixed Pensions

I've been asked many times about the equation for the amount that we assume for a fixed pension when doing an analysis projecting constant inflation-adjusted payments for life. The correct amount should be the present value of the pension multiplied by the ratio A divided by B where

$$A = \text{Pmt(Real return, Life expectancy, } -1 \text{ Present value)}$$

and

$$B = \text{Pmt(Actual return, Life expectancy, } -1 \text{ Present value)}$$

However, few laypersons know how to use financial equations, so I've found that you can get quite a practical answer by simply multiplying the pension by Age/100, where the age we use is dependent on whether the pension quotation is a present value or future value. If the quote is a future value, use your current age in the equation. If the quote is a present value (today's dollars), then simply use the age to retire. That accounts for the same thing as the more elaborate financial equation above, namely, it provides some savings out of the fixed pension to help counter future inflation and provide reasonable inflation protection for a fixed pension as a source of income.

After retiring, the retiree could continue to again use Age/100 as the adjustment for a fixed pension, but this time the age is always whatever is the current age at the time. A 70-year-old would therefore be able to spend 70 percent of the after-tax value of a pension, while an 80-year-old would be able to spend 80 percent of the after-tax pension. The remainder is saved to provide for a net inflation-adjusted amount for life. This assumption is slightly conservative as shown in Figure E.1. For example, at age 65, the Age/100 gives 65 percent as affordable spending while the more accurate equation with 25 years life expectancy and 5 percent return gives 72 percent.

When the fixed payment quote is given in future dollars, use the approximation of age divided by 100 again—but this time use the current age. Figure E.2 points out that this provides a somewhat optimistic assumption about the future value of a pension when there are many years until retirement as in this case for a 30-year-old person with 35 years until retiring, although it is fairly close for a lower retirement life expectancy. Chapter 3 points out the hazards of using an employer's pension quote without discounting it because of the many things that can happen to a pension over many years. A reasonable discount would likely overpower any optimism in the Age/100 assumption.

Fixed Pension Theory at 65
Age / 100 vs. Financial Formula
Factors for age 65 and 3% inflation

Life Expt.	Age 100	Return in Retirement		
		4%	5%	6%
20	0.65	0.75	0.76	0.76
25	0.65	0.71	0.72	0.73
30	0.65	0.67	0.68	0.69
35	0.65	0.63	0.65	0.67

FIGURE E.1 The Age/100 factor is generally lower than that given by the more accurate financial equations which are more sensitive to retirement life expectancy than the future return.

Fixed Pension Theory at 30
Age / 100 vs. Financial Formula
Factors for age 65 rtmt., 3% inflation and
30 years old now

Life Expt.	Age Now	Return in Retirement		
	100	4%	5%	6%
20	0.30	0.27	0.27	0.27
25	0.30	0.25	0.25	0.26
30	0.30	0.24	0.24	0.25
35	0.30	0.22	0.23	0.24

FIGURE E.2 The Age/100 factor is higher than that given by the more accurate financial equations. However, someone who is as much as 35 years from retirement should probably discount the quote in addition to using the Age now divided by 100 factor.

Of course, as the person gets closer to the year for getting the pension, the Age/100 approximation becomes more accurate. A pension projection may not have much meaning for a very young person. It is dependent on both continued employment and an employer who continues to provide pension benefits—neither of which may have a high probability. This is something that you have to consider when entering pension values either for COLA pensions or fixed pensions.

Investments

We assume that pre-retirement wages, new savings, and retirement expenses increase at the same rate as inflation. We are looking for a level of retirement income (expenses plus taxes) that can last at least 25 years before investments are exhausted.

We use three planning models: The nominal model is flanked on either side by a more conservative model with 1 percent less return and a more aggressive model with 1 percent more return than the nominal model. It is not a simple matter for a retiree to change returns by 1 percent either way without large changes in risk—unless the changes can come from using higher or lower-cost funds or advisor fees.

The nominal model is based on 50 percent stocks, 40 percent long-term corporate bonds, and 10 percent money markets. This is a reasonable allocation for many who will be using this analysis. Those who are far from retirement and invest very aggressively may do better than even our aggressive projections. That is, however, a big "may" as many recent aggressive stock investors confirm. On the other hand, those who invest mostly in CDs and bonds, and/or pay exorbitant advisory or fund loads may find our conservative assumptions too optimistic. If you are uncomfortable with any of these assumptions, use one of the more detailed planning methods from www.analyzenow.com. These allow you to specify allocations and costs.

Since investment returns, especially inflation-adjusted returns, are really impossible to predict, we must rely on historical indexes to represent securities. Our source of annual returns is Global Financial Data. In this case, we have used the S&P 500 index for stocks, short-term treasuries for money markets, and long-term AAA corporate bond indexes for the rest of investments.

To account for fees and costs, we subtract typical values of 1.5 percent from stock index returns, 0.3 percent from short-term treasuries, and 0.5 percent from long-term corporate bonds. These costs net to 0.98 percent for the overall portfolio. By historical standards, savvy investors using low-cost index funds may do somewhat better while those who know little about investing may fare worse.

In addition, we account for success rates, dollar cost averaging and reverse dollar cost averaging. Assuming 50 percent historical success rates before retirement and 80 percent after retirement, the net real (inflation-adjusted) returns are 4.1 percent for new deposits, 3.3 percent for existing savings, and 0.3 percent in retirement after deducting costs and accounting for success probability assumptions.

If the statistics for returns and inflation would be the same in the future as they have been in the past, with the nominal case you would have had a 50 percent chance of getting enough money to retire and an 80 percent chance that the investments would last as long as 25 years. Using a 50 percent historical rate before retiring is acceptable because you may well be able to work longer if investments don't pan out or retire earlier if investments do very well. Using an 80 percent historical chance of your money lasting 25 years helps ensure that you will have reasonable income if you live a few years longer. If we used a 50 percent historical success rate for retirement, the investments would last about 36 years as

**Retirement Years
if spend the same inflation-
adjusted amount each year**

Pre- & Post-Retirement Returns	Success Rate in Retirement	
	50%	80%
1% Less	30	22
Nominal	36	25
1% More	51	29

FIGURE E.3 The number of years your money would last depends highly on the risk that you are willing to take. These numbers reflect historical conditions. The future may be quite different.

shown in Figure E.3. Historical success rates may be far different than future success rates, so it pays to be conservative.

Gap Adjustments

To account for the gaps between the age of retirement and the ages to start Social Security and pensions, we assume that the gaps are funded with investments that have an after-tax return equal to inflation. The amount required to fill the gap is simply the future annual payment in today's dollars times the length of the gap.

Again assuming the return equals inflation, we calculate the affordable spending penalty by dividing the resulting investment by the retirement life expectancy which is the same result that you would get using the more complex financial equations. This provides a result that is approximately equal to reducing the total investments at retirement by the investments to fill the gap.

Income Taxes

We do not do an after-tax analysis in the pre-retirement analysis for several reasons. One reason is that few people can estimate what they would need for a spending budget in retirement, but they can get a reasonable idea of what the future might be like if they see how retirement gross income would compare to current gross income. Another reason is that it is very difficult to tell what tax rates will be many years in the future.

We infer a tax simplification when all retirement investments are in deferred tax accounts. This is slightly conservative over a period of years. To illustrate, suppose that we started with $100,000 and added new savings at $10,000 a year increased by inflation of 3 percent each year for 10 years. Assume investments have a return of 8 percent before retiring and 6 percent after retiring. If the deferred tax account draws were taxed at 20 percent and taxable returns were taxed at 15 percent, and the after-tax draws on both accounts were $21,750, the taxable account would last 20 years and the deferred tax account would last 18 years. If the tax rate on taxable returns was also 20 percent, then they would both last 18 years. Thus considering all investments over a long period of time as being in deferred tax accounts is generally going to be conservative when predicting the number of years that investments last.

F

Post-Retirement Assumptions

Social Security

We adjust affordable spending from Social Security when future payments lag inflation by an incremental inflation shortfall. For example, if inflation was 4 percent last year but Social Security increased only 3 percent, there would be a 1 percent shortfall. This is one of the proposals to help reduce the future Social Security deficit. The simplified equation for affordable spending is

$$(1 - (0.4 \times \text{Life expectancy} \times \text{Inflation shortfall})) \times \text{Social Security}$$

This equation also provides a good approximation without having to use a computer or supplemental table (See Figure F.1).

**Social Security Approximation
as a percent of
an accurate computer analysis
100% is perfect**

Life Expectancy	Inflation Shortfall			
	1%	2%	3%	4%
10	101%	101%	101%	101%
20	102%	103%	103%	101%
30	104%	105%	103%	97%

FIGURE F.1 This is a comparison of a simple formula with an accurate simulation of the cumulative amounts of Social Security when the actual inflation rate is 4 percent and Social Security fails to keep up by the amount of the inflation shortfall.

Tax Rates

We simplify the tax computations by using one rate throughout. This is because tax laws change virtually every year, and the swings can be large depending on the economics and politics at the time. Tax rates are not predictable; although the common wisdom is that they have to go up from where we are today.

We use a rate that is based on income tax divided by adjusted gross income, not taxable income for two reasons: (1) This seems to vary less than what happens to individual components; and (2) because we apply that rate to the elements that make up adjusted gross income. For example, we apply that rate only to the part of Social Security that is taxable. We also exclude tax-exempt income from the tax calculation.

COLA Pensions

We suggest that people modify their COLA pension amounts when they are subject to a cap that has a maximum inflation adjustment. We use the same assumptions here as those used to develop Figure 3.2 in Chapter 3; namely, the results are based on the actual history inflation starting in

1965. There is, of course, no way of telling what will happen to inflation in the future, but the starting point of 1965 is conservative from an historical perspective.

Fixed Pensions

We use an approximation to represent affordable spending from a fixed pension. The simplified equation for affordable spending in this case is

$$\text{Fixed pension payment} \times \text{Age} / 100$$

We want to compare results with the theoretically more accurate financial formula that we have approximated with Age/100. The more accurate equation is the ratio: A divided by B, where

$$A = \text{Pmt(Real return, Life expectancy, Present value} = -1)$$

and

$$B = \text{Pmt(Return, Life expectancy, Present value} = -1)$$

In this case, the computer results are dependent on returns, inflation, and that life expectancy changes with age. Therefore we are going to look at three situations that use IRS publication 590 life expectancies from Figure 5.2: (1) a single person; (2) a married couple of equal ages; and (3) a married couple with a five-year age spread. Figure F.2 shows results for those three cases when returns are 5 percent and inflation is 3 percent.

Figure F.2 also shows that the Age/100 predicts lower affordable spending at age 55 than the more accurate financial equations. This is more conservative than the financial equations and is at a time when it is important to be somewhat conservative with a fixed pension. On the other hand, it is more optimistic late in life, but the long years of inflation has already made a fixed pension less significant than the remaining resources, and the underspending at younger ages would have built up more savings to compensate.

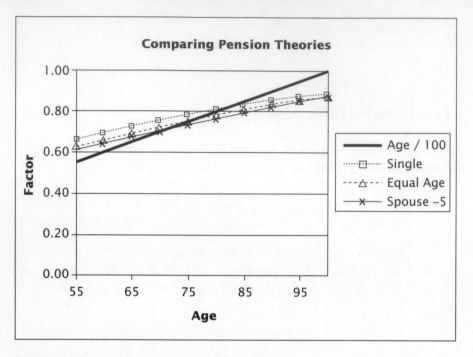

FIGURE F.2 The simple Age/100 approximation gives good results during most of a retired person's life.

Investments

We subtract ordinary income taxes from deferred tax accounts, capital gains taxes from taxable accounts, and no income tax from tax-exempt accounts. In effect, this is equivalent to assuming that all investments are in deferred tax accounts at different tax rates. Over a long period of time, this simplifying assumption is slightly conservative compared to using after-tax returns for taxable investments.

The next thing we do is make a first estimate of affordable spending from investments by dividing the investment balance (after subtracting taxes and reserves) by life expectancy. This gives the results equal to that which you would compute from the financial equation with zero real return:

Affordable spending = Pmt(Real return, Life expectancy, – Balance)

Then, we make an adjustment to Balance divided by Life expectancy to provide for other than zero real return. The resulting approximation for affordable spending is

$$(1 + (0.5 \times \text{Life expectancy} \times \text{Real return})) \times \text{Investments} / \text{Life expectancy}$$

Figure F.3 shows that this simple equation is a suitable substitute for the more accurate computer-derived results. The percentage at the intersection of each life expectancy and real return is the result from the equation above divided by the more accurate computer analysis. 100 percent is perfect. Even at the extreme of 30 years and 5 percent real return, the equation is only off by 9 percent. Importantly, it is always slightly conservative.

Investment Spending Approximation
as a percent of
an accurate computer analysis
100% is perfect.

Life Expect.	Real Returns			
	0%	1%	3%	5%
0	100%	100%	100%	100%
10	99%	98%	98%	98%
20	99%	98%	97%	94%
30	99%	98%	95%	91%

FIGURE F.3 The simplified equation divided by computer results provides surprisingly good results for affordable spending from investments at different real rates of return.

Appendix

G

Rebalancing Worksheet

This Rebalancing Worksheet in Figure G.1 shows how to determine the amount you need to move from bonds to stocks or vice versa to maintain an allocation between specified limits. Include stocks, stock funds, and investment real estate equity in cell (C). (See Chapter 7 for an example calculation.) Steps E and F assume that you will key your allocations to the rules in Chapter 7, *Allocation Rules Rule*. You can, however, insert your own rules in those steps for allocation limits.

If there is too much fixed income in cell (G), then transfer cell (K) from fixed income to equities. If there is too little fixed income in cell (H), then transfer cell (L) from equities to fixed income.

247

Rebalancing to Allocation Targets

Letters in parentheses ( ) refer to entries, e.g., (A) is entry in A

Total Investments	Fixed Income	Equities	Instructions
A	B	C	Break total investments into 2 parts: Fixed income & Equities
	D		% Fixed Income 100 x (B) / (A)
	E		My age now. This is the upper percent limit for my fixed income. See Chapter 7, Rebalancing.
	F		(E) – 10 This is the lower percent limit for my fixed income. See Chapter 7, Rebalancing.
	G		Too much fixed income: If (D) greater than (E), enter (D) – (E), else enter 0.
	H		Too little fixed income: If (D) is less than (F), enter (F) – (D), else enter 0.
	J		Percent to get to target allocation (G) + (H) + 5
	K		If (G) is greater than zero, sell this much fixed income and buy equities: (A) x (J) / 100
	L		If (H) is greater than zero, sell this much equities and buy fixed income: (A) x (J) / 100

FIGURE G.1   Rebalancing to allocation targets worksheet.

Replacement Reserve Worksheet

When you are young, it is hard to save for replacements at the same time that you are making loan payments. By the time you retire, however, you should have worked your way into using this time-tested method by accumulating sufficient replacement reserves. (For more information, see Chapter 6.)

For example, if you were planning to buy an automobile and estimated the current replacement cost (less trade in) at $20,000, and your normal service life for a car was five years, you should be saving $20,000 divided by five years, which is $4,000 each year.

If you had the car for two years, your reserve should already be two years times $4,000 which is $8,000. You would include the $4,000 in your budget and the $8,000 should be part of your investment reserves.

When you have finished your calculations in Figure H.1, you have both a number that has to be covered by your affordable spending budget (column E) and the amount you should already have accumulated for a replacement reserve (column F).

Replacement Reserves

A	B	C	D	E	F
Description	Cost to replace	Normal service life	Years in use now	Annual Savings B / C	Reserve size now D x E
Car less Trade					
Roof					
Furnace					
Water heater					
Carpets					
Painting					
Electronics					
			Totals		

FIGURE H.1   Replacement Reserves Worksheet

If you subtract the tax-adjusted amount in column F from your investments before you enter a net investment value in a retirement analysis, the retirement analysis calculates the amount that you can spend for everything except the items you included in the replacement reserve. The reason, of course, is that you have already set aside enough money to cover replacements by the time the items useful lives are over. However, if you have to replace an item before saving enough for it, you overran your budget.

If you update this analysis every year, you account for whatever inflation has taken place. Theoretically, the current balance of your reserves are increased by a return equal to inflation. Your actual results will be somewhat different as will the year in which your roof or whatever has to be replaced. These uncertainties are relatively small compared to the overall assessment of the amount needed to be saved each year and the necessary balance in reserves.

You can make the worksheet example shown in Figure H.1 as short or as extensive as you feel is helpful. Competent home owners associations usually have very extensive lists that can be many pages of single-spaced type. Those who do not provide for replacements subject owners to irregular and often surprisingly large assessments.

Figure H.2 uses a simplified example of how the replacement reserves would change over a 10-year period for a $1,000 replacement of, say, a hot-water heater tank with a 10-year life. The calculation in each successive year produces a new cost-to-replace, a new annual savings amount and a new amount for the reserve size. Only at the end of year 10 is the actual reserve large enough to purchase the new hot-water tank.

In actual practice, inflation will not be constant as assumed in column B and the saving account in column G will vary as well considering that returns will not be equal to inflation as in the example. It is important to understand that the *cost to replace* (column B), the *annual savings* (column E), and the *required reserve* (column F) are all values used in your plan at the *beginning* of the year. The actual savings (column G) is an end of year value.

Replacement Reserve Example

3% Inflation
3% Return

A	B	C	D	E=B/C	F=DxE	G
Start of Year	Cost to replace	Service life	Years in use	Annual savings	Required reserve	Year end savings
1	1,000	10	0	100	0	100
2	1,030	10	1	103	103	206
3	1,061	10	2	106	212	318
4	1,093	10	3	109	328	437
5	1,126	10	4	113	450	563
6	1,159	10	5	116	580	696
7	1,194	10	6	119	716	836
8	1,230	10	7	123	861	984
9	1,267	10	8	127	1,013	1,140
10	1,305	10	9	130	1,174	1,305
11	1,344	10	10	134	1,344	1,478

FIGURE H.2 Example replacement reserve calculations over a 10 year period for a single item, say, a hot-water heater tank.

NOTE

Tax note: If you are already retired and the replacement funds have to come from a deferred tax account, you must increase the reserve amount from this calculation to account for the taxes that will be due on withdrawal. The same is true if you are not retired and use the method described in Chapter 3 and Appendix A. To make the tax adjustment, divide the amount in column F by the quantity (1 − Tax rate). For example, if your tax rate was 20 percent and the amount of cash you needed from reserves was $8,000, then you would actually need to withdraw $8,000 / (1 − 0.20) = $10,000.

So if you actually had a separate savings account for the water heater, you would have to wait slightly longer than the end of the service life unless you had higher returns than inflation or made deposits earlier in the year. This is really a case of looking into too much detail, because the fact is that almost any item that has to be replaced will have a service life different than you assume. The main point is that if you use this replacement reserve concept, you are much less likely to have to borrow money for replacements, and, to the extent that your savings outpace inflation, you will enhance the remainder of your retirement funds for other expenses.

You should note that there are some computer programs such as the Simplified and Dynamic programs on www.analyzenow.com that allow you to make special entries for items you will have to purchase in the future. If using one of these programs, you do not subtract replacement reserves from investments because the program will do this for you implicitly for the items that you enter. However, you still might want to make the calculation above to determine the size of a reserve savings account if you want such funds separate from your other retirement resources as well as the annual contributions to a replacement investment account.

Glossary

401(k)   stands for the applicable part of tax code that authorized employers to offer savings plans with deferred-tax benefits. Deposits are tax deductible, but withdrawals are fully taxable and are subject to constraints similar to regular IRAs.

AARP   formerly called the American Association of Retired People, but now just known by its initials. This is an organization that lobbies for the elderly as well as offers newsletters, insurance, and other products.

adjustable rate mortgage (ARMs)   a mortgage with an interest rate that is adjusted periodically, often starting with a very low teaser rate that is soon followed by adjustments according to some interest index.

after-tax basis   the value of something as if you had to pay taxes on it today. If wages, it is your gross pay less state and federal income tax. If it is a deferred tax investment, it is the total amount less the taxes that you would pay if you liquidated the account now.

allocate   to specify the percentage distribution of different kinds of investments.

annuity   a tax-deferred investment issued by an insurance company and often marketed by mutual funds. Investment selection and withdrawal rules vary, but unless you withdraw the funds before some specified age, all eventually annuitize, that is, convert to periodic payments as with an immediate annuity.

autopilot   a device in an airplane or system that controls without human input. In an airplane, an autopilot is designed to smooth the flight in gusty air. In a planning program, it is those equations that smooth spending budgets from year to year.

breakeven age   the age when there is no economic advantage of one choice over another or the age where the better choice switches between two alternatives.

consumer's price index (CPI)   a federal measure of inflation. This index is based on the price of a "basket" of items that is supposed to represent the purchases of the average person. The index is ratio of the current prices to the price in some past reference year.

cost of living adjustment (COLA)   wages or benefits may be adjusted according to an index, usually the consumer's price index (CPI) or some other index that measures inflation.

debt   an obligation to someone else usually backed by collateral. A debt is equivalent to a negative investment, often at a rate that is higher than most people would get from their portfolios.

downsizing   selling a more expensive home and buying a less expensive one in order to get cash and less expensive operating costs. This is often a better alternative than getting another loan on home equity.

employer's savings plan   this may be a 401(k), 403(b) or a number of other plans that are "qualified" by the IRS as tax-deferred accounts for employees to save for retirement. These have age requirements similar to IRAs but differ in allowable contributions.

executor   the person identified in a will to see that the terms of the will are fulfilled. This may require assistance from professionals in investing, taxation, law, and accounting as well as former employers and the Social Security Administration.

full-retirement age (FRA)   this is a Social Security reference age that now depends on your birth date. It used to be known as your normal retirement age when it was fixed at age 65 but now extends all the way to age 67 for younger generations. The change was one of what ultimately will be many ways the government reduces its unsupportable obligations to the elderly.

Great Depression   the most tragic economic situation in the United States that followed the stock market collapse in October of 1929. Numerous companies failed, prices plummeted, unemployment was widespread, and many people went hungry.

home equity   the part of your home that you own. Home equity is the current market value less the current indebtedness. If you have a mortgage, you own the equity and the lender owns the rest.

hybrids   a mix of different kinds of investments in one fund. Hybrids have a specified distribution of stocks and bonds that are rebalanced frequently to preserve stated distributions.

immediate annuities   a contract with an insurance company that, in exchange for a lump sum of money, will make lifetime payments on a regular basis. These may be either fixed, have cost-of-living adjustments, COLAs, or be based on other kind of an index. Pensions are really immediate annuities, most of which have fixed payments and some have COLAs.

index funds   a fund with the same distribution of securities as the index it represents. The first index fund was one that had the same percent distribution of stocks as the S&P 500 index that represents the 500 largest capitalization stocks in the United States. Costs are very low because the fund does not have to do any stock or bond picking, which is done by the publisher of the index. Now indexes are published for many different kinds of securities. Mutual fund companies emulate many of these.

inflation   a measure of increasing costs for the same items. Inflation is usually measured by changes in the consumer price index (CPI), which is based on a "basket" of items that are supposed to represent the kind and proportion of things consumed by the average person. Specifically, inflation is the cost growth (this year's costs less last year's costs) divided by last year's costs.

IRA   stands for Individual Retirement Arrangement. This is the most common of deferred tax accounts. They are administered by financial institutions such as mutual funds and brokerages. There are a number of stringent requirements subject to strict regulations such as the earliest age to take out money (59½) and age to start mandatory withdrawals (70½). (Roth IRAs have major exceptions to these rules.) IRS Publication 590 thoroughly covers associated regulations and life expectancy tables used for withdrawals.

laddering   time-wise diversification. This is the intentional staggering of maturity dates for bonds or CDs so that approximately the same amount of principal comes back every year over a period of years. You can also ladder immediate annuities by purchasing approximately equal amounts each year over a period of years thereby getting larger payments as you age.

life expectancy   the additional years to live for a specified group of people all the same age. This is the number of years where 50 percent of the population dies earlier and 50 percent lives longer. The older the person, the shorter the life expectancy. The way it is defined, you cannot outlive life expectancy because you still have a life expectancy no matter what your age may be.

long-term care insurance   an insurance policy to cover living and medical expenses in an approved facility (and sometimes home care). Important considerations are amount per day, possible premium increases, inflation protection, home care alternative, total days covered, and pages of fine print.

Medicare and Medicaid   these are government insurance programs to partially assist people with medical bills. Medicare is automatic for 65 year olds who register with the Social Security Administration. Medicaid is free care for the indigent.

Medicare Part B   coverage of most doctors' services. Its costs are deducted from Social Security benefits. Until recently everyone had the same monthly amount, but in the future Part B costs will be higher for higher income people.

Monte Carlo analysis   a statistical analysis involving a large number of trials of randomly drawn values. In financial analysis, the values are usually historical daily or monthly returns on investments. The result is the probability that investments would have been exhausted in a certain number of past years. Caution! It represents what happened in the past, not necessarily what will happen in the future.

pension   an annuity that makes lifetime payments to a retired employee and, as a lower-paying option, to a surviving spouse.

Pension Benefit Guaranty Corporation (PBGC)   a quasi-government corporation set up to insure employee pensions in case the employer fails to fund its pension trust. It collects insurance premiums from employers and makes pension payments if necessary in accordance with its own rules.

phase-out of deductions   an effective tax increase because high income people cannot take the full deductions from income because their deductions are "phased out" as their income increases. Most wealthy people are allowed only the standard deduction in spite of what might otherwise be substantial deductions—especially for charitable contributions.

planning   a strategy and actions to get to an objective. In finance, it is a projection based on some assumptions about the economy, resources, saving and/or spending that provides an estimate of future financial status.

professional help assistance from a person certified and licensed. The central figure in financial planning is usually a Certified Financial Planner (CFP), but may also be (or assisted by) an accountant or lawyer.

real estate investment trust (REIT) this represents ownership in a company that may own and operate income producing real estate or finance mortgages. The REIT may have a very specialized kind of real estate ownership or be diversified. There are REIT funds that have stock in numerous REITs. Unlike dividends, returns from REITs are taxable at ordinary income rates.

rebalance to redistribute the amount invested in different kinds of investments so as to be in accordance with specified allocations.

replacement reserves cash or other investments set aside to replace major items that wear out and have to be replaced infrequently such as a roof or automobile.

required minimum distributions (RMD) after age 70½, retirees are required to start distributions from deferred tax accounts that have to equal or exceed the RMD specified for their age in IRS Publication 590. The "divisors" used to calculate RMDs originally were life expectancies but now imply longer lives.

returns short for return on investment. The return from bonds is interest and sometimes capital gains or losses. The return from real estate is rent and capital gain or loss. The return from stocks is dividends and growth reflected in either unrealized capital gain if you have not sold yet or actual capital gains (or losses) from the sale. Return is the sum of annual principal growth (or loss) plus dividends, interest and/or rent. It is most often expressed as a percentage growth over a one-year period.

reverse mortgage a contract with a lender that allows you to recover part of your home equity. It may make regular payments to you or give you a line of credit. The debt against your home increases with each payment and time as interest accumulates. These are subject to stringent government rules and often have costly provisions.

reverse-dollar cost averaging the opposite of dollar cost averaging. This generally adverse effect on returns is the result of regular withdrawals that cause selling more shares when prices may be down and fewer shares when prices are high. Few projection methods alert users to this common problem in retirement.

Roth IRA tax-exempt investment with special rules. With few exceptions, Roth IRAs are limited to lower income workers. They are not subject to required minimum distributions (RMDs) after age 70½, but they are subject to early withdrawal penalties. Some employers offer Roth savings plans.

severance package an offer or contract for supplemental retirement benefits. This might include a lump sum of money or an annuity and/or medical or other benefits. These are fully taxable as earned income and so have Social Security and Medicare deductions.

today's dollars   a measure of future values that adjusts for inflation. In financial terminology, today's dollar is the present value of a future value that has been discounted at the rate of inflation. It generally takes more future dollars to buy something than it does in today's because inflation reduces the value of each future dollar.

Treasury inflation-protected securities (TIPS)   these are bonds issued by the Federal government with principal adjusted for inflation. The adjustment is taxable every year as ordinary income, so TIPS are better investments for deferred tax accounts than taxable accounts.

Index